Some Schools

C J (Jonty) Driver

A John Catt Publication

First Published 2016

by John Catt Educational Ltd,
12 Deben Mill Business Centre, Old Maltings Approach,
Melton, Woodbridge IP12 1BL

Tel: +44 (0) 1394 389850 Fax: +44 (0) 1394 386893
Email: enquiries@johncatt.com
Website: www.johncatt.com

ISBN: 978 1 909717 97 8

Set and designed by John Catt Educational Limited

Contents

The portrait of Jonty Driver by Andrew Festing on the cover is reproduced by kind permission of the artist himself and of the Governors of Berkhamsted School.

About the Author

C J ('Jonty') Driver was for many years a teacher, in Africa, Hong Kong and England, in comprehensive, international and independent schools. He is now a full-time writer, living in East Sussex, but travelling regularly to his country of birth, South Africa.

After qualifying as a teacher at the University of Cape Town (1958-62), he was President of the National Union of South African Students, 1963 and 1964, and was held in solitary confinement under Ninety Day Detention by the South African police in 1964. Refused the renewal of his passport while a postgraduate student at Oxford, he became stateless before getting British citizenship, though he remained a prohibited immigrant in South Africa until 1991. He taught at Sevenoaks School (1964-5, 1967-73), where he was Housemaster of the International Sixth Form Centre. He then became Director of Sixth Form Studies at Matthew Humberstone Comprehensive School in Cleethorpes before becoming Principal of Island School, Hong Kong (1978-83). He was Headmaster of Berkhamsted (1983-9) and then Master of Wellington College (1989-2000).

Jonty Driver has been an honorary senior lecturer in the School of Literature and Creative Writing at the University of East Anglia since 2007. He was a judge of the Caine Prize for African Writing in 2007 and again in 2008. He was a research fellow at the University of York in 1976 and more recently has held residencies at the Liguria Study Centre in Bogliasco, at the MacDowell Colony in New Hampshire, and at the Hawthornden Writers' Retreat near Edinburgh. He has governed a variety of schools and has been a Trustee of the Beit Trust since 1999.

He has published five novels (the first four of which were re-issued by Faber Finds in 2010), two biographies, a memoir, an essay in autobiography, and seven collections of poems, the most recent *Citizen of Elsewhere*, Happenstance Press, 2013.

Acknowledgements

I am grateful to those friends who have read this book in the various stages of its development, and especially to John Bowers QC (who helped particularly with the chapter on Matthew Humberstone School), John Guyatt (long-serving schoolmaster at Sevenoaks School), John Clare (who manages that difficult combination of being rigorous in criticism and yet supportive of the whole endeavour), John Davison (whose own recent history of Berkhamsted School was especially helpful), Colin Niven (my successor as Principal of Island School and a friend ever since), Jonathan Smith (writer and schoolmaster) and Jane Mercer (a deputy head at Island School and another long-term friend). Derek Bingham of JCEL has been a thoughtful editor.

I am grateful to my successor's successor at Wellington, Anthony Seldon, for his generous foreword. It is not always easy to try to tell the truth without being unkind to the living or unfair about the dead, but I hope I shall be forgiven for not concealing my own errors of judgement – and for having had strong opinions about professional competence.

Those who know me personally will not need reminding how lucky I have been in being married to someone who combines love, loyalty, a sense of perspective, and an independence of mind and spirit. My children too have served to remind me that "you're not a Headmaster at home, Dad".

Foreword

I first encountered Jonty Driver in a *gîte* close to the river Dordogne in Southern France in August 1970. I was travelling south to the Mediterranean coast in search of enlightenment with three sixth form friends. Jonty Driver was a folk hero to all of us. He was the complete epitome of cool and everything we aspired to be. His first published novel, *Elegy for a Revolutionary* (you can't get a much cooler title than that) had been published by Faber, no less, the year before. In every sense of the word, he was a giant of a man, and visiting him in this idyllic setting felt like a pilgrimage.

He had first come to public prominence when President of the National Union of South African Students in 1963-64, with a high point being his 90 day detention at the hands of the government. He subsequently had his passport refused and his writing banned. He sought refuge in the UK, teaching at the most chic school then in the country, Sevenoaks, where he was a legend across the school. There was nothing about this man that was not inspiring. Goodness knows what he thought when four bedraggled students turned up at his door in France. But Jonty and his multi-talented wife, Ann, in no time had whisked up a meal for us, full of nourishing local Dordogne produce and tastes.

I followed Jonty's career closely over subsequent years, years he describes with such poignancy in the pages of this book. He writes beautifully about schools, a subject that fascinates all of us, but which is rarely written about well. His range of experience is mind-boggling. After working at Sevenoaks, an independent school, he went to what was then

South Humberside to be head of sixth form at a pioneering state school. He subsequently became Head of three very different schools: the Island School in Hong Kong, serving predominantly ex-pats, then back to the UK to become Head of Graham Greene's old school, Berkhamsted, and finally, Master of Wellington College.

As one would expect from a poet and a man of letters, he writes pellucid prose, free of the jargon and anachronisms. In a profession that is bedevilled by obfuscation, he writes about schools with a delightful honesty and directness, in a style that reminds me of the other great postwar Headmaster-cum-writer, John Rae.

It was an incredible thrill when I was appointed the head of the school which Jonty had served with such distinction as its leader at the end of the 20th century, Wellington College. Without his encouragement and advice, I never would have applied, nor been successful in that application, nor been the kind of kind of head that I was. I owe him everything.

Jonty has written an important book which should be read by all who care about schools. No one else has had such a combined impact on politics, schools and literature. It is a remarkable story.

Anthony Seldon

Some Schools

'The achievements of exile are permanently undermined
by the loss of something left behind.'

Edward Said, *Reflections on Exile*

'I suspect that at root Britain – or perhaps I should say England –
does not care as much about education as other countries.'

Claus Moser

'Confusion and complexity are generally a truer way of looking at
things than certainty and simplicity.'

Bernard Porter, *British Imperialism: What the Empire Wasn't*

'Conrad had very strongly the idea of the Career. A Career was
for him something a little sacred: any career. It was part of his
belief in the ship-shape.'

Ford Madox Ford, *Joseph Conrad, A Personal Reminiscence*

Introduction

In my professional life, I was variously a President, a Housemaster, a Director, a Principal, a Headmaster and a Master. I have also been a Fellow (several times), a Governor (often), a Chairman of Governors, a Visitor (twice), an Advisor, and an honorary Senior Lecturer. Once, for a short and happy time, I was in the United States a Colonist. Twice, I have been the Ordinary of school chapels. I have never been a Professor, though I have always envied the French notion of the *professeur*, the all-round teacher in school, college or university. When I talk about the people in charge of schools, the term which comes most easily to me is Headmaster or Headmistress, and the easiest way of abbreviating and generalising that appellation is to use the word 'Heads'.

Two of the best chairmen of governors I ever worked for were women; both delighted in calling themselves 'chairmen', though there was no mistaking their gender. I have done my best to be scrupulous about the terms I use, although I draw a grammatical line at using a plural pronoun when the subject is a singular 'everyone' or 'someone'; 'someone' is 'he' or 'she', never 'they'.

When I talked to my pupils collectively, I always addressed them as 'Gentlemen' or 'Ladies' or (collectively) as 'Ladies and Gentlemen', perhaps especially when I thought they didn't deserve the courtesy of those titles. When I talk about them, it still is as 'boys and girls'. Some of them are 'students' already, as they will – one has to hope – all become if and when they get to the university; but it is not a term I find easy to apply to school-children. 'Scholars' I shall always be inclined to think of as (first) those who are clever and fortunate enough to have won scholarships and (secondly) those who have studied subjects long and hard, and know more than most what they are talking or writing about. 'Learners' I regard as condescension, though I suppose it means much the same as 'pupils'.

I worked in both single-sex and co-educational schools. Sometimes, when I talk about 'boys', it is because the school I am referring to had boy-pupils only; sometimes it is because I am referring only to boys in a co-educational school. I have had less to do with girls-only schools than with boys-only or co-ed, but our daughter was in a girls-only secondary school and I was for many years first a governor of Benenden School (for girls), and then founding member of its advisory board (chairman and, I add proudly, by my own design the token male). I was also a governor of Farlington School (for girls only) for five or six years, and chairman for four.

I tend to use the word 'teaching' to apply to what happens in the classroom, laboratory or workshop, not least because I want to hang on to a concept of all-round involvement and commitment in schools, way beyond the statutory hours required – and therefore cherish the title 'schoolmaster' above all others. 'Schoolmistress' should have an equal force, although, given the nature of our culture, the all-round schoolmistress is a species even harder to find than the all-round schoolmaster. Though it seems long-winded, I shall use the term 'schoolmasters and schoolmistresses' rather than just 'teachers'.

'Professional' should be an accolade, applying to someone who works until his or her desk is clear, without paying too much attention to the clock. If the desk is clear by three o'clock on Wednesday, he can get away to play a round of golf; if the desk isn't clear at six o'clock on Friday, she works until it is – or takes the work home, or resolves to come in on Saturday morning. Payment for overtime makes the work into a job; not worrying too much about the pay helps make the work into a profession.

Chapter one

Sevenoaks, Oxford, and Sevenoaks again

My first teaching post in England was at Sevenoaks School in Kent. The position had been offered me without interview, indeed without my even applying, because of the good offices of Robert Birley, formerly Head Master of Eton, then visiting Professor of Education at the University of the Witwatersrand, who admired the work being done at Sevenoaks (he had served on the council of Voluntary Service Overseas with the Headmaster of Sevenoaks). The general view of friends and family was that the 20-month stint I had done as president of the National Union of South African Students (NUSAS) was long enough; I was so much in the public eye for my outspoken attitudes to apartheid – indeed, had managed to earn the personal opprobrium of the Minister of Justice, J B Vorster, including direct attacks on my views and my character in the South African Parliament – I was probably doing NUSAS no good, and was in line to have my passport confiscated, and probably gain a banning order too.

So I accepted by telegram the offer, booked myself on the Union Castle liner leaving Cape Town for Southampton on 13th August 1964, and wrote a letter of resignation, explaining that my position would be taken over by the vice president, still my closest friend and eternal ally, Maeder Osler, who had already been elected president to succeed me in January. I had for weeks been expecting to be arrested as part of the general round-up of the African Resistance Movement, even though I had never been a member; but when it hadn't happened I assumed the Security Police had realized they couldn't prove involvement on my part, even though politically it would have been useful to do so.

In the event, I was arrested at midnight the night before the liner left, and held under the Ninety Day law, which allowed detention without charges being laid nor recourse to lawyers, in solitary confinement. I was held for a week before I was taken from Woodstock police station to Roeland Street police headquarters for a long session – some ten hours, I seem to remember – of questioning. With their usual heavy sense of humour, the police chose to question me on what they knew was my 25th birthday.

That detention is not part of this narrative. It is enough to say the Headmaster of Sevenoaks, L C Taylor – known as 'Kim' – kept the post open for me, told the newspapers he was doing so, but quietly found a replacement in case I didn't appear. The substitute was an ex-pupil of the school, Timothy Langdale, who had taken a First in history from St Andrew's and was currently taking his bar-exams (he has recently retired from a career as a celebrated Q C). In the event, I was released from detention a few days before the start of the academic year and, using the passport I had managed to hide away when the police detained me, flew to England in time for the start of term.

Kim kept Tim Langdale on the staff, too. I had been due to teach English, history and Latin, and was delighted to find Tim would do the history and some of the Latin; my knowledge of English history was rudimentary, though I could manage elementary Latin. We were each given a bed-sitting-room in No 9 High Street, just over the road from the school; the top floor was occupied by R B Hanson, Richard, sometimes called Hank, an English teacher and the housemaster of a day-house, a long-haired bachelor with a passion for ballet and no enthusiasm for games, who became a life-long friend.

Did we have a cleaner? I don't remember. Did we have an arrangement about sharing the costs? I don't remember. I do remember it was the Headmaster's wife, Sue Taylor, who showed me the room, with its bed, table, chair. There was no bedding – and I had none in my one suitcase. I had no money either; when I had tried to change at the airport what little South African currency I had, it had been refused. So the Headmaster's wife lent me sheets, blankets, a towel, a pillow.

The three bachelors in No 9 got lunches in the school dining room. Once a week Hank would cook an evening meal (a small ham, boiled cabbage, boiled potatoes); Tim would sometimes cook leathery omelettes and thin sausages; sometimes we would go to a local pub for delicious sandwiches; and I guess I did my share of the cooking; but, to tell the truth, I remember very little of the detail of that year. You don't do five weeks in solitary confinement without damage. Years later, the ex-wife of one of the housemasters at Sevenoaks said to me, "You know, Jonty, you were quite mad in those days: you were there, all six foot four of you, but you weren't all there."

There is a kind of record of that in a sequence of poems published in the *London Magazine* in 1965, called 'Through Tall Fires'. I don't think they are particularly good poems, but re-reading them now I remember especially the aggravation of the weekly practice-night of the bell-ringers at St Peter's down the road – that, and the constant nightmares, where policemen would once again come thundering into my bedroom to wake me with their questions. I remember Richard Hanson saying to me, over a drink in the local pub one evening, "You woke me again last night, shouting in your sleep." Sometimes, when the bleak English winter and the apparent smallness of life got too oppressive to bear, I would take off into Knole Park next to the school, and walk through the wet bracken and the woods round the edge of the park until I knew weariness would help me sleep. Later, I found an English girlfriend who owned a car, and sometimes on Sundays she would drive me down to the Kent coast so I could look across the sea and imagine the distances of Africa.

I'm told I went into my first class – Sevenoaks had one entry at 11, one at 13, and this must have been a class of 11 year-olds – scowling and saying, quietly, "I take it you know I've just been released from gaol. I'm not going to have any trouble with you lot, am I?" I remember that class – and a remarkably able sixth form class – with especial affection; in my book-shelves I still have the present the sixth form gave me at the end of the year: *The Elegies and The Songs and Sonnets* of John Donne, edited with an introduction and commentary by Helen Gardner, Oxford at the Clarendon Press, 1965, and tucked into the front of the book is a list of names:

> This book was presented to C J Driver on leaving Sevenoaks School, July 19th 1965... J.Cook N.Powell G.Jenkins C.Steel A.Cole P.Reynolds *et al.*

One of them (now Professor Jon Cook, of the University of East Anglia) is still a friend; Neil Powell is a poet and biographer; and occasionally I run into another of that clever class. Most of them will remember me mainly because I was so addicted to smoking I couldn't get through a 40-minute lesson without sneaking to a window for half a Woodbine.

I must have coached rugby too; I was reminded of this recently when an elderly man came up to me at a memorial service to tell me the first sentence he had ever heard me speak. I had been helping coach the U14s. Apparently I poked my head into the scrum and said in what was in those days still a strong South African accent, "Now, listen you blokes, you're going to have to get your arses down."

In the summer there was cricket. I had failed to turn myself into a cricketer at school but had read coaching manuals and some cricketing autobiographies, had done some coaching in my father's school, and knew I was fairly good at that, even if I wasn't much of a practitioner myself. However, there was a staff team – named after a Roman schoolmaster, Orbilius, as the Orbilians – and I was welcome there, at any rate in the friendly matches against village sides in the early evenings or on Sunday afternoons (though not when the Orbilians borrowed some of the better schoolboy players so they could compete in the local league).

The first over I bowled for the Orbilians on the delightful ground under the walls of the great house at Knole found me out. In my enthusiasm to prove I could bowl fast I lost all sense of a run-up and ended by bowling 13 times, mostly wides or no-balls, to complete a single over. Fortunately, the captain forgave me, and I was invited again to play, even to bowl, even in due course to open the bowling. On warm summer afternoons, when the pitches were hard, I would sometimes manage to bowl straight enough to take a wicket.

か～ら

Jonty Driver Detained at Midnight

MR. JONTY DRIVER, president of Nusas, was detained at midnight after Security Police searched his flat in Harfield Road, Kenilworth. It is presumed that he is being held under the 90-day clause.

Mr. Harry Wilson, one of the two men with whom Mr. Driver is staying, told the *Cape Times* early this morning that he had arrived home at about midnight, just as four men in plain clothes were taking Mr. Driver away.

"I said goodbye to him, but he said nothing."

The flat had been searched, but as far as he knew nothing had been taken.

A POET

This is Mr. Driver's second term of office as Nusas national president.

Mr. Driver, 24, was a brilliant student at the University of Cape Town. He has a B.A. Hons. degree and a B.Ed. degree. He is also a recognized poet, his works having been published both in the Republic and oversea.

Mr. Kenneth Parker, a friend of Mr. Driver and a former vice-president of Nusas, who was at the flat last night, said: "We were supposed to go for a drink at 11 o'clock and we were waiting for Jonty, who was having dinner with friends, to come home. He arrived at 10.45 p.m. and we were just about to leave when Detective-Sergeant Van Wyk, of the Security Branch, and three other plain-clothes policemen arrived."

SEARCHED FLAT

"They searched the flat for one and a half hours and took several Nusas documents. They then left, taking Mr. Driver with them.

"I asked Sergeant Van Wyk why he was being taken away. He said that he was being held under the 90-day clause."

From the Cape Times, *August 1964.*

19

After the end of the summer term, I stayed on in Sevenoaks because I had nowhere else to go; while I had managed to get entry to a post-graduate degree at Oxford, and a place in my father's old college, Trinity, I had very little money, even with what I had managed to save from my schoolmaster's salary. Robert Birley had again used his good offices to get me an annual grant for two years from the Sir Ernest Oppenheimer Memorial Trust, but I couldn't draw on that until September – and anyway it was only £600 a year. I spent some time staying with a South African friend in Oxford and, in due course, Winston Nagan found two undergraduates who were looking for a third person to share a small cottage on Osney island, blissfully looking out on to the Isis. More boats than cars went past our front door. That became my home for the next two years.

Going back to university aged 26 – after two years' working full-time for NUSAS and a year's teaching – was a strange experience, though I loved Oxford and Trinity, and was lucky in my teachers, and even luckier in that Maeder Osler had finished his year as president of NUSAS and had come to Oxford too. My two years there are not really part of this story, though I came away with an enhancement of my academic qualifications from the University of Cape Town, namely a BPhil in Modern English Studies (it was upgraded to an MPhil a few years later).

↾⇀

There were two great changes in my life while I was at Oxford. When my South African passport expired late in 1965, I sent it to the embassy in London for renewal. After some months, I enquired. The embassy had sent it – someone explained – to Pretoria for renewal. Eventually, with a friend to accompany me just in case some attempt might be made to hold me inside the embassy building, I went to London. I explained to a pleasant clerk at the counter it had been months since I submitted my passport for renewal.

He seemed genuinely surprised, and disappeared into the rooms behind. Soon he was back, looking thunderous. He had discovered he was dealing with a dangerous subversive. No, I wasn't getting my passport back. A moment or two later, a man we recognized as a security policeman we had had dealings with the year before arrived to stare at us. "Look," I said to the clerk, "if you won't give me back my passport, how am I going to get back home?"

"We can issue you with an entry-permit," the clerk snapped. We had heard of one-way exit-permits, sometimes given to trouble-makers to get them out of the country, but never before of an entry-permit.

"Would an airline accept an entry-permit to let me board a 'plane?" I asked, fairly sure I knew the answer.

I was, in effect, stateless. There would be no more 'going home' for me, at any rate until apartheid came to an end and, if I was honest with myself, I thought that system so entrenched it wouldn't end for many years.

Fortunately, someone mentioned to me that, if I hurried, I could register under the British Nationality Act of 1948, as amended by the Commonwealth Immigrants Act of 1962 and the South Africa Act also of 1962 (the date when South Africa left the Commonwealth) and, by that means, after five years' residence in the UK, achieve British citizenship merely by 'registration'. This I did, and in September 1969 I duly became British – well, more or less.

The second great change was that, at a party in London on New Year's Eve, 1967, I was taken by a girl-friend from the University of Cape Town to a party in a flat on the edge of Chelsea. As I was introduced to the hostess – a slim, dark-haired and dark-eyed young woman in a silver lamé dress with silver lamé stockings and silver lamé shoes, and a pony tail – I knew with weird certainty I would marry her and told her so the same evening, though she thought I was merely joking. However, I persevered and, as soon as I had finished my degree, we married, and will stay married for the rest of our lives. There is no 'more or less' about that.

The end of my time at Oxford, the certainty I wouldn't be returning home, and impending marriage, meant I needed a job. Vague ideas of emigrating to the West Indies were rendered futile by my being stateless, and an enquiry to a contact at the British Council made it plain my political past and lack of citizenship would be impediments in achieving a decent career in that direction. There weren't in those days the proliferation of creative writing courses in universities which have provided careers for a good many hopeful writers. I was sensible enough to know that poetry on its own wasn't a career, even if I achieved regular publication.

Ann Hoogewerf was, by then, ensconced as press officer for Granada Television in London, so we needed to live close enough for her to commute. By chance I ran into Kim Taylor in Oxford. Almost without thinking, I asked if there might be a chance of a post back at Sevenoaks from September 1967. I was so used to Kim's decisiveness I half-expected an answer there and then; however, he grinned at me, said he never appointed people in the street, and anyway there were people he would need to consult – a new head of the English department, for instance – and it might be sensible if I applied in writing.

Summoned to a interview with the English department, I found myself getting on very well with John Adams, who had moved from Bristol Grammar School to take charge of English at Sevenoaks: not an easy task, given the disparate talents he had assembled in his charge. However, he must have approved, because in due course a letter came offering me a post; at that stage of the year, no school accommodation would be available, so Ann and I would have to find somewhere in Sevenoaks to live – difficult in what even then was an expensive area, especially as most residents commuted to London.

∾∾

At first, going back to Sevenoaks seemed almost like a retreat. It may have been the closest place to a home I had in England, but I was going to have to be a schoolmaster first and foremost. Any writing I did would need fitting into the interstices of a busy life, especially as I was now married. I wasn't interested in getting involved in South African exile politics; after my experience of the real kind of politics in South Africa, what went on in London seemed to me merely futile and often unpleasantly personal. I would try to keep my friends and avoid my enemies.

In fact, teaching English throughout the school, coaching games seriously (I ran Colts rugby for a season, and then was promoted to coaching the Second XV and, in the summer, took charge of junior cricket), helping in the International Sixth Form Centre, being married and, in 1968, becoming a father, kept me busy. Moreover, Cyril Connolly, whom I had met in South Africa in early 1964, and who had been kind to me during my first years in England, had suggested a short story

Jonty with Form 2C at Sevenoaks in 1965.

I had written read like the first chapter of a novel; it became my first novel, *Elegy for a Revolutionary*, published by Faber and Faber in 1969. It was banned in South Africa even before Penguin published it as a paperback. Three more novels followed: *Send War in Our Time, O Lord* (also banned in South Africa), then *Death of Fathers* (set in a school not unlike Sevenoaks), then *A Messiah of the Last Days*. There were poems, too, some of which were published.

Sevenoaks was a great school to teach in, particularly in those years under Kim Taylor's inspired leadership. Kim, with an elder brother also nicknamed Kim, had come from India to prep school and then on to Sevenoaks. Their father had died when young Kim was only nine and, from then on, school was – even more than it had been – effectively home; their housemaster and his wife at Sevenoaks became surrogate parents – and, in due course, perhaps even more than that, because by the time I got to Sevenoaks Ernie Groves had become Kim's Second Master.

In the days when the Taylor brothers were pupils, Sevenoaks was not the celebrated place it has since become. 'Jimmy' Higgs-Walker, the Headmaster appointed in 1924, had (it was true) made significant changes, opening day-houses and expanding the sporting side of the school; but it was still a small, boys only, minor public school which served in part as the local grammar school, with an 11+ entry paid for by Kent, and an entry from mainly local prep schools at 13+.

Young Kim had been a great success. A big boy, tall, strong, and very bright, he rose to be head of school as well as captain of rugby and of boxing. He had been just about to take the entrance exam for Oxford when war was declared; so he went home to his mother in India and there began teaching, aged only 17, at St Paul's, Darjeeling. In 1942 he was commissioned into the Indian Army and sent to Burma to fight the Japanese.

After demobilization, he taught for another year at St Paul's, before finding a passage back to England to take up a place at New College, Oxford. He didn't get the blue for rugby he had hoped for, but did get a blue for boxing; he told me once he had thought it might help him get a Headmastership if he had a blue, so when he didn't get one for rugby he made sure he got one for boxing, though by the time I got to Sevenoaks boxing had vanished as a school-sport.

More importantly, he got a First for history. Both the schools he knew best had made him sure he wanted to be a school-teacher, but he went off to the USA first, on a Commonwealth Scholarship, to take a degree in psychology at the University of Chicago. It was there he met Suzanne Dufault, whom he would later marry, and who was an important part of his successful career: she was lively, forthright – indeed, outspoken – and very attractive.

Kim's first teaching job in England was at Repton. In 1954, still only 32, he was offered the Headship of Sevenoaks on the retirement of Jimmy Higgs-Walker. Although he himself always gave credit to Higgs-Walker for what he had achieved, actually Kim Taylor transformed Sevenoaks within half a dozen years. Some of what he did is described in *Experiments in Education at Sevenoaks* (London, 1965) by Bob White, Neil Patterson, *et al*; it is summarized in Brian Scragg's masterly history of the school (Bath, 1993).

The Voluntary Service Unit (VSU) was a development from Kim's enthusiasm for Voluntary Service Overseas (VSO), on the national committee of which he served. The trouble with VSO was that by its very nature it offered very few boys and girls the chance to do social work abroad. Kim was convinced there was enough local need for masses of boys and girls to learn about service not by precept but by direct hands-on experience. Kurt Hahn, founding Headmaster of Gordonstoun, and Alec Dickson of VSO, came to talk to the school, and Kim appointed a young historian, Neil Patterson, to run VSU.

At first, it concentrated on caring for the young and the old, but year by year added more and more expertise, the initial 20 boys having grown to more than 100 by 1964, and other local schools being involved: manning school crossings; visiting old people to garden, wash up, clear and decorate; helping in local hospitals and in schools for the blind, ESN, physically handicapped and emotional maladjusted, even in a Borstal.

At the HMC Conference in 1962, Kim had urged other schools to set up their own Units, and dozens of schools came to see what was being done, and to emulate the scheme. By 1972 the VSU had grown so much its management was funded by the Kent County Council, and a town Volunteer Bureau was set up in parallel with the school's VSU.

Kim's internationalism was also behind the setting up of the International Sixth Form Centre (always called the IC) in 1962. While overseas pupils had been coming to British schools for many years, more and more were now applying from abroad to do their A levels so as to get entry to British universities. Yet they were often older than their British equivalents, and weren't likely to fit easily into normal boarding houses. On the other hand, one wouldn't want to isolate them from their fellow-pupils in a separate house.

Hence the IC always included about a third of home-grown students, two-thirds from a variety of other countries. Though they were all full members of the school, the IC had its own form of limited self-government, whereby the house was run by an elected committee and regular house-meetings, rather than by prefects appointed by the housemaster.

A third experiment was the Voluntary and Independent Scientific and Technical Activities (VISTA). Kim had been introduced by one of his governors to Gerd Somerhoff, an expert in artificial intelligence who was doing post-graduate work in Oxford and also running a 'Science Club' at the Dragon School, aimed at enlivening science teaching by directing it towards engineering and technology. Kim persuaded Somerhoff to join the staff at Sevenoaks by promising him that a Technical Activities Centre (TAC) would be built there to his own specifications.

Somerhoff was passionately convinced that most science teaching stifled invention and experiment. Even though there was beginning to be more work in laboratories (particularly by the Nuffield methodology), the teaching of sciences was inevitably corralled by curricula. Yet, for a generation at least, boys had been building models, usually with instructions supplied. Now, the teaching and the model-making would be combined, but the boys would have to learn the principles for themselves, starting from scratch. Building of the TAC started in 1963, and by 1965 it had a national reputation. Within a very few years, the largest single entry into any profession from the school was engineering.

The change in the school came not simply from the 'experiments' but from Kim Taylor's preparedness to back the people he had chosen to appoint (for instance, Bob White in an art department which became so

The enlarged International Sixth Form Centre in 1973. Casey McCann is third from the left; 'Rawsie' the Matron, is next to Ann Driver, holding son number one is on the author's lap. Two along is Peter Parkhouse, an additional tutor.

successful Sevenoaks was one of the two schools in the country where boys could do their foundation diplomas before going on to degree level at art school). It helped that the numbers were going up (in 1956 there were 451 boys, 88 in the sixth; by 1960 there were 557 boys, 196 in the sixth), so he was adding to the staff rather than merely replacing people as they left or retired.

The new staff gave energy to the older, and the uncommitted got short shrift. When Ernie Groves retired, Kim was able to appoint as second master another man who had taught him: the redoubtable Jack Robinson (whom I remember especially because he once shut me up in a staff meeting when I was being boring about boys not wearing raincoats and then coming damply into class by saying, "Small boys dry quickly").

Brian Scragg explained some of Kim's quality in his history of the school:

> Those who worked with and for Kim Taylor at this time tend to remember him for what he was rather than what he did, as a remarkable force de la nature rather than an efficient leader clocking up one solid achievement after another. The many innovations which attracted so much attention in the sixties, and gained ... for Sevenoaks School the reputation of daring pace-setter ... seemed ... to flow as it were naturally from a man capable of making Staff Meetings occasions to be looked forward to. He worked very hard, and those about him were expected to do the same, but they were also expected to share his excitement, his restless refusal to believe things couldn't be better.

I would add to that: Kim wasn't working from a master-plan. He was an extraordinary opportunist (and that applied to his skills as a fund-raiser too): he seized the moment, improvised, put the right people in charge, let them get on with the job in hand, encouraged them. What he had was a vision of the possibilities. Schools had to be fun, had to be expansive, had to be imaginative. Oh, they needed order and discipline too (I've never forgotten Kim's telling me that Sevenoaks was only about 10% experimental; 90% was, he said, a traditional public school); but he got those old things straight enough for there to be room for the new. All the same, is it just my imagination that makes me remember his saying once to me that, actually, he rather believed in change for the sake of change?

෨෧

In 1965, in a re-shuffle of the senior staff, the founding housemaster of the IC was promoted to be Under Master – what in most schools would be called the deputy head – although he continued to run the IC. In 1968, to my delight, I was invited by Kim to take over as housemaster. Since Ann had given up all but part-time work for Granada Television after the birth of our son, the appointment had material advantages: we lived in the IC rent-free, although hardly comfortably, as our bedroom and bathroom were in the old attic, our kitchen – shared with the boys – three floors down at one end of the Victorian hotel which had been made into the IC, and our sitting room and my study the other end.

At that stage, the evening meal was sent down from the school and, as the custom then was, our own provisions were paid for by the school. (The living arrangements changed while we were there: the school built an extension to the old hotel, which included extra accommodation for more boys and a flat for the housemaster and his family; and instead of the school's simply paying all the grocery bills for all the boarding housemasters and their families we were given a more sensible allowance.)

Looking back on the experience now, I am torn. On the one hand, it was a marvelous step in my own career. Of course, for an ex-president of a National Union of Students taking over an international boarding house in 1968 of all years the times were fraught with contradictions. Whose side was I on anyway? Was I now the voice of authority? But the bedrock of the IC was its experiment in participatory democracy.

The housemaster of the IC did, it was true, have the power of veto over decisions of the weekly house meeting; but it was a power almost never to be exercised, though its existence could act as a brake on excessive silliness. In fact, I vetoed only one decision of the house meeting in my five years as housemaster, when a clever boy with an extraordinary ability to rile me proposed that, to express its disgust at the inequality of giving house-colours, everyone in the house should be awarded house-colours even if he was as weedy on the games-field as the speaker himself. I was tired after a hard day, and anyway fed-up at what I saw as never-ending bolshiness. I think my cross veto surprised even myself. Was it important? Of course it wasn't. If it had been otherwise, I might have argued more coherently.

On the other hand, I don't think I was that good an appointment. I was too young, I was too recently married, we had just had our first son, I was too committed to my own writing, and (most of all) I got the distance between myself and my charges wrong. Oddly enough, that centred on nomenclature. Ever since I could remember, I had been called Jonty by almost everyone and in almost every situation; even the South African newspapers often referred not to Jonty Driver but simply to Jonty.

For some of the overseas boys, a first name was much more important than the family name. My wife called me Jonty; other staff called me Jonty; wouldn't it be merely pompous to call me 'Mr Driver'? So I made the mistake of saying the boys in the IC could call me Jonty there in the house, though at the main school they should call me Mr Driver, and refer to me similarly.

Of course, especially the overseas boys forgot; so if a senior member of staff asked an IC boy where his housemaster was, he would be told "Jonty's coaching rugby on Solefields". Ann was Ann, not Mrs Driver. Of course, there were schools where staff and pupils were on first name terms – Bedales, for instance – but Sevenoaks, so go-ahead in many ways, so advanced, so experimental, was still in some ways a very formal school. To some of the more elderly and conservative staff, the IC was anyway an awkward experiment – and boys who were encouraged to be democratic in their boarding house often assumed the same freedom applied in the classroom.

There were other tensions between the main school and the IC. For instance, the selection of the overseas pupils was done mainly by the ex-housemaster of the IC, now the Under Master. While I was consulted about which English boys might make up the one-third which comprised the home-grown contingent, I was merely informed which overseas boys were coming. I thought my South African background and my Oxford experience of Commonwealth students made me rather better qualified to make those judgements than what I regarded as merely 'the school office'.

Sometimes, of course, disastrous decisions were made. There was the Arab boy, already 18 when he arrived nominally for two years to fit him for entrance to a British university; his father – who had a huge pan-Arab job across three Middle Eastern countries – was wealthy, powerful and entirely imperious. He didn't think his son would like sharing a room; after all, at home he had his own flat (and, we discovered, a staff of servants to wait on him). Well, here in the IC all boys shared rooms; each had a bunk, a desk, a lamp, some wardrobe space, and anything which didn't fit could be kept in a trunk in the box-room. In that case, said the father, he would pay for two places in the house, so his son could have more room. That wouldn't be possible, the housemaster replied. Places were at a premium; every place had been taken.

The father left and the boy stayed, though not for long. The first weekend he managed to get an 'uncle' in London to invite him to stay; he didn't come back when he was meant to. Warned about his conduct, the next weekend he took off without permission and didn't come back until Tuesday. When he did, he presented himself to the house-tutor with a request to be referred to the school-doctor. He seemed to have caught gonorrhea, he said; the weekend with an uncle had actually been with an air-hostess. Usually, I was protective of my charges, even when they erred; this time, I was glad the Headmaster and Under Master thought a mistake in admission had occurred, and the father was persuaded his son might complete his education elsewhere.

Mostly, however, the boys from overseas were a delight and the difficult job of choosing them without (generally) the chance of prior interview done very well. Certainly, some of the international boys were outstanding in one way or another, a few were intellectually brilliant, and nearly all of them interesting: Robert Bideleux from Brazil; Nolo Letele from Lesotho; Chai Chinamano from Zimbabwe; Taye Teferi and Berihu Mohammed from Ethiopia; Mosh Rewane, one of the sons of Chief Rewane of Nigeria; Johnny Cholet-Cohen from Iran; Peter Szarf, whose parents worked in Italy – but which country did he come from? Was it Sweden? Piero Carydis from Cyprus; Michael Demetriades, also from Cyprus; Harry Hadimoglou, one of the Schillizi scholars from Salonika (and perhaps the cleverest of all the clever boys we had); the Zisman brothers from Peru; Felix Ordeig from Spain; Haysam El Dalati from the Lebanon; Chris Khamis from Palestine; Robert Chew from Hong Kong, who became so much part of the family that we asked him to stand godfather to our daughter when she arrived; Keith Monserrat from East Africa; Kevin Sacco and Bill Baker from the USA; Mike Marshall from Kenya, who caused a problem by arriving with several live snakes concealed around his person. "No, you can't keep them in the IC", I told him. "You'll have to persuade the biology department to look after them for you…"

At some stage, the school seems to have lost most of the records of those days and tracking boys who were with us for only a year or two before going home is tricky, to say the least. Occasionally, one of them will turn up at a reunion, or someone will come up to me at an airport to say, "Hullo, Jonty, do you remember me?"

"Good heavens, is that really you, Felix Ordeig?" I say, if I happen to remember a name and if the years have dealt kindly with him.

Or a letter will come out of the blue. 'My family and I live in New York now; if you are ever here, do let me know and come to stay.' So I did. And here is another letter, from someone I thought might have rejected most of what I thought the IC stood for.

> It's 41 years since I left the IC and I'm not sure you remember me from then but I do think of my days there often… I learnt a great deal at the IC and think that through most of my life so far I have stood by the principles and values we tried to respect there. I've retained my radicalism and campaigning spirit, a little slowed by age – I turn 60 next year – but have also engaged with the establishment through regeneration work, always trying to reduce poverty and help those at the bottom of the heap… This has turned out to be all too serious a letter so I'll sign off by wishing you a great and joyous Christmas and New Year and by letting you know that I still think happily about my times in the IC and the support, guidance and thoughts you gave me…

One of the few boys I positively disliked in those five years, about whom I said to the Headmaster near the end of the boy's time, "It's him or me, sir. Either he goes to live with another member of staff or I shall be up on a manslaughter charge…", came up to me at a reunion at the school. I didn't (I confess) recognise him; but I noted he was a charming, intelligent man who had clearly benefited hugely from his education in the IC. Then I learned his name and was remorseful I hadn't found more to like when he was in my care.

There are others I'd like to know what happened to, but I can't track them: Wendell Jeter, for instance, who came to us from New York. He arrived several days before the beginning of term, but wasn't at all worried. He wasn't sure what subjects he would study for his A levels, nor indeed what A levels were. I can't remember now who was paying his fees; I'm not sure he knew himself. Am I right to remember his father was dead? He was a Methodist, he said, and close to a Methodist minister in New York, who seemed a surrogate parent. I'm not sure I knew the term 'laid back' then, but whenever I hear it the person who comes to mind is Wendell.

Most memorable are the details of his departure from the school. I am fairly sure he was with us for a year only, rather than the usual two years; that did take the academic pressure off him as well as off his teachers. At the end of the term, just before he was due to leave, he suddenly disappeared. A couple of his friends thought he had said something about going shopping in London.

Later that day there arrived an envoy from American Express, a retired British policeman. Had we any acquaintance with one Wendell Jeter, he asked sternly. We had. Were we aware he had obtained an American Express credit card and was making some purchases from mainly Bond Street shops? We explained he had almost no money, and was only 17. How had he got hold of an American Express card? Someone in the USA had stood surety for him, the ex-policeman explained. But – I asked – was it usual practice to issue a card to a 17 year-old? False pretences. Was he sure? Mightn't it have been a cock-up by American Express? And how had Amex found out? Oh, said W. Jeter had gone to Asprey's to order some jewelry to be delivered to the aeroplane for him to collect.

There was still no sign of Wendell. We fed the officer from Amex tea and sandwiches, and waited. As the evening turned into night, the official said he was going to summon the police. I said he was welcome to do so if he had to; while we were waiting for them to arrive, I would compose a letter to the newspapers to warn all independent school housemasters and housemistresses that Amex had issued a 17 year-old schoolboy with a credit card on what seemed a dodgy surety. In the circumstances, he agreed to wait a little longer. In fact, he had just settled down for the night in his car in the forecourt of the IC when a taxi drew up: Wendell had taken a taxi from London, rather than catch the train.

It turned out he had cashed in his airline ticket and had had a marvellous time using the money to buy things he needed: a tweed sports coat, beautiful Italian shoes, silk shirts and ties, and – when the load of parcels grew too much to carry easily – a suitcase to carry the goods in. He had used the Amex card to order another airline ticket to take him home. The visit to Asprey's for jewelry – was it for his mother? I think so – had been done on the spur of the moment, when he saw the wonderful displays in the windows. When we tried to explain that a credit card required its possessor to have the means to pay for what he or she had bought, Wendell said he knew he had 'social security' funds waiting for him in New York. He was a little shame-faced about the surety he had obtained, but he knew he would be able to set that right.

In the end, the Amex official seemed to realise that he was dealing not with a criminal nor a confidence trickster, but with an innocent. Moreover, Amex itself had issued a card to someone underage. So he would be content if the card were handed over. The jewelry wouldn't be delivered. The airline ticket ordered on the Amex card was cancelled, too.

I had already alerted the Head. Now, I had to persuade the school to pay for the boy's airline ticket, while I tried to get back the cash he had spent. Could I persuade the shops the goods were undamaged? The Head said I could have the day off school (we were close to the end of term). I dressed as I thought an indigent schoolmaster should, in an old sportscoat, grey flannels, brown shoes, took a train to London, then worked my way round various Bond Street shops.

The managers – all of whom seemed to be rather snooty young men with highfalutin accents and well-cut pin-striped suits – agreed to let me talk to them somewhere private; as soon as we were out of the actual shop, they all turned much more human, often losing their posh accents as the door closed. I explained. Could they possibly take their goods back, and give me the cash? I think there was only one slight quibble: the Italian shoes (I hadn't realized shoes could be as expensive as that). Fortunately, the soles were unmarked and, in the end, the manager gave me the cash. The last thing to be handed back was the suitcase. Of course, I couldn't get the London-Sevenoaks taxi-fare back; but I had almost covered the cost of the airline ticket which took Wendell away from us and back to the USA for someone else to care for.

He did come to see us again a couple of years later; I can't remember what he said he was doing then, but he looked prosperous.

Another very different example was Mustapha Ali Djamgoz, who came to us with a scholarship from OPOS (Opportunities for Overseas Students). The only son of a Turkish shoemaker in Nicosia, Cyprus, who had died some years before, Mustapha didn't really want to come to us at all; he wanted to go straight to university. He had already spent a year effectively out of school, serving with Turkish Cypriot militia patrolling their bits of Nicosia. He insisted, glowering, he would take his A levels in a single year. The science staff weren't keen but, in the end, by allowing him to take just two and not three A levels (maths and physics) and to attend classes with both the lower and the middle sixth, we managed to devise a workable timetable for him. Towards the end of his first term, he applied through UCCA (as it then was) and was offered a place by Imperial.

What turned Mustapha from an angry and ambitious loner into a more human boy was our eldest son, then aged three or four. One day, we found Mustapha crawling across the lawn, with Dominic on his back, laughing and urging his mount to go faster. From then on, Mustapha became a member of the family, always welcome in our kitchen, often staying with us for holidays.

The OPOS scholars were meant to return to their home countries once they had finished school; there was little for Mustapha back in Cyprus, and there was no money for his university studies. In those enlightened days, overseas students paid the same fees as British undergraduates. He found a holiday job, and somehow we scraped together from friends, relations and scholarship funds enough money to see him through Imperial. Success there helped raise scholarship money and, in due course, Mustapha became Dr Ali Djamgoz and then Professor Ali Djamgoz, an authority on the physics of eye-sight.

The problem with the English boys was that, too often and in general, they were less mature than the international boys. I didn't always please the other housemasters by trying to recruit from their houses boys who I thought would cope better with the demands of self-discipline. No sensible housemaster would want to lose a boy whom he had been watching grow up for three years and whom he had in mind to be a prefect, possibly even head of house; on the other hand, he'd be quite happy to lose a trouble-maker.

So sometimes I used almost to 'do deals' about whom I would take from the other houses: if I take him (difficult boy), would it be all right if I took him too (potentially a star)? Of course, there was a cachet attached to taking on a tricky boy and helping him make a success of his sixth form years. There were several boys who might be thought to come into that category: perhaps the most celebrated is the film-director, Paul Greengrass. As far as I remember, it was John Adams, the head of English, who persuaded me to take Paul into the I C. I can't now remember what his difficulties had been, and he certainly wasn't the easiest person to live with; but even then his creative intelligence was apparent.

❧◈

We were fortunate, too, in the staff we had. For much of our time there we had as matron Beulah Rawston-Smith, 'Rawsie' as our children knew her, and as I think the boys called her too. When the number of boys we had room for went up from 28 to 45, and the housemaster's flat was added to the building, we needed a resident matron, which Rawsie became.

A long-serving Portugese couple lived in a flat next to the garage; above them was another staff-flat, usually occupied by someone to act as extra house-tutor, which gave the resident house-tutor and me some back-up and the occasional evening off-duty. After my first few terms as housemaster the resident house-tutor was replaced by Casey McCann, who stayed on all the time I was housemaster, and longer.

It surprised me to be reminded Casey wasn't one of Kim Taylor's appointments, because he was in his way so typical of the kind of person Kim would have risked: Irish by birth, upbringing and education, and – dare I add this? – temperament too, Casey had spent a miserable time working in a London maintained school before escaping to Sevenoaks, where he quickly established himself as a very lively, constantly busy member of the staff, though – unusually in that staff room – he had absolutely no interest in games.

He was a committed member of the Labour Party, and saw no problem in becoming first treasurer and then chairman of the local party while working in an independent school – the abolition of which most members of the party would have argued for (except perhaps those wealthy enough to send their children to one of them).

That Casey was homosexual by inclination, if not in practice, was obvious I think to everyone. I have never had a problem with the fact that some of the best schoolmasters and schoolmistresses are gay. Homosexuality is no more necessarily connected to paedophilia than heterosexuality is. The problem with paedophilia is as much to do with the abuse of power as it is the abuse of sexuality. In a sense paedophilia is on the same moral plane as rape: rape isn't simply to do with sexual gratification, it is intended to humiliate the person raped. For me, what is most immoral about paedophilia is its abuse of power, of an adult over a child, of a teacher over a pupil. Of course rape and paedophilia are sexual; but they are also intrinsically associated with the abuse of power.

As far as I know, Casey's sexuality was never directed towards his pupils. There was a kind of openness about it which was, in a way, almost innocence. I suspect Casey liked danger, that he was the sort of homosexual who went in for 'rough trade': in other words, that he wanted to put himself into danger, rather than subjecting others to danger.

The manner of his death, years later, supports this view. Casey was by then Headmaster of St Paul's School in Sao Paulo, Brazil, and about to retire. At his request, I had become involved in the search to find an adequate successor for him and, eventually, the lot had fallen on one of my ex-housemasters from Wellington. After he had been appointed, he had been invited by Casey to spend some time in Sao Paulo, orientating himself to his new role, the term before Casey actually retired from Brazil to the flat he had bought for himself in Barcelona. After a week of constant shadowing, Casey had said to Rashid Bennamar he thought they probably needed a break from each other. Rashid could have the rest of the weekend to rest and recuperate. They would meet again at the school on Monday morning.

On Monday morning, Casey's driver waited for Casey to appear as early as usual to be driven to school. When he didn't arrive, the driver went in search of him and found Casey dead in an armchair, ankles and wrists bound, his mouth gagged securely. Had he been asphyxiated in the course of a sexual game? Had he died of a heart-attack? There were two whisky-glasses set out on a side-table. There had been no theft, and there was no evidence of violence. No one was ever charged with what may have been merely an accident, not a murder. No one will ever know what happened, except the person who wasn't there any more to be questioned.

I am once again way years ahead of the chronology of my story, but I needed to explain why Casey figured large in the I C. He stayed on as house-tutor after I had left, and eventually rose in the hierarchy of the school to be Under Master, and in many ways a flag-bearer of continuity in the school. He understood the imaginative originality of the school from the inside and I for one expected him to see out his career there, though others close to him thought he was becoming increasingly frustrated by being Under Master and not the Headmaster himself. All the same, what seemed like a sudden departure to become Headmaster of an international school was in some ways a surprise, though clearly his years in the I C were crucial preparation for that role. I am sad he didn't have the long and busy 'retirement' from Headmastering I have been lucky enough to enjoy.

&

One of the compromises the first housemaster of the I C had made with the boys concerned smoking. A tree-sheltered area of the garden was designated as 'the smoking-patch' and the boys had provided themselves with some derelict furniture there. Provided the boys didn't ever smoke in the house itself, the housemaster and the house-tutor wouldn't raid the smoking-patch; boys could smoke there with impunity. With hindsight, one may see that, because it was the most social place, boys who otherwise may not have smoked were encouraged to do so, just by being attracted there.

In those days, the housemaster and house-tutor themselves were smokers; most of us were. The evidence linking smoking and cancer (not to mention heart-disease) wasn't as well-known as it should have been, even then. Moreover, smoking in secret in the house itself would have been dangerous for other reasons, as the building was undoubtedly a fire-hazard, especially in the attics which had been converted into bedrooms. (When I asked the person who installed the fire-escape mechanism – a sort of sling on the end of a thick rope which got lowered to the front drive from the housemaster's flat on the fourth floor – if he would test it out, he refused point-blank, on the grounds that it was far too dangerous.)

One of the new problems which began to loom large in those years of my housemastering (1968-1973) was the ever-increasing use of cannabis ('pot' is too friendly a name for me to use happily). About the smoking of tobacco I couldn't afford to be other than libertarian: I had for years been addicted to my pipe and tobacco (Boxer B in South Africa, St Bruno Roughcut in England); when I could, I smoked Gauloises cigarettes, though more usually it was Woodbines; when I was flush, I smoked panatela cigars (the long thin sort).

However, about cannabis I was and am ignorant, although utterly illiberal. I had seen enough of what in South Africa is called *dagga* not to be easily persuaded it was non-addictive and (even taken in moderation) merely as pleasurable as alcohol. In the Cape there had been a class of deteriorated addicts known as the '*dagga*-smokers' (in fact, they were probably alcoholics as well). It was also a fact that, in South Africa, *dagga* was associated with violence, not with peacefulness. However, even if it did turn out that cannabis was peace-provoking and harmless, it was – unlike tobacco – illegal. Possession was against the law; trading in the substance was likely to result in gaol.

I think it was in my fourth year as housemaster that my wife came into our bedroom looking worried; I had already retreated to bed after a long day of teaching, games-coaching and duties, and the lights in the boys' part of the house were nominally out (the time for 'lights-out' was set by the weekly house-meeting itself, but almost impossible for anyone to enforce: if a boy wanted to go on working late, he would merely turn the lamp at his desk on, and stay up all hours. Some of the ambitious overseas boys worked as hard as the most punctilious university students in search of a First).

She had heard a noise coming from the third floor and had gone to investigate; she had found three boys smoking, leaning out of the window of their room. She had ticked them off, said she would report them to me and to the house-meeting; but then she mentioned the smoke had smelled strange.

I went to investigate. Clearly, they had paid no attention to Ann's warning – and it was at once apparent they were smoking cannabis, and were already pretty much out of their minds. I took the remains of their roll-ups, told them they were fools now in deep trouble, and sent them to bed. Next morning, I informed the Head and the Under Master what had happened; the three boys were suspended from school, and Casey and I set about finding the source of the drug.

One of the boys suspended confessed the cannabis had been given them by an overseas boy who had smuggled it into the country when he came back from home to school. We interviewed him. He was a convincing liar and, after a time, the house tutor said we should believe him to have handed the whole supply over to the smokers. For some reason I didn't believe this.

After hours of questioning, I asked him, suddenly, "Will you take Casey to where you have hidden the rest of the stuff?" Yes, he would, he said. There was a tin hidden behind the cistern in one of the upstairs bathrooms and, in it, a solid block of what I supposed to be cannabis resin.

Did we let the three smokers back into school after their suspension? I think they were about to take A levels, so we probably did. Was the supplier expelled? I think we persuaded his parents to withdraw him from the school so he wouldn't have the stigma of expulsion.

I shall return to the topic of cannabis/marijuana/*dagga*/*hashish*/the weed/pot, whatever one wants to call it, in later chapters. I think I may have smoked *dagga* myself, once, on a train from Cape Town to Johannesburg, with a crowd of young men, some of whom had just been released from what we called in South Africa a reformatory, a prison school for young offenders; I knew some of them because I had played rugby for a university team against them. One of them gave me a hand-rolled cigarette which tasted very odd; I had already drunk a good share of a bottle of vodka, and the effect of the cigarette was to make me suddenly and violently vomit, I thought out of the train window, but unfortunately it was shut, not open. The consequence of that stayed with us for the rest of the journey, and is called 'aversion therapy'. I drank no vodka for years after that, and never again tried *dagga*.

I guess the subject will go on being debated for a long time. I would not myself favour legalization, and am inclined – for good reasons, including unhappy experience close to home – to think the evidence linking early-onset schizophrenia and other mental illnesses with the protracted use of marijuana likely to be proved. However, whatever the arguments, whatever the doubts, of one thing I am certain: smoking marijuana is not a good way to revise for exams.

ॐ

One of the most enjoyable aspects of running the I C was the termly 'international evening', when the boys would help prepare a supper of their national dishes for a large number of guests, and would then talk about their home-countries. Guests might be friends from other houses, members of staff whom the boys liked especially, the occasional governor, local parents who entertained the boys over weekends and during holidays, their guardians or parents, and so on. Sometimes, the 45 boys and the five or six staff would find themselves entertaining as many guests as there were hosts. The old pots and pans of the hotel which the I C had been before the school bought the building came in useful then. I would buy large flagons of dry sherry to hand out to the guests beforehand, hoping the boys were not helping themselves too liberally behind my back.

Over the years, we heard some memorable talks: the Greek scholars telling us about their homes in Salonika (one of the boys used to carry his shoes to school so he didn't wear them out too quickly); Mosh Rewane telling the tale of his uncle coming to give away the medals at his school sports-day in Nigeria and, after he had done so, stripping off his jacket, tie and shoes, and rolling up his trousers, to show that he could jump higher than the boy who had won the school high-jump; two Cypriot boys, one Greek, one Turkish, on the tensions in Nicosia – it turned out that they had faced each other across the barricades; Nolo Letele on Lesotho; Chris Khamis on Palestine; and more.

Inevitably, it is the disasters of the meals we served which we remember better than the delicious successes. We were having curry for an Indian evening. Ann – an expert maker of curry because of her family background – had with the help of the Indian boys and Rawsie made, the day before, two huge pots of curry, one with chicken, one with vegetables. They had been put in the store-room, waiting to be re-heated.

Shortly before the guests were due to arrive, I wandered into the store-room and lifted the lids on the pots. They were bubbling away merrily. "That's odd," I said, calling Ann. "I didn't know this table was a heater." It wasn't: both pots of curry had fermented overnight. Rather than poison our guests, Emilio had to bury the curries in a flower-bed, and we used the rest of our entertainment allowance for the term buying every scrap of curry the local Indian restaurant could spare.

For the U S evening Mrs Baker, mother of Bill, had sent over recipes for peanut soup and Brunswick stew. Uncooked peanuts were hard to find, and the sort we bought broke every liquidizer we could borrow. The soup consisted of stock leavened with some milk, in which little lumps of roasted peanuts were to be found. The main ingredient of Brunswick stew seemed to be squirrel. I'm not sure what Ann used as a substitute.

And there was the famous evening when we were serving to our guests an enormous dish of Middle Eastern food; the boy carrying the dish tripped on a step as he was carrying it out from the kitchen and deposited the lot (rice, meat, vegetables, raisins, pine-nuts, spices) on the lino floor. "Quick," said Ann, "before anyone notices, shovel it back on to the dish". We served it and nobody but us knew that it had come off the floor; and fortunately nobody was ill as a result.

≫≪

I would probably have stayed longer as housemaster of the I C than the five years I did, if there hadn't been two changes of Headmaster in those years. First, Kim left and was replaced by Michael Hinton, who until then had worked in state schools, most recently as the successful Headmaster of Dover Grammar School. It should not have come as a shock to the school that, after 14 years, Kim Taylor decided to move on. We knew the course he had set for the school was so defined it would be almost impossible to deviate; and he wasn't leaving education, as he was becoming director of the Resources for Learning project funded by the Nuffield Foundation, in the process of which he wrote *Resources for Learning*, published by Penguin in 1972.

I thought he would probably go back to running a school after a year or two, and it is now known he was one of those interviewed to succeed Chevenix-Trench at Eton in 1970. It was probably a good decision Taylor didn't get the job, as what Eton needed then was someone to steady the discipline and pull the housemasters back into line, which is precisely what Michael McCrum, the man appointed, did so successfully. Still, I can't help imagining how Eton might have changed under Kim's passionate guidance.

Instead, he went to Paris to work for the OECD (principal administrator of the Centre for Educational Resources and Innovation); next, he spent five years in London with the Independent Broadcasting Authority as head of Educational Planning, and latterly he became director of the Gulbenkian Foundation. In 1976 he accepted an appointment as a governor of Sevenoaks School, keeping well clear of the Head's responsibilities, but taking an especial interest in the International Baccalaureate, of which he was an enthusiastic proponent.

The first part of his retirement was spent nursing his wife, Suzanne, through a long illness. After her death he moved from Sevenoaks to Chichester, to be nearer children and grandchildren. He lived there eight years, doing occasional stints as a door-keeper in the cathedral, writing letters in his immaculate italic script, and reading especially history, always with pencil in hand.

When Kim was 90, he came back to Sevenoaks to be the main speaker at the 50th anniversary of the founding of the I C: he spoke without referring to his notes, still as lucidly as ever. A year later, having talked to a grand-daughter over the telephone at lunch-time, arranging for her to come to tea, he settled down to read; when she arrived, she found him in his arm-chair, a book on his knees, as if asleep.

Two stories from those days at Sevenoaks may help illustrate why so many of us thought so highly of Kim, indeed, why I still regard him as being the paradigm of what a Head should be. I was talking to him one day outside his house in the middle of the school when a master came rushing up: Willie Bleyberg, a brilliant teacher of chemistry but a schoolmaster with a Teutonic sense of school rules who often spent his Saturday evenings doing the rounds of local pubs to catch day-boys breaking 'lock-up time'. He was brandishing a half-empty half-jack of whisky which he had found secreted in the wainscot of the library in the Manor House. When Kim had quietened Willie down and sent him off to dispose of the rest of the whisky in his lab, I said to Kim, "You didn't seem that worried, sir."

"Good heavens, no: a half-bottle of whisky isn't the worst thing that can happen in a school".

"What is the worst?" I asked.

The answer was instant: "Oh, bullying."

Second story: one of my charges in the I C was the captain of rugby, a superb all round games-player but (I thought) also clever enough to get to a good university, if only he would do some work. Nothing I did could persuade him, and I was under constant pressure from his teachers – they were failing to get any work out of him at all. Eventually, I asked the Head for help. "All right", he said, "Send him to me."

I tracked the boy down, took him by car to the main school and walked him to where the Headmaster was doing what he often did in the early afternoon: weeding the flower-beds. I stood the far side of the lawn while the boy went over to Kim. Kim straightened up, said something briefly, then went on weeding. The boy stood for a moment, then turned to walk back past me, saying not a word. When I next saw him, he was at his desk working. Reformation was instant – and in due course he got his A levels and a place at Oxford.

"What did you say to him?" I asked Kim a day or two later when it became clear that, whatever his words had been, they had worked a magic I had been entirely unable to muster.

"Oh," he said, "I just told him to stop being such a bloody fool, and to get down to some work."

A good rule of thumb for those put into positions of leadership in any profession is this: if you can, succeed someone who wasn't too successful. Succeeding Kim was always going to be a hard task, and very quickly it became apparent that Michael Hinton, for all his virtues and previous success as a Head, was not a good appointment. Partly, and unpleasantly, this was a matter of social class: in the main, Sevenoaks saw itself as being on its way upwards to the ranks of the really smart schools; the chairman of governors – the hereditary chairman, mark you – was Lord Sackville; Knole was the school's neighbour, and the catchment area was increasingly expensive; the day-boys (for in those days it was still a boys-only school) tended to come more and more from wealthy middle-class and upper-middle-class homes.

True, Sevenoaks wasn't as smart a school as Tonbridge; but it was beginning to attract the children of London intellectuals, not just the locals. While Hinton was a clever man, with a First in history from Oxford and a doctorate, he was clearly not smart, and it was quickly apparent his wife wasn't going to be a Sue Taylor. Essentially, he was 'grammar school', rather than 'public school'.

It was true that, until about 1983, half those entering the school at 11 were on 'County places' (that is, had their fees paid by the Kent County Council), and the school therefore still had a larger proportion of the 'middle/lower' element of the middle class than in later years. It is possible one of the reasons for the appointment of Hinton had been that Sevenoaks might have followed the example of Cranbrook School, also in Kent, which remains a maintained school (though parents of boarders there pay boarding fees). Instead, when the County places were abolished, Sevenoaks kept up its numbers by going co-educational throughout (there had been some girls taught there in previous years).

Perhaps as important in the debacle of the appointment was that Michael Hinton was a convinced evangelical Christian (in later life he was ordained as a clergyman), and he thought the school had been allowed to drift into a broad and lazy agnosticism.

I was among the last members of staff to accede to the view this had been a mistaken appointment. I thought Hinton's connections with the state sector a thoroughly good thing; but he was so clearly unsuited to his new role, and so many of the staff I liked most were opposed to every move he made, that in the end I had to shrug my shoulders and agree it would be best if he left. While he was clearly a good, kind man, he certainly seemed to lack any sense of humour.

Geoffrey Gilbert, the master in charge of woodwork – a brilliant woodworker himself – had spent years building a wonderful old-fashioned pipe-organ which had been installed in the main school hall, Johnson's Hall. Geoffrey was a small, precise and meticulous man, very good at his job. After the installation of the organ, the Headmaster stood up in front of a full school assembly to say he was sure we would all want to join him in "congratulating Mr Gilbert on the erection of his magnificent organ". I give the schoolboys credit; they swayed like a field of wheat under a passing breeze, but no laughter was heard. Three or four staff left hurriedly, coughing. I put the whole of a handkerchief into my mouth.

What actually transpired between the new Headmaster and the governors will probably be kept secret for ever; but after four terms Michael Hinton announced he would be leaving at once to take up the headship of a large comprehensive school in Weston-super-Mare. For two terms, until the appointment of a new Head, Brian Scragg as Under Master was acting Head. The Hintons' elder son had already taken his A levels and was on his way to university; the second son, David, who had a year to go, asked if he might join the I C. This he did, and coped manfully with the obvious difficulties involved, although we tried to make sure there was as little commerce between him and the acting Head as possible.

Hinton's successor was Alan Tammadge, a maths teacher by training, who had previously been Headmaster of Abingdon School. He was a more conventional appointment and, in many ways, a great success. His wife, Rosemary, was as actively charming and busy in the school as Sue Taylor had been. Two things were quickly apparent, however. First, the way Ann and I were running the I C wasn't likely to appeal to him (and looking back now I am not at all sure he wasn't right to be critical).

Secondly, I was becoming more and more doubtful I wanted to spend the rest of my career teaching in independent schools. Perhaps I should follow Hinton's example and go to work in a comprehensive school.

Tammadge made it clear he would like to appoint someone else to run the I C, but would be glad if I stayed on in the school, as an English teacher and an all-round schoolmaster; in our discussions he told me how valuable he thought I was as an English teacher. He forbore to tell me I wasn't what he wanted in a housemaster. To encourage me to leave the I C but stay in the school, he offered the family the occupancy of a lovely private house owned by the school the other side of Knole Park.

Housing was a problem. House prices in the south-east were going up very, very fast; we hadn't bought a house when we married in 1967, but had rented accommodation. If I hadn't been made a housemaster in 1968, we would then have bought a house; instead, I put some piddling sum each month into a savings account. By 1973 that had accumulated into what wasn't even enough for a deposit on a mortgage. If we wanted to buy a house we would have to move. I devised a *cv*, then worked out which areas of England still offered houses we could afford, and started to apply for jobs in comprehensive schools – but they had to be jobs at the level of a 'senior teacher', or we couldn't afford to move at all. The perks offered a housemaster – free housing, a food-allowance – made the apparently lowly salary at Sevenoaks much more than it seemed.

I forget how many times I was short-listed, and how many times the spokesman for the appointments committee kept me back to say, "Mr Driver, we were very interested in your application; and you interviewed well; but you have no experience of comprehensive schools." At that stage, the job having been offered to another applicant, all I could do was shrug and hope I hadn't missed my train back to London. There would be no point saying what I wanted to gain was precisely that experience in a comprehensive school. Once, I was actually offered a job; but it was to be head of Year 5 in a big comprehensive school in Derbyshire – and I wanted to keep my connection with the sixth form, so turned the job down.

I had just printed off a second 100 copies of my *cv* (I reckoned that showed how determined I was to find a new job) when I was offered a post in a comprehensive school, on a senior teacher's salary. By then Ann, who had imagined herself living variously in Somerset, Devon, Suffolk, Yorkshire – and I forget where else – had stopped bothering to ask even where I was going. Loyal though she was, she would have been content to stay in Sevenoaks, close to her mother and sister in Chislehurst, and with lots of friends and all-round support in the school community. I telephoned from the station to tell her I had been offered a post as director of sixth studies of a new comprehensive school.

"Where?" she asked.

"Oh, Cleethorpes. It's a lovely old Victorian town, slightly decayed, but beautiful." It was, too, at any rate as I saw it that spring day: the station overlooked the Humber estuary, and the tide had been in when I arrived. The Humber stretched broad and peacefully over towards where Hull wasn't visible, the spring-time sun shone, the air was balmy, and there were no tourists. As an immigrant from South Africa, I had no idea of its status as a music-hall joke-town; all I knew was that D H Lawrence had brought his girl there, and they had kissed (well, at least kissed, and maybe a bit more – with Lawrence it's often hard to tell) under the pier.

"Have you accepted?" she wailed down the telephone.

"Yes, I have. We shall be able to afford a decent house here."

Chapter two

Matthew Humberstone Comprehensive School

When I took Ann to see Cleethorpes, I showed her where I thought it would be sensible to buy: in the new suburbs on the edges of the town, with their small red-brick detached bungalows, each with enough space between for a single row of daffodils, a tidy, tiny lawn in front, a concrete yard and small garden behind. "I couldn't bear to live in one of those boxes," she said. So we bought a hardly habitable, indeed semi-derelict three-storey, seven-bedroomed house, formerly a boarding-house, just up from the sea-front, the end house in a terrace. It had been empty for two years and, although it had seemed cheap to us after Sevenoaks, we realized soon enough why it hadn't sold: it had been overpriced. We lived there until December 1977 and must have been among the few house-owning couples in the U K not to make money out of rocketing house-prices.

Our sons went to the local primary school. After the enlightened primary school in Sevenoaks, Thrunscoe Junior School was a tough place, not only for pupils; there was (literally) a sign on the driveway leading to the front entrance, 'No Parents Past This Point', and when my wife called on the Headmistress to offer her services, for instance in helping listen to pupils' reading, she was told the only way she could get involved in the school was by taking a qualification as a teacher and applying for a post. No, there was no parents-teachers' association; she didn't believe in them. She ran the school, as directed by the local educational authority, not the parents.

In fact, within the limitations of that kind of attitude, it was a reasonably good school of its type; and the teaching was solid enough, if hardly imaginative. Inevitably, however, our eldest, tall for his age, skinny, clever, gregarious and used to having lots of friends, but with the evidence of the effete south in his accent, quickly came up against playground bullies. He wasn't inclined to back off or back down, but wasn't very good at fighting. So, to his mother's horror, I took Dominic into the garage, spread an old blanket on the concrete, and got down on my knees in front of him.

"This is how you protect yourself," I said, picking up my fists and using forearms and elbows to protect chest, throat and chin. "You've got long arms, so you use your left fist to jab at the other boy's face: aim for the nose and the mouth, because that hurts. Jab, jab, jab…" I demonstrated. "If they try to hit back, you've got the protection of your arms. Jab, jab, jab with your left, then, when their hands go up, whack them as hard as you can with your right fist, aiming at their solar plexus or their hearts." It was a straightforward version of the skills of the boxing ring I had been taught myself at prep school.

My wife was furious, and sure what I had done was not merely immoral but dangerous. Wouldn't it be wiser for her to beard the Headmistress in her lair to complain our first-born was being bullied? "Well, if this doesn't work…" I said. However, the next evening, Dominic came back from school grinning with happiness. "It works, Dad," he said. "I had three fights in the playground, with the boys who bullied me, and I won. One of them had a nose-bleed, too."

The worst sort of bullying isn't the physical kind that happens in most school playgrounds; but often the best way of dealing with this is the old-fashioned way. If you can, thump the bully – and then make sure you don't become a bully yourself. I suppose I must be glad schools no longer teach boxing, but I do regret the basic skills of the boxing ring aren't available to everyone. I am glad I was taught to box, and I have no compunction I taught my sons the same skills; if our daughter had ever been bullied physically, I would have taught her too. I know the Queensberry rules are little use against blades or boots, or where one lad has to fight against three or four, but they have uses, even then.

I shall return more than once to the question of bullying in schools, and how one deals with it. However, a first step is to realize that bullying is a blanket term for all sorts of nasty behaviour. The one-on-one thuggery of the playground is usually a minor problem; how often have teachers broken up a fight in a playground between two boys (sometimes even between two girls), only to see them next day the best of friends?

The thuggery that involves a group's picking on an individual – because he or she is different in some way – is harder to deal with; but in my experience there aren't that many pathological bullies, and usually one may intervene early enough to make the bullying group understand what it is doing, and why it is so hurtful to the person being bullied.

The bullying of younger or smaller pupils by older or bigger ones is harder to deal with, partly because too often the bullies think they are actually enforcing some sort of benevolent social code. "We're trying to make her understand how we behave here," is a usual self-defence. Again, the forceful application of reason is generally enough to get a change in behaviour. Verbal bullying by a group – sometimes name-calling, sometimes its opposite, the 'sending to Coventry', the deliberate exclusion of the person being bullied – is even harder to deal with, but again can usually be stopped before it gets too damaging, by quick intervention and (where possible) the involvement of the person being bullied in explaining what is so hurtful about the name-calling or the exclusion.

The very occasional pathological bully – that is, the kind of bully who can't help himself being a bully, who gets some kind of perverted pleasure out of cruelty – needs dealing with swiftly and rigorously: and, in just the same way that society at large needs prisons into which criminals can be removed so that they aren't damaging to that society, so a school must be able to exclude or expel an unrepentant and unreformable bully. It doesn't solve the problem for the individual bully; he still needs help, in the same way as a criminal needs help if he is to reform – but that isn't the school's own problem. I have come across social workers who think that all exclusion, all expulsion, whatever the reason, is wrong; but I think they are just being sentimental, or haven't actually had to deal with the occasional immoral monster who does turn up in a school.

Mostly, and fortunately, most bullies in a school are merely occasional bullies, and can be made to behave decently. A properly structured school, with observant staff and sensible rules about behaviour, should be able to prevent bullying – or, when it does occur, to stop it quickly, by discussion, education and, if really necessary, punishment of the offenders.

My own way, as a Headmaster, was to gather all those involved in an incident of bullying together as a group in my office, with the staff involved there too. Quite often, some of the pupils would have to sit on the floor, or perch on the edge of tables. I'd keep them waiting for some time, while they settled and while I watched. (One small pointer at that stage would be at someone who giggled; nearly always that would be someone involved in the bullying. "Outside," I would say. "And stay there until you can control yourself.")

When any giggler had returned, I would ask, quietly, "Well, gentlemen, why do you think I've got you all together like this?" (The staff of course had been warned not to join in at that stage.) I don't remember ever having to wait that long before someone – usually a nice boy, often a possible leader in reformation – would say that someone in the group was unhappy, and (after more talk) that X or Y was being bullied. Discussion would ensue. Sometimes, someone would say that the boy being bullied brought it on himself; nearly always, unless he was a very shrewd bully, that would be said by a bully himself – and with any luck someone in the group, who knew that what was happening was wrong, would say so. I knew of course who was being bullied, and I nearly always had a fairly clear idea who the bully probably was; I could have dealt with that directly, and forcefully; but that wouldn't really have cured the problem, indeed, might have made the bullying more secretive and therefore worse.

Sometimes, though not often, a bully would at that stage own up to his offence; if he did, the problem was really not hard to sort. More likely would be a grudging admission that the group had been unkind, and

The Staff XV versus the Matthew Humberstone School 1st XV in 1977.

that everyone had a part to play in improving things. A ploy I sometimes used at that stage was to form a committee, with the nicest, morally strongest boy in the group as chairman, the boy being bullied as the secretary, and the boy I suspected as the main culprit as the treasurer. The committee was to report on the happiness of the group daily to the tutor – occasionally even to me personally, if I was sufficiently worried.

What I couldn't do – what no Head can do – was to solve problems which hadn't been reported. I have a vividly unhappy memory of two parents at Wellington saying to me they had removed their son after spending a year watching him being intolerably bullied in his boarding house. Had they told a housemaster? No. They certainly hadn't told me. Why hadn't they? They were afraid of making the situation worse, they said. Perhaps they were right to think someone should have known, and I had some harsh words to say to the housemaster afterwards. Yet to allow bullying to continue, when one knows about it, is an ultimate cowardice. Perhaps I was wrong to teach my son how to retaliate with his fists; but if that hadn't worked, if the bullying had persisted, my wife would have been in the Head's office very quickly.

ৡৈৰ

Matthew Humberstone Comprehensive School was formed by the amalgamation of an old-established but slightly weary grammar school (Clee Grammar for boys) and Beacon Hill Secondary Modern School, co-educational. It was on two sites, the junior part in the old grammar school buildings, the seniors (13-18) in the more modern buildings of the secondary modern. The fifth and the sixth forms shared a new, very plain, red-brick building, of no architectural merit whatsoever: the sixth form had a large dining room which doubled up as a work-space, a common room, lavatories for boys and girls, and I had an office opposite the front door. In all, the school was to have about 1700 pupils; my sixth form was going to number 180. There were a few girls who had been in the secondary modern school, but mainly the pupils were boys, and mainly from the grammar.

The amalgamation of the schools – effectively speaking, the closing down of an old grammar school, under its long-serving Headmaster, who was bitterly opposed to the whole idea of comprehensive schools – had caused anger and resentment especially among some of the staff of the grammar school. Although everyone had been promised the security of his or her job in the new set-up, what a number of the grammar school staff had decided to do by way of protest was to delay their resignations until the last possible moment, thus making it almost impossible for replacements to be found for the start of the new school year.

The result was that we began the academic year in 1973 17 staff short of our proper number. Many of those should have been teaching the top streams, and simply weren't there. The result was that everyone on the staff had more periods to teach than he or she should have had. For instance, I had been told I would be teaching about two-thirds of a normal timetable, to give me time for administration such as careers advice and especially for dealing with university entrance. Instead, I had a full timetable of English teaching, with barely a period off during a busy week, even though I was dealing with a large sixth form, two years of it, most of them doing three A levels, and most thinking they would go on to university or some form of higher or further education.

I had also been given, as a sort of initiation test ("Let's see how this public school laddie deals with the real world..."), one of the more difficult classes in the school: 3N, it was called, a 'bottom stream' class from the old secondary modern. It was never a very large class, never more than 20, I think. I taught the class for nearly three years and learned a great many things from it. Of the boys in the class, only one didn't spend some time away from school during those years; all the other boys were away for at least a time, one after the other, because they were having a spell in approved school – 'borstal', they called it cheerfully. A couple of them were clever boys, and I wished I could have taught them sooner; but of course the clever boys were those who tended to get into the worst scrapes, or to commit the clever crimes.

The only boy who was with me all those years without a break was one Paul Hind. He was a small, skinny boy, a shrimp essentially, not wicked, but undoubtedly ESN – 'educational sub-normal'. He had indeed been in a special unit, but was reputed to have been such a handful there that the local educational psychologist had been called in to upgrade his

IQ to just above the limit for classification as ESN – so Paul had been moved to the secondary modern. He got into trouble occasionally for sexual misbehaviour – he had been found with one of the girls – but wasn't really a bad boy at all; however, he was almost unteachable, in any normal sense.

I don't think, in nearly three years of teaching him, I had the remotest intellectual influence on him at all. I did learn how to keep him sitting still in his desk; and I discovered he loved being read aloud to. Occasionally, when I was weary of trying to do the normal kind of teaching, I would say, "Today I'm going to read to you." Paul would at once be at his desk, eyes fixed on my face, and for once silent. Best of all? Dickens. There was something about the flow of the words, their rhythms, that entranced Paul. I'm not sure how much he understood, but he listened.

Even when he wasn't entranced, even when he wanted to wander around the classroom, disrupting the work I was trying to get the others to do, he never missed a day of school. I asked his head of year why. He grinned and shrugged. "I'm not going to give you the details, Jonty, but I promise you: home is worse than school." Only twice in three years was I driven beyond patience; once, I sent him out of the classroom to see his head of year, knowing perfectly well that the result would be a caning.

Yet there was nothing else I could do. Or, rather, there was: so next time Paul went beyond my limits, I grabbed him by the shirt-front, and picked him up in the air to bang him bodily against the blackboard. The board broke, and Paul's shirt tore. "Oh, sir, look what you've done," he said, pointing at the tear. "My Mam will give me a hiding for that when I get home." At the end of the lesson, I took myself off to the head of year to confess.

"Next time", he said, "Just send him to me."

"But you'll beat him, "I replied, "and it won't do any good."

"At least I won't be charged with assault…" he answered, gently.

I often wonder what happened to Paul; one of the penalties of moving jobs as I have done, so abruptly, so diametrically I suppose I should say, is that I haven't kept in touch with ex-pupils as I might have done if I had been steadier in my profession.

I mustn't give the impression that 3N were all like Paul Hind. They weren't. A few of them were perfectly intelligent children, some of the girls especially. Two of the girls I tried very hard to persuade to stay into the sixth form; one of them was I suspected very bright, but she had had an undiagnosed cleft palate until her teens, which made everyone think she was mentally deficient because she had spoken so oddly. An operation had fixed that, but couldn't undo the years of educational neglect.

I tried and tried to persuade her at least to stay on in school long enough to take her CSEs; she would certainly have got a Grade 1 for English, and I thought she could get a good grade for A level English too. But she wouldn't; she had a brother in work, and she could get a job with him, she thought. However, one of the '3N girls' did stay into the sixth form for a year: she became quite a family friend, because she lived near us and liked taking our dog for walks. Gloria Morland, she was called; she turned out to be talented in art, and ended with a decent qualification which I hope helped her into employment.

The staff of the secondary modern school included some outstanding all-round schoolmasters; and the survivors from the grammar school staff were, in the main, equally good too. In the long run, the resignations from the grammar school helped settle the new school, and meant that good appointments could be made. It helped, too, that in both schools there was a tradition of excellence in games; it was nothing special that almost every year at least one boy from one of the schools would play football for the national schools' team. The secondary modern school had fielded a team made up of some boys and some staff in a local basketball league.

Keen games-playing continued in the new school. Football was always excellent. The grammar school had had a good cricket team, also playing in the local league, and that too continued in the comprehensive school; several of the staff were enthusiastic cricketers. In the summer, the staff would play friendly fixtures around the county. With the help of some of the other games-players on the staff, we began a rugby team, and even played a staff *vs* students match, though after I had tackled one of the students so vigorously he had to be carried off with concussion we gave up that particular activity.

One may make too much of the importance of games in a school; but part of the success of the new school in those years depended on staff – not just PE staff – prepared to give up their free time (including weekends) to coach games, to play games with the boys and girls, to umpire or referee, and to take teams away to play other schools. Seeing 'the other' outside the context of the classroom changed attitudes. It was harder for a young man to cheek an economics teacher when he knew that, in the afternoon, the same teacher would probably hit his first ball for six over long-on.

What mattered most, of course, was the quality of teaching in the classroom. In every department there was at least one excellent teacher, and in some departments more than one: all three science departments were strong, Joe Gregory in chemistry especially so; Peter Greenfield in maths; Mike Andrews in history; John Wilson in English; Keith West in economics; Tom Robinson in art; John Fraser and Jan Dann in PE. I was lucky enough to have several of them as sixth form tutors, and there was some admirable academic teaching.

We recruited some excellent teachers too; an especial friend was Trevor Millum, an English teacher with a doctorate from the University of Birmingham. The strong discipline of the secondary modern school helped keep good order in classrooms, too. The heads of year in the middle part of the school – Years 3, 4 and 5 – stayed with their years as they moved up, giving continuity which horizontal systems of pastoral care in schools often fail to provide: Euan Griffiths, Headley Atkins and Owen Roberts were the heads of year, and all fine schoolmasters.

The Headmaster – brought in from outside to try to heal some of the rifts created by the amalgamation of the schools – was an experienced administrator from Newcastle, David Johnston. He had run a big comprehensive school there, but had moved south after a divorce; he and his new wife had chosen to live (as a matter of policy) in a village outside the catchment area for the school. I liked David Johnston, I suppose partly just because he had been brave enough to appoint me, and I learned much for him in the four years I served under him.

Not everyone on the staff felt as I did: he was a tough-minded, fierce man, with bristling black hair and firm opinions. His nickname was 'the Mole', because he was thought to leave his office too seldom; and even I was quite surprised at how rapidly after the end of the school day he managed to get out of the school gates and back to his new wife in Caister. However, he gave me a great deal of support, and I was disappointed when he moved back north, though his successor, Bernard Beacroft, was admirable, too.

About the deputy head, a 'gross fat man' called Len Field, my feelings were different. Very quickly, I realized he was a bully. Almost the first thing he said to me was that I had better realize, if I had intended to come to this school to write a novel about it, I wouldn't get away with it (my third novel had been set in a school not unlike Sevenoaks). I remember thinking, immediately he made the threat, 'Now here is someone with something to hide.' I am fairly sure he was instrumental in putting me to teach 3N, thinking a failure there would show me up.

Two of the girls in 3N soon let me know about Len Field's habits. There was little sophistication to get between them and a teacher once they had learned to trust him or her. "You know, Mr Driver", they told me, "Everyone says you should never accept a lift from Mr Field, not in the front seat and never on your own. It doesn't matter whether you are a boy or a girl…"

Yet it wasn't until some thirty years later that, at last, Len Field was prosecuted for paedophilia, convicted and sent to jail where he died six months' later. How did he get away with what he did for so long? How did we – the teaching profession, and those who governed the teaching profession – let him get away with it? I did in fact try to do something about Len Field's nastiness: I mentioned to the Head the rumours about his deputy's behaviour. I remember the reply that getting rid of a member of staff was very difficult: he or she had to steal school money, be drunk on school premises, assault a pupil at school or while on duty. There was nothing we could do about Len Field unless there was some positive evidence from school itself.

As it happened, shortly after that complaint, I heard that Len Field had beaten one of my sixth formers for some offence which usually I would have been expected to deal with in my capacity as director of sixth form studies; Len made little secret of the fact that he relished beating boys. I confronted him to check the truth of what he had done. "I'm going to the Head now," I told him. "You can come with me if you want."

I suspect there had already been trouble between David Johnston and his deputy over the subject – or a similar subject – beforehand, because the Head was abrupt and direct. He told Len Field firmly that he was not in future to beat any sixth formers. Even if I hadn't won my war – because there were very few on the staff who thought like me that discipline could be maintained without the threat of caning – I had at least won my battle. From then on, Len Field didn't beat sixth formers, at any rate while I was there. I wish I had been able to keep him away from all children for always.

ॐॐ

At the same time, I must say that, on the subject of paedophilia, our culture has become often more than a little hysterical. The sort of experimental sexual exploration that children get up to with each other ("if you show me yours I'll show you mine") is not paedophilia. The next step ("If you don't show me yours, I'll thump you") is bullying, and despicable; but it isn't paedophilia. An adult who comforts a child who has fallen over in the playground and grazed a knee, by picking her up and putting her arms around her, isn't a paedophile. I remember once, when I had to expel a boy from school because he had been caught stealing, and he was heartbroken – because he couldn't understand how he had managed to do anything so foolish when he knew what the consequence would be – the only way I could think of comforting him was to put my arms around him and hug him to my chest while he wept. His parents were there in the room, and if they thought I was wicked to hug their poor malefactor of a boy suffering from what was almost certainly some form of kleptomania… well, they would have been welcome to have had me sacked. You can love a child, even a damaged child, without wanting sex with him or her.

An adult's making sexual advances to children isn't something new; what's new is the awareness of how common it has always been. When I was a boy, I became for a while an enthusiastic Boy Scout. The

60

scoutmaster was one 'Skip' Millin, who was training to be a priest at St Paul's Theological College. I think he was quite a good scoutmaster, energetic and kindly. However, it was widely known among the boys that, if you sat next to Skip round the camp-fire of an evening, he would slid his hand up your thigh to feel you up – and, if you didn't move away, more than that. Was one expected to reciprocate? I've no idea; I made sure that I never sat next to Skip, though there were boys who seemed to enjoy doing so.

I do know that Skip's proclivity was known to adults, because my father once took me aside to check that, on my visits to see my scoutmaster in his study at the Theological College (I was working towards becoming a Second Class Scout), nothing untoward happened. Being my father, being the man he was, he was deeply embarrassed to be asking. "No, Dad, of course not," I re-assured him. "If it did, I wouldn't go." I wasn't an innocent; I knew perfectly well what my father was asking about.

I lost touch with Skip when I lost interest in scouting, which I did aged 13. Years later, I heard that, after he had been ordained, he had become a chaplain on South African railways, and had there been found out for homosexual activity on trains and sent to prison.

Part of the moral problem we seem to have created for ourselves is this: we think it wrong to confuse what a person is with what he does. There are male homosexuals in teaching, and no doubt some of them are also paedophiles, that is, they would like to have sex with boys. If they don't do what they want, they are no more dangerous than heterosexuals who might like to have sex with their girl-pupils, but who wouldn't dream of putting their desires into practice. I have taught some very attractive sixth form girls; I taught and interviewed girls on their own, and never bothered to get a chaperone to supervise my teaching or interviewing.

Once only, many years ago when I was still a young Headmaster and teaching an A level literature class, I was marking a sixth form girl's essay and she came to stand behind me to see precisely what corrections I was making. When I realized that she was pressing her very beautiful breasts against my back – and I was sure knew quite well what she was doing – I stopped writing and said to her, "My dear, I think you had better go to sit the other side of the desk". She did, and nothing more needed to be said.

Yet our culture also seems to think that we should 'find fulfillment', that we should do what we are. That pretty 17 year-old girl was letting me know that she really fancied me – and (surprise, surprise) I really fancied her too. Yet, if I had acted on that fancy, I would have deserved not just to lose my job, but to be forbidden to be a teacher.

Similarly, how wrong it was, nearly all of us now maintain, that once upon a time a homosexual who went to bed with another man in the privacy of his own home should be prosecuted for doing so. Of course, if that is what you are that's what you should do. By acting out your desires you are more of a real person. Isn't repression of desire likely to lead to trauma? Yet there are times when the repression of desire is the only proper way to treat it.

As far as I am concerned, the prohibition on sexual activity between adult and child needs to be applied just as much to sexual activity between teacher and taught of any age, not just with those under the legal age of 16, and I have therefore welcomed the extension of the law to the notion of the abuse of public office. I remember once meeting a woman who was divorced from a husband who had, she told me, seemed to think it was part of his function as a teacher of sixth form girls to initiate them into the pleasures of sex.

I think she assumed that I, as a specialist teacher of sixth formers, might have behaved in the same way. She certainly wanted to know if I thought there was any justification for that view – and for her ex-husband's behaviour. No way, I told her: if I had my way, the prosecution of school-teachers who seduced their pupils, even if they were said to be grownups, would be as automatic as it is of so-called paedophiles. A teacher has power over those he or she is teaching; to persuade them into sexual activity is an abuse of that power.

Of course there are cases of teachers falling in love with their pupils, and of that love being reciprocated; some very happy marriages have been made as a consequence – but any decently moral person in that situation removes himself or herself from the power involved in the relationship before any declaration is made. A man who falls in love with a sixth former whom he is teaching should resign his post and go elsewhere until she is capable of making up her mind she wants a relationship with him.

Do I sound old-fashioned? Good. I am delighted the law seems to have taken a similarly old-fashioned position. Myself, I wish the prohibition I advocate extended to the relationship between university teachers and their undergraduate pupils.

࿐

One of the reasons for the success of the amalgamation of the grammar and the secondary modern schools was the presence of some very clever and forceful boys. I remember names like Nick Meaney, Andy Roper (who won an Open Scholarship to Trinity College, Oxford, and there got a First), Robert Ingham, Bernard Abrams, Chris Walton (son of two local Head-teachers), Mark Baker, Mark Smith, Ian Townsend, Frank Appleyard (a judge now) and Alan Buckle (who became the senior international partner in a worldwide accountancy firm).

One of the cleverest and most influential was John Simon Bowers, a QC specializing in employment law, a part-time judge and, from September 2015, Principal of Brasenose College, Oxford. John was the only son of a Jewish couple, refugees from continental Europe, who for many years ran a corner-shop in Grimsby. He was a keen member of the Labour Party, and very much in favour of the movement to comprehensive education, so disinclined to join those who regarded the closure of the grammar school as a disaster. Indeed, I don't think there were many pupils who didn't agree with John.

From someone, John heard I would be keen to get involved in the local Labour Party (under the influence of Casey McCann at Sevenoaks, I had joined the Labour Party there). I had not confessed to anyone yet that part of the reason for my enthusiasm for local Labour was the discovery Cleethorpes was in the constituency called Louth, the MP for which was Jeffrey Archer. I had friends who had been at Oxford with Archer, and from one of them, who had been a successful athlete at Oxford himself, I had learned not everything Archer said was necessarily truthful.

John Bowers came to call on me. He stood at the front door of our house on Rowston Street, just off the sea-front. "I gather you are interested in working for Labour, sir," he said. Yes, I was. "Would you rather canvass or write?" he said.

Well, I replied: I'd love to try my hand at canvassing, but I somehow think a southerner with still quite a strong South African accent might not necessarily be taken that seriously by the voters of Cleethorpes. Since I was a published poet and novelist, perhaps I'd better volunteer to write.

John grinned at me, and produced from behind his back a shoe-box full of envelopes, and a voters' list. "Good," he said. "Would you please write addresses on these envelopes?" It was thus hardly a surprise when John won an Open Scholarship to read Law at Lincoln College, Oxford, nor when he got his First.

There were more than a few clever boys in the sixth form, then and later. I keep saying 'boys' not because I am being sexist, but because I am being factual; there were a few girls in 'my' sixth form, but they had come up through the secondary modern school, and only some of those few were academic. The girls' grammar school had become part of another local comprehensive school, known as Lindsey. Both schools were fortunate in getting the full range of talent: there was no tradition of boys or girls being sent away to boarding school, and the local independent school in Grimsby was hardly a challenge intellectually. In the five years and a term I was there, only one boy was taken away from Matthew Humberstone to be sent to an independent school – and actually he would have done just as well academically if he had stayed with us as he did wherever it was he went.

Another thing I realized very quickly was this: in my first term there was a parents' evening, to talk about university entrance. The sixth form weren't required to wear uniform (a great relief after Sevenoaks, where I had been in constant disagreement about enforcing the rules, especially in the evening. The boys in the IC were allowed to wear their own clothes in the house and the garden, but if they went up to school again, for instance for their evening meal when central feeding was brought in, they had to change back into uniform.)

There was however in MHS a dress code for sixth formers: jackets and ties were obligatory. I stuck to that myself, but for the parents' evening thought I wouldn't bother, especially as it was a warm autumn evening. I went back to school early to prepare my talk; as the parents started to arrive, I realized that most of them were very smartly turned out: suits, collars and ties for the men, smart dresses for the women. There I was, in open-necked shirt and flannels. I sneaked round the back of the school-buildings to the Head's office. He was as usual in a suit. "Do you by any chance have a tie I could borrow?" I asked, sheepishly. He grinned at me as he handed over a spare tie; I had learned another lesson.

While more than some of these parents were working-class, and almost none of them (even those whom one might have called 'lower middle class') had university educations of their own, the fact their children were in a sixth form was a big step forward for the family. Most children in the area left school at 16; a good many – for instance those in 3N – left the moment they could, not bothering to stay after the Easter holiday to take the exams for the CSE or GCE (these were the days before the merging of GCE and CSE).

What jobs there were didn't require certificates or, if they did, the College of Further Education would provide the necessary qualifications on day-release. If their children could get A levels, and even better if those A levels would take them to the university or to a polytechnic or to a college … well, then, this was the big chance. The sort of clever idleness which had made teaching at Sevenoaks sometimes less than pleasurable hardly existed in Matthew Humberstone School. Not all the youngsters there were as clever as John Bowers; but there were clever pupils, and they did work – and the not so clever worked hard, too. Only once in five years did I have to call parents in to tell them that their son was wasting his time and their money: he was doing no work at all, he wasn't producing homework – they'd do better to take him away and put him in the local technical college or make him find a job. They did so without demur.

In those days, before any kind of academic league table, the most significant standard wasn't merely entry to the university, but entry to Oxford and Cambridge. John Bowers's Open Scholarship – and two other boys in that year getting offered places at Oxford if they got decent A level grades – was useful, but the new sixth form could hardly take credit. In 1976 came the real coup: that year, seven boys got places at Oxford, two of them with Open Scholarships (and both the Open Scholars got Firsts in due course). Even old Colin Shaw, the retired Headmaster who hadn't set foot in the school since the dissolution of 'his' grammar school, was magnanimous enough to come to see me in the sixth form centre to offer his congratulations.

To tell the truth, I hadn't done that much, except that I 'knew the system' and was able to give to teachers and pupils a greater confidence in their own capacity. I had been at Oxford myself, I knew some people who taught there, I knew the kind of references they liked to get, and I tried to make sure our pupils applied for the right courses and for colleges which would welcome them. What was more I knew from my Sevenoaks experience and from being at Oxford for two years that most of the boys and girls going to Oxford and Cambridge weren't Open Scholars likely to get Firsts; they were sound, intelligent youngsters likely to get 2:1 degrees if they worked reasonably hard. The old grammar school habit was to direct only the brightest of the bright towards Oxford and Cambridge; the independent schools knew the hurdles weren't necessarily as high as they seemed. It is (I suspect) still this lack of essential confidence that is a main reason maintained schools don't get their fair share of the rewards of entry to Oxford and Cambridge.

Of course, as long as there are more excellent candidates than there are places, the system will go on having some of the elements of a lottery. Tutors for admissions in the Oxford and Cambridge colleges will usually (provided they can be quoted off the record) acknowledge this: from the dozens of excellent candidates, they choose those they really want to teach – and it is hardly a surprise that those chosen do well, so well that the tutors say, "How well I chose; look at their success". But honest tutors will admit that, if they had chosen eight or ten or twelve others equally worthy from the candidates in front of them, instead of those they did actually choose, they would have had equal success.

I did work hard at university entrance – and I imposed on my sixth form tutors the same demanding stipulations about the quality of the references they wrote as had been applied to me at Sevenoaks when I wrote about the boys from the IC – and if necessary I re-wrote the tutors' drafts until they seemed to me good enough. References had to be truthful, not merely generous; I wanted our sixth form to have a reputation for the quality of the applications it submitted. The boys and girls were not allowed to fabricate personal statements that made them out to be better than they were (unlike the pupils, I knew how quickly a decent interviewer tracks down half-truths and exaggerations), and I needed to know they had done serious research about the courses and institutions they decided to apply to.

There was of course the normal load of teaching – 'normal' after the first year, at any rate: I usually taught (shared with someone else) two A level English literature sets, and one O level set, usually for two years, as well as 3N. However, at least as much of my professional energy went into trying to make sure that the sixth form curriculum included courses that would benefit and interest boys and girls who, in the old days, wouldn't have dreamed of staying for any time longer in school than the law insisted on.

I had never been keen on the notion of general studies; even the name repelled me: in my experience, the studies which were valuable were always particular, not general. The general studies A level mattered not at all to those dealing with admissions to the university, so I discouraged pupils who wanted to take it because they thought it might make their university applications look stronger. Instead, the sixth formers were offered what I called particular studies, which were either supplementary to their A level subjects (so, for instance, a girl doing physics, chemistry and biology to A level in the hope of getting to a medical school might add a course in mathematics) or complementary (a boy doing three Arts A levels might do a course in human biology).

I knew, from the experience of teaching so-called general studies literature courses at Sevenoaks that, if I wanted even clever sixth formers to treat these courses as seriously as they treated A level, an exam at the end of the course which led to a qualification would help motivation. The existence, through the local Examinations Board, of the Certificate of Extended Education (CEE) – a logical extension of the Certificate of Secondary Education (CSE) – gave this scheme at least a temporary validation. It had the added advantage of providing certificated courses for the pupils from the old secondary modern stream which gave them a goal if they joined the sixth form for a single year. The alternative for them would have been to repeat O level GCE or CSE courses which they had already tried and not done that well in.

We all put a great deal of effort into the CEE courses for the five years I was at Matthew Humberstone, though in the end the venture became a cul-de-sac when the A/S system was introduced. Properly certificated and examined, the CEE could have been an end in itself, useful both for those for whom A level was a step too far and as a way of broadening the far too narrow scope of the three A levels that were the minimal entry requirements of most universities.

We were especially lucky in a connection we made with the politics and education departments at the University of York. Because of my South African political background, I said I would be very keen to help the politics and education departments at York with some research into the feasibility of political education.

There was resistance to the idea, of course, the assumption in this country always being that all politics means party-politics, and that any attempt to provide political education in schools would be associated with left-wing conspiracies to corrupt young minds. But anti-apartheid politics couldn't be dismissed as merely left-wing, and so we were allowed to co-operate. Thus came into our lives the extraordinary personage of Haleh Afshar, a diminutive, very clever, beautiful, funny and fierce Iranian by birth (though she likes to be called 'Persian'), married to Maurice Dodson, a New Zealander who lectured in maths at York. Haleh is now Baroness Afshar, sitting firmly on the cross-benches of the House of Lords.

I had other connections with the University of York, because a friend from London, Christopher R Hill, had become the first director of the Centre for Southern African Studies. Through Haleh Afshar I met Ian Lister, Professor of Education, and was invited to talk there about the experience of moving from an independent school to a maintained.

Looking back on my career as a schoolmaster, I see those five years at Matthew Humberstone as being, in some ways, the most exciting of all. The hunger of the boys and girls to succeed, the delight they showed when they achieved university or college places, the enthusiasm of almost all my colleagues, the co-operation of parents in the education of their children, were I think unmatched in any other school I worked in. Why then did I leave when I did?

To explain that, I need to mention what was happening in my literary career. Between 1969 and 1974 I had published four novels; although they had been well received (and the first had also been published in the USA and then by Penguin), they hadn't sold well enough to make a move to full-time writing even worth fantasising about. In 1974 Bill Webb, then the literary editor of the *Guardian*, asked if I would become, with Robert Nye and Angela Carter, one of the regular reviewers of novels; each month he would send me a parcel of a dozen books, sometimes more, almost never fewer. I could choose five or six to write about, in about 1000 words. I read fast, and I enjoy reading almost all novels. The income was a useful supplement to my teacher's salary, especially as Ann didn't at that stage have a paid job.

Cyril Connolly warns in *Enemies of Promise* that the closer a job resembles the writing one should be doing, the less writing one does. Reviewing novels – which I had hoped might broaden the possibilities – meant I had less and less time for writing. Poems still turned up occasionally, and even more occasionally were published. Novels – and my desire to write them – slid away.

Reviewing for the *Guardian* did, on the other hand, mean new quasi-literary opportunities came my way. I got involved in the Lincolnshire & Humberside Arts Association, and became chairman of its Literature Panel. I was invited to serve on the Literature Panel of the Arts Council, under the chairmanship of Roy Fuller (whom I had admired as poet and novelist ever since I had read the poems he wrote about his South African wartime experiences) and David Johnston was good about giving me the occasional day off school to attend meetings.

I met Ian Hamilton, and got on well enough with him to be invited to write occasionally for *The New Review*; it helped that Ian had shared a house in Oxford with two of my old friends, Ben Bradnack (on the staff of Sevenoaks with me) and Norman Bromberger (President of the Student Representative Council at the University of Cape Town when I went there in 1958). Matthew Humberstone School sixth form began to be included on the itineraries of tours organised by the Arts Council to send writers into schools: visitors included Piers Paul Read the novelist, Danny Abse the poet, John Arden the playwright, and others less well-known.

David Johnston's generosity about giving me leave of absence did not extend to letting me join one of the Arts Council tours myself, when I was invited to do so. However, when early in 1976 I was offered a Research Fellowship in the Centre for Southern African Studies (CSAS) to enable me to write – with the blessings of his widow and children – a biography of the South African radical politician and editor, Patrick Duncan, David Johnston persuaded the governors of the school – and got permission from the LEA – to let me have the summer term as a sabbatical, on full pay.

By beginning at York at the start of the Easter holiday, and by working there until the end of the summer holiday, I managed to get almost six months clear of school-teaching. The earliness of A level exams in the summer term, and the fact that all but one member of 3N left at Easter, meant that my pupils' work didn't suffer significantly, and colleagues at MHS rallied round to cover the classes I was missing. We let our house fully furnished, which meant we could afford to rent a small graduate house on the campus at York; and the children went very happily to the local primary school in Heslington. Most importantly in terms of the quality of the eventual biography, a grant from the Leverhulme Trust enabled the CSAS to employ for two years as my research assistant Tom Lodge; it was the beginning of his considerable career as an academic. Without his work, I don't think I could have written the book at all.

For most people, the summer of 1976 is memorable mainly because the weather was blissful. Ann and the children enjoyed being on campus and in Yorkshire; we all made interesting friends, with whom we explored the countryside on bikes we had taken with us or had borrowed; when we picnicked, it was warm enough to swim in streams. I accepted invitations to give lectures in three departments: education, English and politics. I had an office in Heslington, and spent hours – indeed, days and nights – reading the materials from the Duncan papers that Tom Lodge had sorted in the University. Then, with Tom Lodge providing the solid chronological basis I needed for the biography, I settled to write, sometimes working right through the night. By mid-August I had a first draft of the book done. There was much work to do still, checking, re-writing, cutting; but the basis was there for the serious political biography I had envisaged all along.

Unfortunately, it was not the sort of book that Faber & Faber had envisaged and, when I made it clear that I wasn't going to rewrite as the editors thought I should, the firm declined to publish. In the end, it was Heinemann Educational Books which published the book in 1980.

To stay on in the university was a temptation. I was interviewed for a joint appointment in the English and education departments; in a way, not being offered the post was a relief. I think my wife and children would have liked to stay on at York, but I was by no means sure I wanted to give up school-teaching. I had in fact been offered, at about the same time, a post at North-Western University in Chicago, but had turned it down. There was no security of tenure attached, we would have to pay our own passages to the USA, no housing was on offer, and was I really that keen on the research I would have to do – and publish – if I were to make a career in the university? So it was back to Matthew Humberstone School and Cleethorpes.

While I was enjoying my work at the school, and was proud of what we were managing to achieve there, I knew I wasn't going to stay for the rest of my career. I was dumbfounded when the LEA announced it planned to bring all 16-19 education under the aegis of the College of Further Education (FE) in Grimsby. The sop offered me was the Headship of a new coeducational school for ages 11-16 in one of the middle-class villages bordering Cleethorpes. Did he not understand – I explained to a deputy director of education who had been sent to sound me out on my reaction to the plan to 'rationalise' all sixth form teaching – that I was essentially a sixth form specialist? I loved teaching boys and girls of that age, when they emerged from the often tricky years of puberty into the beginning of adulthood.

Intellectually, it was nearly always the period when youngsters grew most quickly. Good teaching then set them up for ever. Good guidance – was I not after all a 'director'? – would get them into suitable universities and colleges. And I was interested in all children, not just clever children, getting an academic education; I did not want only the clever to get A levels, while the rest were shunted off into vocational courses fitting them to be plumbers and hairdressers. I disliked the very thought of an 11-16 school because it would limit the horizons of too many children.

One of the local friends I had made was Bev Joicey, one of Her Majesty's Inspectors of Schools, with a particular interest in art. He and I had worked together on the LHA Literature Panel, and had produced an anthology of local poems and photographs. He thought I might enjoy being an HMI, and introduced me to other HMI. The job did have its attractions; it was better paid, it had a status in the teaching profession at large, it would offer the chance to see more of England than the narrow confines of a catchment area around a maintained school – and, of course, lurking in my imagination was the example of Matthew Arnold.

Nevertheless, I was also hankering for the international. Ann and I were both, in our way, strangers to England, she because of her childhood in India and her father's Indo-German background, I because of South Africa. Did we want our children to grow up thinking that England was the centre of the known universe? What about my trying for the Headship of an international school? As well as applying to be an HMI, I began to look more carefully at adverts for international schools.

Chapter three

Island School, Hong Kong

The interview for the Principalship of Island School, Hong Kong, was held in London. The short list consisted of three men who were already Heads of comprehensive schools, one who was the deputy head of a big comp in London, and me. Unusually for those times, the first day was to be a group-interview, where all five of us were to meet for a discussion with the two interviewers: the Revd Geoffrey Speak, formerly Principal of the celebrated Anglo-Chinese school in Hong Kong, St Paul's College, first Principal of Island School, and now Secretary of the English Schools Foundation in Hong Kong; and a senior civil servant, Seamus Rainbird.

The deputy head (a nice man who did in fact end up running an international school) rather handicapped himself in this competition by arriving late, even though he had less distance to travel than anyone else. However, I seemed so much junior to the other three – in terms of age as well as experience – I thought it unlikely I would get anywhere. I decided that, for the time being, I would sit back to let everyone else do the talking; it was clear the three senior men quite agreed mine was a right decision, since my occasional comments were treated by them as irrelevant.

Yet the more I heard about the school, the more interesting it seemed; and the more I heard from the experienced Heads, the less impressive they seemed. One of them, in particular – clearly someone used to protracted silence while he finished saying what he had to say – was pompous and platitudinous. Finally, after I had caught half a glance pass between the interviewers, after the p & p Head thought he had completed a discussion by saying, "What I always say is that (long pause) a comprehensive school is (long pause) nothing if it is not (long pause) a community", I decided that, on the second day of the interviews – these conducted individually – I might try to make a sprint from the back of the field, which is clearly where I had positioned myself.

I can't remember much of the detail of the second interview, but I do remember being asked why I had said so little on the first day. Was I actually interested in the job? Yes, I was. I hadn't however thought the discussion revealed much. The platitudes had rolled out, and weren't really useful in thinking about what schools were for.

The interviewers brightened, and the tone lightened. Quite soon I was asked what I thought of the other candidates – not a question one is usually asked in interview. I answered honestly: the man who was a deputy head already had done for himself by arriving late, and the other three seemed to me either hidebound by conventional attitudes or even platitudinous. The interviewers sat back in their chairs, and we began to talk about the kind of things we should have discussed the day before.

At some stage, I remember being asked – by the clergyman – if I minded a question about my own religious views. I did not, and explained that, typically for the son and grandson – indeed, great grandson too – of clergymen, I veered wildly between desperate atheism and religious observance. He said he knew exactly what I meant, and shared – even as a clergyman – the complexity of my attitudes. We also managed to talk more about Island School and the population it served, what kind of staff it managed to attract, the major problems it faced, and plans for its future.

The upshot of the second day was that, back in Cleethorpes, I had a telephone call saying I was going to be offered the job from January 1978. I didn't accept there and then, which would be my usual habit; could I please wait for the actual offer to arrive? I needed to talk to my wife and children.

A complication was that, shortly before this, I had been called to London for an interview to be one of Her Majesty's Inspectors of

Schools. Friendly HMIs I had talked to told me that, once you had got as far as interview, you were seldom turned down; but I was by no means sure I wanted to be an HMI, attractive though the position seemed. Did I really want to be sent where I was required, rather than have the power to choose? While I admired the work HMI did, I didn't think the anonymity required of the prose-style of their reports would suit me. Was I really by nature an 'inspector'? Wasn't I rather an 'activist', a doer? Shouldn't I be better running an actual school, rather than inspecting lots of schools?

In the event, I made such nonsense of the interview the decision was taken for me. Sheila Browne, formidable Chief Inspector, snapped at me, "What do you think about the education of women?" I knew the fact I had taught fewer girls than boys was a weakness in my *cv* but I knew, too, I thought the education of girls should be exactly the same as the education of boys. Unfortunately, what I said in flustered reply to what seemed essentially an adversarial question was, "I don't think much of the education of women". My interrogator closed down, and my attempts to explain what I meant sounded merely feeble.

Still, I had said I would accept a post as an HMI if I were offered it. A telephone call to the HMI office elicited clear advice: if I had been offered a job elsewhere I should accept it. Although the failure rankled, I knew it was a good decision, for the Inspectorate and for me: I would have been a hopeless inspector.

And so to Island School, Hong Kong. Why had I applied there? I used to make a facetious reply that, when I pushed a knitting needle through a globe, starting with Cleethorpes, Hong Kong was where it emerged – and to be sure Hong Kong was almost as different from Cleethorpes as anywhere could have been. Moreover, the job was well-paid, and the expatriate terms offered (free housing, an annual gratuity, biennial trips home to the UK, and so on) attractive. But I didn't apply because I wanted to go to Hong Kong or because I hoped to become wealthy; it was the school itself I liked the sound of.

Until 1967, the secondary education of those children of British expatriates who weren't shipped back to boarding schools in the UK was provided by King George V (known as KG5) in Kowloon. There were also a number of primary schools in Kowloon and on Hong Kong island itself, providing an alternative to British boarding prep schools, a German-Swiss school on the Peak, an American International school above Repulse Bay – and at some stage a Japanese school was added, and a French school, originally 'Embassy' schools, but catering for the expatriate business community too.

Sometimes British families anxious to avoid the boarding school option would use these schools, but in general KG5 was the choice of most British families, though military families had the option of the 'army school', St George's in Kowloon, and a few British families managed to find room, especially for their clever daughters, in the ferociously academic Anglo-Chinese schools.

Originally a pressure group to encourage the Hong Kong government to provide schools for the ever-increasing number of expatriate children, the English Schools Foundation (ESF) became what was essentially a local education authority to set up and manage new schools for English-speaking pupils. In 1967, what became in future years its flagship school, Island School, was established, at first in the premises of the old British military hospital above Victoria Barracks, on the Mid-Levels of the island, but then in six purpose-built inter-linked tower blocks on sloping land about the size of a football pitch, grouped around three of what in England might have been called 'quads' but in Hong Kong were called 'atriums'. The one immediately below the Principal's office window had seats on one edge under shady trees, where pupils often sat to eat their lunches. There was a small tuck-shop run by a marvelously friendly Chinese man called universally 'Greg' selling pot-noodles, burgers, sandwiches, buns, snacks and soft drinks of all kinds.

The school was intended to cater for 1400 pupils, co-educational, from ages 11 to 18; the sole entry qualification was reasonable ability in English, though in fact Chinese pupils were allowed entry only with the permission of the Education Department (and that was never given unless it could be demonstrated that the pupils had 'lost their characters', that they had been educated out of the colony for long enough to fall sufficiently far behind others of their age-group when it came to knowledge of the characters of the Chinese script).

By 1971 it was clear Geoff Speak's dual role as secretary of the ESF and Principal of the new secondary school was impossibly demanding; so a new Principal was found, leaving Geoff Speak to run the ESF. Ronald Rivers-Moore had previously run a large grammar school turned comprehensive in the south of England, and was a pleasant, competent man coming to the end of his career as a Head-teacher.

During the holidays before I took over, Ann and I were invited to spend a week with Ronald and his wife Sheila in their flat in Stanley, and enjoyed what was essentially an unexpected holiday; since the school itself was on vacation, we saw almost nothing except its buildings, and met very few staff. Ronald was a keen sailor, and ran a small business on the side selling day-boats of a particular class.

We spent a pleasant day sailing with our hosts, except I foolishly wore shorts and didn't plaster my legs with suntan oil, so spent the return flight to Heathrow trying hard to stop my trousers touching my skin.

I had discovered very little about the school. Most of what Ronald wanted to tell me was how he got into work in the mornings through the heavy traffic from Stanley to Mid-Levels. What he did was to ride a small motor-cycle. A brief survey of the traffic was enough to persuade me I wouldn't follow his example. Ronald promised a briefing document would be sent; when eventually it arrived in England it was a 20-minute tape, mainly about how to get from Stanley to the school in the mornings.

When I arrived in the school in January 1978, I discovered that Roland Rivers-Moore had left me several problems he hadn't dealt with before leaving. First was that a sixth form dance had gone badly wrong: some sixth formers had encouraged friends from English boarding schools to gate-crash what was meant to be a party for Island School only; drink had been brought, and several people had been very drunk indeed.

Sorting that was simple. At the end of the first school-assembly, I asked the sixth form to stay behind and then come forward. I perched myself on the edge of the stage to say there would be no more dances until they themselves had come up with a code of conduct for future dances. Of course, what they came up with – by the end of a week – was much tougher than anything I could have imposed by direct rule.

The other problem was worse. Some idiot had thrown a bottle into the school swimming-pool. There was a considerable drought; if we emptied the pool, we would not be allowed to refill it. The PE staff thought most of the broken glass had been swept up, but couldn't be sure. I decided a Hong Kong summer without a pool would be a worse disaster than a cut foot.

I had hardly seated myself at the desk in the Principal's office when a third problem manifested itself. My secretary told me there was an irate businessman on the line, not a parent of the school, but furiously demanding to talk to me. After I had persuaded him to stop shouting, and had explained that this was my first morning in the school, he told me he had seen a bus of European school-children, and one of them had been 'mooning' – sticking his or her naked backside out of a window as the bus went along a crowded street.

I would find out soon enough, he said, how disgusting the Chinese would consider that kind of behaviour. It was utterly appalling, and something needed to be done at once ... What kind of school did I think I was running? And so on, and so forth. A moment of inspiration made me ask him to tell me precisely where he had seen the incident: that would help identify the route of the bus. I took his telephone number and promised to let him know when I had dealt with the problem.

The school bus service – a considerable venture in a day school of nearly 1400 children on a crowded island – was run by the very active Parent-Teachers' Association (PTA). During my first visit I had met the remarkable parent who was in charge of this operation. I telephoned her. Was this one of our buses? I asked. On that route? No, she said. Much more likely to be a bus taking children to the American International School in Repulse Bay. I telephoned the Principal of that school. Oh, dear, he said: yes, one of their pupils had a problem. He would do his best to sort it out. Would he like to telephone the person who had complained? No, he wouldn't; please, would I do so? With pleasure, I said.

A fourth problem I couldn't do much about, initially at any rate. There was gossip going around the expatriate population that discipline in the school was seriously awry, and the specific rumour on which this gossip was based was that a second-year girl had gone at break-time to the top of one of the tower-blocks, and there had observed a sixth form girl fellating one of the sixth form boys.

Right from the outset, the story seemed to me so improbable, so out of character with the kind of mischief I knew sixth formers might get up to, that I had no compunction in saying it must be untrue, and very likely a deliberate attempt to damage the reputation of the school. Sixth formers might have been smoking up on the roof, but sexual misbehaviour in broad daylight, in full Far Eastern sunshine, in open view of others … no, it had to be a lie, probably a malicious lie. There was – I had already discovered – gossip about Island School; but it wasn't about sexual misbehaviour, rather it was a claim that KG5 was 'the grammar school' and Island School 'the secondary modern'. That I had previously been in a comprehensive school might have contributed to that notion.

With the help of the senior woman on the staff, a deputy head, Jane Mercer, we tracked down the name of the girl who (it was said) had observed the incident. However, she was on leave with her parents. Until she came back, we couldn't ask her anything. Denial might quell the gossip, but the salacious no doubt continued to spread the detail.

Eventually, the girl came back from leave. Jane Mercer interviewed her. Had she seen something? she enquired. No, said the girl, apparently mystified. What had happened was that she had been stopped by a sixth former from going up to the roof of one of the tower-blocks. She had seen nothing, but had mentioned to a boy in her form she had been stopped. Loftily, he had explained to her what had probably been happening.

Now the boy was interviewed, gently. Had he seen anything? No, he hadn't; nor had the girl told him she had seen anything. It was … well, not pure imagination, but impure imagination on his part; and it transpired his mother had been giving him some graphic lessons in sex education. A few days later, the same boy brought into school a vibrator; he was showing it to other pupils in his form when the form-teacher interrupted, confiscated the vibrator, and brought it to me, gingerly wrapped in some of her tissues.

I hid the vibrator in a drawer, and asked my secretary to arrange for the mother to come to see me. When she did so, I gave her the vibrator back, and suggested that perhaps some of the lessons she had been giving her son were rather too graphic for a boy of his age (he was 12). She had given him the vibrator, she explained, because he got bad migraines, and by using it against his aching forehead he gained some relief.

The vibrator went into her handbag, she left, and the rumours came to an end.

ॐॐ

In general, however, the problems in the school weren't to do with pupils or their parents, but with a multi-talented but ill-disciplined staff. Ronald Rivers-Moore was actually a rather kindly and gentle man, who had told me he didn't attempt to run staff meetings as meetings. He would merely let everyone gather in the staff-room, would sit himself down in their midst, and then allow them to raise any topic; he made no effort to chair the meeting, telling me he regarded it was a group therapy session. Before the end of my first meeting, I realised that 'blood-letting' would be a better metaphor.

"Are they always like that?" I asked Jane Mercer.

"That was peaceful," she replied.

Next day, one of the more co-operative members of staff (who had solved the problem of my refusal to ride a motor-bike in Hong Kong traffic by offering me a lift from Stanley into school each day) told me about a John Cleese training film called *Meetings Bloody Meetings*, which a friend in business had shown him. I arranged to see it for myself. The next staff meeting was held in a lecture theatre, and the sole business was this wonderful, funny, wise film, in which John Cleese is arraigned as an incompetent MD in a court run as he runs his meetings: no agenda, no minutes, regular absences and so on.

From then on, there were no staff meetings without an agenda, previously published. I chaired the meeting. When my own conduct was the subject for discussion, I handed over to the deputy head. Everyone attended (except those excused by me for what I required to be good reason). Minutes were kept. No one spoke before being asked to do so. A guillotine on discussion was enforced. No matter could be raised under AOB which took more than two minutes – or it would go on the agenda for the next meeting (if you ever want to disrupt a peaceful meeting, wait for AOB and then raise a stinker). I can't claim that peace broke out; but I hope I still have a reputation as a chairman of meetings, punctilious to the point of judicial.

Part of the problem with the staff was in fact created by the man who should have been a main ally in the establishment of good order: the long-serving deputy head, Neil Harding, a clever mathematics teacher, astute with finance, brilliant in dealing with technical problems like timetabling and, when he chose to be, charming and good company, but often abrupt and rude, especially to other members of staff, sometimes to the point of brutality.

This was despite the fact he was a practising and devoutly evangelical Christian, on the charismatic edge of the churchmanship of those times. Once I had made it privately plain to him I wasn't going to be bullied – by him or anyone – we established a *modus operandi*; he was good enough at his job to make that possible, even if we were never going to be more than colleagues.

Our relationship was complicated by the fact that Neil, his then-wife and three children lived in what was meant to be the Principal's house. Because the Rivers-Moores had brought no children with them, they had handed over the house – formerly the living quarters for the medical staff of the old military hospital – and had gone to live in a rented flat in Stanley. We liked Stanley, and made friends with several of the other inhabitants of Sea & Sky Court (rents there were cheap, and so the block had attracted several journalists and academics).

However, the flat which had sufficed the Rivers-Moores was too small for us and three children and Ronald had been right to dwell on the difficulties of commuting from Stanley to Mid-Levels. There was no way we could turf the Hardings out of their home, so we found a slightly larger flat elsewhere in Stanley. It wasn't until Neil Harding's wife left him, and two of his children moved out too, that he finally let us take over the house, and we went to live within easy walking distance of my job. Although the house, rented from the Hong Kong government by the ESF, was even more derelict than our house in Cleethorpes had been (at one stage, our eldest rigged up a drainpipe inside his bedroom to run water from the leaking ceiling to the verandah which ran round three sides of the house), it was spacious and comfortable, with high ceilings and fans in every room, and beautifully positioned just about the junction of Borrett Road and Bowen Path. Usually only the rich had houses in Hong Kong; we even had a Chinese domestic servant and her family living in the quarters behind the house.

A particular memory of an encounter with Neil Harding in my early days as Principal was my overhearing him one break-time in the staff-room being so unpleasantly unkind to another member of staff I intervened to stop the conversation and asked Neil to come at once to my office. Once the door was closed, I said to him, "Neil, you were being so horrible up there, so vituperative, that I really must ask you this: how can you call yourself a Christian and behave like that?"

"Think how much worse I would behave if I weren't a Christian," he said, turned on his heel and left the office, leaving me unable to say anything. We had very little to say to each other for several days after that. I did learn to see he was himself an unhappy man, in the throes of a marriage disintegrating. It was difficult to be a private citizen in that community.

Fortunately, one of the other tasks that Ronald Rivers-Moore had left me was the appointment of a third deputy head. After interviewing some candidates, I settled on a long-serving English teacher, Mike O'Neill, a cheerful, kindly man, happily married with two children in the school, and a delightfully ebullient wife. His influence – added to the tough-minded good sense and kindly influence of Jane Mercer – made Neil Harding's awkwardness less damaging.

Staff appointments to the ESF schools were even more complicated than staff appointments in most schools. Pensions were not provided but, at the end of each year, a substantial gratuity was paid; some staff chose to use this to build up capital or to buy property, others to keep up their teachers' pensions in the UK, though they had to pay both the employer's and the employee's contributions there, expensive but in the long run sensible (though limited to a maximum of six years).

Up to two-thirds of the staff could be on overseas contracts, that is, they would have housing provided, various allowances, and their flights in and out of the colony paid for every two years. Of those, half were allowed to have dependents, who would be included in the deal. The other one-third couldn't have dependents – which meant, in effect, they had to be single. The rest of the staff, the third one-third, so to speak, were on what were called 'local conditions'; they got no housing and none of the allowances provided for those on overseas contracts.

Because the overseas contracts were for two years at a time, but could be renewed, the balancing of the rights of staff to keep their jobs and the need of the school to have the right staff in place and in time was always a complex operation. Most staff were thoroughly co-operative: when they had decided they wanted to move to another school, or to return home, they would give notice well in advance. However, the annual advertisement in the British press always had to be a little provisional, and the actual choice of staff wasn't just a matter of choosing the best candidate.

For instance, we might be looking for a physics teacher and an English teacher. We could offer both overseas contracts – but one had to be single, and the other might have dependents. Our first choice physics teacher was married with three young children; so was our first choice English teacher. Our second choice in physics was also married with a child; our second choice in English was a single man. So, we got the physics teacher we really wanted, and the second best of the English teachers. But then the physics teacher we thought we were replacing decided he was going to withdraw his provisional resignation, so we had to turn away our first choice physics teacher and be content with our second choice English teacher.

Add to that complexity the fact that we were often selecting staff for both Island School and its off-shoot, South Island School (because numbers had grown so rapidly it had been necessary to begin a new school the term before I arrived – though for my first year the two schools shared premises). I thought the fact the ESF liked to save money by sending not both Principals but merely one to undertake the interviews in London silly penny-pinching: the choice of staff is surely a Head's most important responsibility. This process became even more complicated when, a few years later, KG5 ceased to be a 'government school' and came under the umbrella of the ESF, too.

Finding the one-third of teachers who had to be on local contracts was in some ways even trickier than the overseas appointments. In general, we relied on the wives of expatriate businessmen and civil servants to fill these roles, and the best of them were excellent teachers. Received opinion was that Chinese teachers simply wouldn't manage the discipline required; I had heard too much in South Africa of quasi-racist talk to believe it easily. The non-teaching staff were mainly local Chinese; the financial manager was a brilliantly capable Chinese woman, Vicki Leung, and the other Chinese staff long-serving and delightful. They seemed to get on well with pupils and with the teaching staff. Why should we not be able to find more Chinese teachers?

There was one Chinese teacher on the staff, teaching an introductory course of Chinese studies – and one of the best teachers of French was an Indian woman, a Sikh, Geeta Singh; she had a degree from the Sorbonne and her classes were among the most strictly disciplined in the school (in later years she taught at Yale). So I insisted we should try advertising more widely for local teachers and, when the applications came in, found several Chinese teachers who had excellent qualifications and good experience; we would interview them, I said.

My optimism was ill-founded. Quickly I began to realise that, by and large, the culture of Chinese education was based on a Confucian mode: the wise teacher sat with his disciples at his feet and gave them the knowledge they needed, and this they accepted without question, merely recording it meticulously. Western education was imbued with the Socratic mode: the teacher asked questions, and the pupils learned by trying to answer the questions, in the process of which the teacher would ask more questions, providing doubt as often as certainty.

Of course, that was a simplification; but when I interviewed a Chinese physics teacher, with a good degree from the University of Manchester, I asked him the simplest of practical questions: how would he approach the teaching of Boyle's Law (about the expansion of gases when they are heated)? Every Western teacher of physics would have a ready answer: you'd fix a lid on a tin, stand it on a Bunsen burner, and after a minute or two the air inside the tin would expand to blow the lid off – or variations of that experiment.

This pleasant young man with a good degree from a British university said he would write Boyle's Law on the blackboard and get his pupils to write it in their notebooks and learn it; very likely (I knew already) they would do that more quickly and efficiently than British pupils, because Chinese pupils learned a great deal very fast. But could he (I asked) not think of an experiment by which he could demonstrate Boyle's Law? He did try, and came up with the idea of a visit to a crowded street, to show how people when funneled through a narrow space slowed down … and so on and so forth. Yes, that was how molecules behaved under pressure, but…

So, towards the end of the interview, I asked him (and took to asking the same in other interviews, too, not simply with Chinese candidates) a question that I guess in England would get me into serious trouble. As his class is leaving the room, one of the more difficult pupils saunters at the back of the crowd, then turns to mutter, audibly, "Bloody Chinaman". What would he do? I know what I would do, instantly and quietly. My crooked forefinger would summon the miscreant back in front of my desk. "What did you call me?"

"Nothing."

"Nothing, what?"

"Nothing, sir."

"Next time you cheek me, young man, you will be in front of the Head within five minutes. Is that clear?"

Defiant stare.

"I said, is that clear?"

"Yes."

"Yes, what?"

"Yes, sir."

I know this, because I have done it, or something like it, more than once. My Chinese interviewee had his answer, too. "I wouldn't hear a remark like that".

At a later stage of my time in Hong Kong, I became a member of the association of the principals of the Anglo-Chinese schools – and how instructive that was too. Several of them became friends, and one chose to send his son to complete his education in a school I became Headmaster of back in England. I always remember a discussion at one of the meetings I attended. What did I do, asked a senior Chinese Principal, when I got an anonymous letter? I put anonymous letters straight into the waste-paper bin. Do you not investigate them? came the astonished reply. Never: straight into the bin. But what if the letter contained truthful information? Then it should have been signed. That would not do in a Chinese school. The most serious complaints were the anonymous ones.

One of the major problems of Island School was that the funding we got from government via the ESF was based, as in the Anglo-Chinese schools, on the number of classes we had, and a class was defined as being anything up to 45 pupils. Part of the reason for the original founding of the ESF had been classes in KG5 of 44 and 45. The Education Department had come up with some valiant research to show that the results of large classes were just as good as the results of smaller classes; but of course that depended on largely passive classes absorbing information and then regurgitating it, not on classes asking tricky questions and deducing their own conclusions from experiments, as the so-called Nuffield technology now encouraged, especially in the sciences and maths. So I found myself in the somewhat unusual situation for a Headmaster of trying to keep class-sizes down by limiting the intake into the school.

I hated the fact I was not allowed to accept Chinese pupils without the specific permission of the Education Department; it smacked too much of the kind of rules I had so loathed in my home-country. However, the rules weren't essentially racist. We did have Chinese pupils in the school, making up about 8% of the school-population. The requirement was that they should have been educated out of the colony for long enough to make it hard for them to catch up with what they would have missed in their Chinese or Anglo-Chinese schools. I did occasionally suspect that wealthier Chinese families who wanted their children educated in a 'Western' school but who didn't want to send them off to board in the USA, Australia, Canada, Switzerland or the UK sent them away for a term or a year, then brought them back so as to circumvent the Department of Education.

Of course, when they came back and into Island School, they tended to stay, as did the children of other local families – 'local' as opposed to 'expatriate', who tended to be on shorter term contracts. This meant that the other most stable component in the school-population than the Chinese were the children of Indian families. Many of the British – 'British from Britain' we used to call them – were in the school only as long as their parents' contracts, and often they were on two year contracts.

That meant, as well as the normal turnover of any school (a whole class 'graduating' – to use the useful Americanism – at the end of seven years), there was what we reckoned to be an annual turnover of about 25%, of children leaving and arriving. Most Americans tended to go to the American International School in Repulse Bay, but we tended to get the children of those I thought of as the 'dissident Americans'. We had slightly more girls than boys (the percentage was 52-48) for the obvious reason that British families were more inclined to send their sons away to board than their daughters. We lost a few boys aged 13 who were put in for the Common Entrance exam for the 'public schools' in the UK; but we firmly avoided teaching 'for' Common Entrance, and I made no secret of the fact that I thought 13 too young for boarding school. Sixteen was a more sensible age – but we were skilled at getting children into universities in the UK, and worked hard to gear ourselves better for the requirements of universities in the USA. So why not keep the children in what was clearly an excellent school until they were 18?

Technically, we were a comprehensive school, in that we were required to accept any English-speaking pupils from our catchment area who couldn't go to a Chinese-language or Anglo-Chinese schools. In fact, Island School was more like a direct-grant school in a rich British suburb, and one of the major changes during my time as Principal moved the school closer to that model, in that the rules were changed so that the ESF could supplement the fixed grant which it got from government with fees charged to parents. This enabled all ESF schools to limit class-size to a maximum of 30.

Some of the most interesting decisions of my time at Island School were about admissions. A Swedish sea-captain arrived one morning with his 12 year-old daughter in tow. Please would I accept his daughter into my school, of which he had heard excellent reports? He had been posted to Hong Kong, and had brought his daughter – but not his wife – with him. She looked a charming lass, sweetly smiling as she sat opposite my desk, next to her adoring father. I asked her a question, she looked at him for approval, and he answered for her. "Please," I said, "You are going to have to let me talk to her, because I need to know how much English she has."

I spoke to the girl again. "Are you enjoying being in Hong Kong?" I asked.

"Yes," she replied, brightly.

"How old are you?" I asked.

"Yes."

"I'm afraid that is all I have been able to teach her so far," her father said.

Carefully, and as sympathetically as I could, I explained that I simply couldn't take a child into the school who had no English. All our classes were in English. We had no specialist EFL class. Our classes were large and full, and the possibility of individual attention for a child who had no English very limited indeed.

"I do understand," said the sea-captain. "But, please, could you tell me, where do you think I may send her to school? There is no Swedish school here."

Hearing in my head already what some of the more union-minded teachers would say to me when they discovered I had accepted into the school a child who had, literally, only one word of English, I swallowed and said I would take her. Within a term she was fluent in English; within two terms she was top of her class in virtually every subject. When, after two years, she and her father came to see me to say his company was moving him elsewhere and she had to go too, they were both in tears. I began then to wish I had a small boarding house attached to Island School into which we could shepherd children for the sake of their education.

Of course, not all admissions were as fortunate as that. I learned to be careful about boys brought back from their public schools in the UK at odd stages of their schooling, and learned that, as often as not, 'He wasn't happy boarding' meant 'He got expelled for indiscipline'. Sometimes, I had no choice but to accept them; but more than once their stay was short. I remember one of them who managed, within a week of arrival, to steal a dumper-truck from a local building-site and drive it into the school car-park, wrecking two cars belonging to members of staff. Day-school we might be but our pupils were required to work and to behave. Out of order was out of order, even in what was in many ways a very liberal institution.

One of the worst admissions I ever made was of two girls, not from English boarding-school but transferred from another school in Hong Kong. They were the daughters of a senior civil servant who had died suddenly; their mother was staying on in Hong Kong, and wanted her daughters not to have to commute from the island to Kowloon-side for school. They seemed intelligent, attractive, though clearly somewhat wayward girls, and at a stage of their schooling where shifting schools and exam-syllabuses was not that easy, for them or their teachers; but it became clear their father had been very senior indeed, though quite what his actual role had been was mysterious. I guessed he was probably one of the China-watchers for the British government, or perhaps MI6 or SIS or similar.

Soon after their arrival, I had a deputation from the head girl (appointed by me) and the chairman of the student council (elected by the students). They thought I should know that cannabis was being brought into school and sold to various students. I had already begun to hear gossip to this effect, but this was the first real evidence. I explained how difficult it was to do anything on the basis of rumour or even suspicion.

"Wait a minute," said Sunil Nanda. Within ten minutes he was back, and handed over a solid lump of cannabis resin. I remember being quite surprised at its bulk: four or five inches long and an inch wide, an inch deep, wrapped in silver foil. He had taken it from another student, who had admitted buying it from the sisters whom I had recently taken on. I summoned their mother, and then the girls. I had no alternative but to suspend them from school, I explained, and I thought myself it might be sensible if she was to remove them from the school before I took the next step, which was to inform the police.

The girls had told her, the mother said, they hadn't brought the cannabis into school; they hadn't sold it to anyone. She knew her daughters better than I did; they never lied to her. If they said they hadn't done it, they hadn't.

But they had; by then I had interviewed the boys they sold the cannabis to, and I knew how much the transaction had cost. What's more, I had the stuff in my desk. Pretty well the whole school knew by now. There was no doubt of their guilt; and actually their lying was making dealing with the problem worse, for them and for the school.

I telephoned the police. Would they please send someone to school to collect the cannabis? I didn't like being in possession of an illegal drug. A policeman came, and the cannabis went. I talked to the officials of the ESF, and to my chairman of governors; when they heard the family name, they were suddenly less available to help (in fact, the chairman of governors resigned soon afterwards, perhaps for unconnected reasons). I called the chairman of the PTA, a tough-minded American woman, Nan Robertson, already an ally. She was absolutely on side: the girls had to go. Their lying made that even more necessary. There was no remorse, no compunction, merely obdurancy.

There came a telephone call from the Director of Education. He would like to see me to discuss the problem. No, he didn't want me to come to him, and he didn't want to come to the school. He knew the family concerned well, and was surprised the girls were in trouble; they were always so helpful and charming. Could we meet somewhere more private, perhaps in my home? So we fixed a quiet meeting at home between the secretary of the ESF, the Director of Education, Nan Robertson and myself. At that stage, the Director of Education was still Alex Reeve, a good man, and himself an ex-Headmaster; but in this meeting he was entirely a civil servant, looking for what he thought was a compromise, but what to me looked like a capitulation.

Nan Robertson understood; eventually the secretary of the ESF seemed to; and finally the years the Director of Education had spent in schools made him see why I couldn't possibly have back in the school two girls who would not admit they had done what everyone in the school knew they had. If they had been contrite, I might have had some room for manoeuvre. If they had admitted their fault, if they had told the truth, I might have found some intermediate way of dealing with them, given the family's recent bereavement. But their lying made it impossible, unless we were prepared to undermine the whole discipline of the school.

The girls never came back to the school. Did they in the end tell their mother what they had done? Did she realise they must be lying? I think I must have written a formal letter at some stage actually expelling them, but perhaps that wasn't necessary. What would I have done if I had been told by those who were my employers that I had to re-admit them to the school? I would have resigned, of course, although I had already made it clear I would not have gone quietly.

Oddly enough, years later, at Wellington, I faced something of the same problem, with a Chinese boy from Hong Kong. He was caught shop-lifting in Reading; there was no question he hadn't been shop-lifting, because not only were the goods in his possession outside the shop but there was a CCTV video of his pocketing the goods before leaving without paying. No, he hadn't shop-lifted, he said. We showed him the video. No, that wasn't him. But it was.

I tried to explain to him: don't you understand that, by lying, you are blocking all the exits? I can't deal with this by getting your guardian to pay for the goods, and your apologising, and promising never to do it again, and the shop-keeper deciding to be kind to a foreign boy... No, it wasn't him, he maintained. I showed his guardian, actually his aunt, the video; I asked her if she couldn't get him at least to admit his guilt. He is a very stubborn boy, she told me. So stubborn, I told her, that I was going to have to expel him: not for shop-lifting, though that was enough on its own to merit expulsion – but for persistent lying. Mr Driver, she told me, I don't think you understand how important 'face' is to us Chinese.

In a way, I did understand, I think, because I had learned by then how much the British hate being what they call 'embarrassed', which is really not that different from 'losing face'. Indeed, one of my private theories was that one of the reasons the Chinese and the British got on relatively well together was that they understood 'face' from the inside. There was also the underlying assumption both Chinese and British had: they knew, secretly, that they were the best, but they also quite admired the other for thinking that, actually, they were the best.

⤜⤐

One of the considerable strengths of Island School was the quality of the care given to individual pupils. It was unusual in day-schools in having opted for a vertical system of pastoral care, rather than a horizontal one: that is, all pupils were, on arrival, allocated to a form, which was part of a 'house', in which they would stay for the whole of their time in the school, cared for by form-tutors in the first place, but under the general supervision of a house-mistress and house-master throughout their time in the school.

The intellectual homogeneity of the school-population – because, despite the claims that Island School was a 'comprehensive', the pupils were almost without exception intelligent children from homes which cared about education – was a contrast with the racial and international heterogeneity; this meant that, in a good many subjects, so-called 'mixed ability' teaching was perfectly feasible (though we did find it possible to set the pupils – to separate them into groups according to their abilities – for maths and for modern languages).

There was work to be done to improve the teaching. There were some exceptionally gifted children in the school; they needed not more teaching, but more imaginative teaching. We were given some 'BBC' computers, and set up what I think was the first computer classroom in Hong Kong. An expansion of the library, and the appointment of a librarian, helped. There were a few children who struggled; they too needed special help. There was some pressure to amend the curriculum, for instance to shift to the International Baccalaureate; while in many ways I preferred the range of the IB to the narrowness of O and A levels, the fact that so many of especially the 'British from Britain' pupils would be going back to schools which taught not for the IB but for A and O levels made us decide to stick to the conventional.

We did however need to take account of the fact that more and more pupils – and not just Americans – wanted to go to colleges and universities in the USA. In theory, the system of entry to US colleges and universities was based not on what the entrants knew, but on a broader vision of their intellectual capabilities. In practice, of course, it is almost impossible entirely to separate how well pupils think from how much they know; and of course it helps to know as much as one can about how the tests work before one takes them. The entry to US universities depended on performance in Scholastic Aptitude Tests (SATs), though now the word 'aptitude' has been changed to the more honest 'assessment'; the theory was that the tests showed not so much what a student knew, but what his or her capacity to learn was – 'aptitude' for study.

For years at Sevenoaks, and again at Matthew Humberstone School, I had taught pupils how to get through the Use of English exam, required by some universities to show that pupils could use English well enough to cope with the linguistic requirements of degree-level study. The difficulty of finding people to mark the exam had seen the introduction of multiple choice examinations (not only in Use of English, of course). It was a puzzle that some of the best pupils, capable of top grades in normal exams which required – for instance – four essay-type answers in three hours, suddenly crashed when they faced multiple choice questions.

I set myself to do the exam in this format and quickly spotted the problem: the kind of teaching I did – the sort of teaching I had been taught to think the best – required the pupils to use their imaginations, not to give the answers which the examiners were looking for: to look for the odd angles, the divergent possibilities, the delightful alternatives to the conventional. That was how teachers and examiners could spot star quality; that was what turned a competent B or C grade into an A (these days, when grades are so obviously inflated, the star quality is shown with an actual * attached to the A).

In multiple choice questions, the imaginative answer is not required. The machine marking the paper wants the only answer; the right answer is the one which the examiner wants. Most multiple choice questions actually have as a deliberate trap an answer that is clever but wrong. So, when pupils looked at, say, four possible answers to a question, they needed to ask themselves, which answer is the examiner going to think is the right one? Once pupils were prepared to work in that way, they got the rewards. The SATs were essentially no different, though they seemed very sophisticated.

The decision by the Thatcher government to start charging overseas students full fees rather than the fees charged to 'home' students exacerbated the problem. Now, boys and girls who might automatically have hoped to go to a British university looked instead to the USA, Canada or Australia. When the children of expatriate British families applied to British universities, if they didn't have the wealth to pay 'overseas' fees, they had to demonstrate that they were 'home' students, not always easy to do if your parents didn't own a house in the UK and pay rates on it, or if you didn't have co-operative grandparents to provide a 'home' address. For those pupils who had no hope of proving they were 'home' students, universities in the USA or Australia or Canada became more attractive: fees were often high, but it was more customary for students to work part-time to support themselves – and there were many more scholarships available than there seemed to be in the UK.

What I found particularly distressing was that, under the new dispensation, I myself would not have been able to go to Oxford at all. As it was, I had struggled to find the money for fees and maintenance; under the new rules, I could not have hoped for those two years at Oxford. So, when I was asked quietly by the Hong Kong Secretary for Education if, when I was on a visit to London to interview, I might call on William Waldegrave, then Secretary of State for Higher Education in the British government, I did so more than willingly.

There was no chance, I realised, of getting a change of policy: Thatcherite economic policies were too much in the ascendant for that; however, one could ask for understanding of the particular problems of (first) the children of expatriates living and working in Hong King and (secondly) the genuinely overseas students who would be deterred from applying to British universities. One realised full well that the British tax-payer might feel aggrieved about subsidizing the children of enormously oil-rich Arabs; but what about the clever Malaysian boy whose subsidised years at Imperial College made him forever inclined to trust British standards?

Did my visit have any effect? William Waldegrave was courteous and charming, and clearly understood the case I was making. I think the problems of the marginal 'home' student did get eased; but in the long run the UK in my view lost some of the influence that once upon a time its universities had exerted overseas.

In part, of course, it was the consequence of parochial ignorance. I have never forgotten helping a clever Japanese boy get an offer from an Oxford college to read for a degree in engineering. The grades offered were easily within his grasp; he would, I was certain, get a First at Oxford, as well as a Blue for tennis (he was one of the best young tennis-players in Hong Kong). Unbeknown to me, he had also applied to Caltech in the USA, which also offered him a place and (I think) a scholarship. In some distress, because Peter knew my predilection for Oxford, he came to say he had decided to go to Caltech. I had to write to the College to explain. Back came a surprised letter: very few people turned down such easy offers – and what was Caltech? I couldn't reply to say the fact an Oxford don had to ask what the California Institute of Technology was might just possibly be a reason Peter had not chosen Oxford.

Still, whatever the universities and the examiners lacked in the way of imagination, the vision of education I wanted to nurture placed imagination at its centre. An unused space at the bottom of one of the tower blocks became a studio theatre; while the school had a tradition of an excellent annual production, what I wanted was more school plays, and more children involved. Too many 'school plays' became showcases for a few talented children (and rather too often in my view for members of staff thwarted in their desire to be seen as performers of note); the ideal would be always to have a play in rehearsal and another in production. We didn't ever quite manage that; but the studio theatre enriched a good many lives.

Remarkable was the fact that, of all the schools I have ever been in, as pupil, as teacher, administrator, governor, there was less bullying of any kind in Island School. In part, the quality of pastoral care was responsible for that; but the cause ran deeper, I think. I began to understand that actually there was so little bullying because there was nothing like a social norm against which some pupils could judge others' behaviour.

Newcomers had to be welcomed, because pretty soon you might be a newcomer yourself. Exclusion from the group simply wasn't an option, because the group was so fluid. Name-calling wasn't going to happen when there were so many odd and peculiar names already (I have recently been reminded by a friend there were two sisters in the school whose surname was O'Hara. No, they were Burmese). In my five years and two terms at Island School, I remember only one case of bullying: an Indian girl in her second year in the school discovered that, if she kicked a boy hard in the crutch, he would be in pain. The boys were too embarrassed to complain – and (as we found out after one boy was kicked so hard he had to be taken to hospital) the girl herself was so innocent of any knowledge of anatomy she had no idea why her tormenting of boys was successful. Explanation was required rather than punishment.

The two problems I learned to dread most were anorexia and school-refusal: both seemed like problems for the school, but were in fact almost entirely problems at home brought into school. Often, the school would be the first place where the anorexia would be noticed (in my experience, something which afflicted girls – I know anorexia is not unknown among boys, but I never came across it). Often, women members of the PE staff would bring a girl's dangerous skinniness to the attention of the house-staff.

Parents would be summoned. "It's not really a problem," we would be told. "She is very fussy about her food." We were fortunate that one of the parents was a psychiatrist: Dr Bill Green, the father of seven children, most of whom went through Island School, and one of the sanest doctors I have ever known. When I got really worried about some girl, I would quietly telephone him for advice – and often parents would be happier to accept advice from another parent than they would accept formal referral to a doctor.

Sometimes, of course, the family problem would be so deep-seated it went beyond anything we could manage. Once, when we had failed to persuade a particularly complicated family their daughter was dangerously ill, I found myself having to suspend her from school. The grounds I gave were that I was not prepared to take responsibility for her dying at school. It still took the family another ten days before they managed to get the girl to see Bill Green. He told me that by the time he got her into hospital she was in renal failure: her ankles had been thicker than her thighs, he said, and her back matted in thick hair.

School-refusal was less dangerous physically, but equally intractable – and I had little help in dealing with it. "He is refusing to come to school," a parent would say. "There must be something wrong with your school".

"We have more than 1300 pupils who come happily to this school each day," I would answer. "They don't find anything wrong." How could I tell them the truth? That, in my experience, children who refused to come to school did so because they were terrified that, when they returned home in the evening, there might not be a home for them to return to. Truancy usually meant a problem at school; school-refusal invariably meant a problem at home.

In general, however, the parents of Island School were a delight to deal with. The PTA was a hugely supportive body, first under the chairmanship of Nan Robertson, then under Claire Clydesdale; first one, then the other, moved from running the PTA to chairing the governing council. Both of them were, as it happened, citizens of the USA. I did not like the American International School any more than they did, and had a monumental row with its Principal over the behaviour of two of his boys.

We discovered that one of our Indian girls was being regularly waylaid on her way home by two boys from the International School; their teasing took the form of pretending to lift her skirt. She was desperately shy and very frightened. Eventually, I got from other children the names of the American boys, and telephoned their school to ask for action.

Oh, I was told, we aren't responsible for discipline outside the school-gates. Well, in that case, give me the boys' addresses, or their parents' telephone numbers. Oh, we can't do that. Very well, then, I replied, I shall get the police to escort our girl home after school, and I will hope to have your boys arrested and charged. By the way, the editor of the *South China Morning Post* is on my governing council. Co-operation improved, and I was able to warn the parents of the American boys what would happen if they came anywhere near one of our girls again.

One of the useful practical contributions Island School parents made was manning a First Aid room. There was a constant rota of capable women always there to deal with the minor injuries liable to happen in a big school with cement playgrounds and lots of stairs – and able to pick up the telephone to call a parent to come to collect a child who had insisted on coming to school that day despite feeling nauseous or headachey. In charge of the First Aid room for most of my time at the school was the redoubtable Joan Zirinsky, an Irish Jew originally, who had married in Shanghai a White Russian called Victor Zirinsky, whose family had fled Moscow for Vladivostock, then Vladivostock for Shangahi, then Shanghai for Hong Kong.

Joan had inherited from her father (he had only daughters) the almost sacred post of washing the Jewish dead before their funerals. She knew more secrets than anyone I have ever met, and she kept them to herself, unless there was a danger. It must have been from her I first heard the gossip about cannabis coming into the school; almost every day I would do a quiet wander round the school, and whenever Joan was in the First Aid room I would find myself there, to make sure all was well in the school. When it wasn't, Joan would know.

It was Joan who alerted me to the fact that a fifth form girl was coming into the First Aid room every morning, saying she felt sick. Might it be what one would suspect? It turned out that the girl's parents had gone on leave, leaving her at home alone; every night she had taken to inviting some boys to visit her parents' flat, and they were drinking. Her sickness was because of the alcohol. In England one might have asked social services to have the girl taken into care. In Hong Kong I knew the company the father worked for; a telephone call to the managing director got the father back from leave very sharply indeed. He was furious with me; there was – he said - an amah looking after his daughter. So I told him about the morning sickness, and what we had at first suspected. Collapse of indignant parent...

In some ways, Hong Kong was for the Driver family socially a kind of upside down mirror of what Cleethorpes had been. I realised that very early on. At the end of my second term, the A level exams were in full swing; one of the invigilators slipped out of the exam hall to summon me to look at a sixth form boy who was clearly having a crisis of some kind: he had been sitting at his exam desk for more than an hour, and had not written a word. It was a two-and-a-half hour exam; I knelt down next to the boy to say to him, "Look, old chap, don't worry; if you can, try to get something down on paper, because that way we can explain to the examiners. But a blank paper won't help…" There was no response; he didn't move, nor did he pick up his pen.

I went back to my office and rang the boy's home. No, his mother wasn't there; she was back in England, and his father was looking after him. I telephoned the father's office; he was boss of a major Hong Kong operation. After some protracted argument, I got hold of this man's PA. He couldn't possibly speak to me, she said; he was busy in an important meeting. Busy he may be, I said as quietly as I could: but this is the Principal of Island School, and I think the son of your boss is having a nervous breakdown, and if his father is not here in half an hour to collect his boy at the end of the exam there will be trouble of a kind you cannot begin to think of. You interrupt your boss's meeting to tell him that, or I shall not answer for the consequences.

The poor boy was collected; next thing we heard was that he was back in the UK, and in a mental hospital. Apparently there was a history of mental illness in the family; the mother was herself often in hospital.

A few months later there came a letter from The Duke of Edinburgh's private secretary. He thought I should know that an ex-pupil of mine – he named the boy – had written an obviously deranged letter to The Duke saying various things about what I was up to. It turned out he had also written to Mrs Shirley Williams, then Secretary of State for Education; she had referred the letter – which she and her Education Department took literally – to the Director of Education in Hong Kong, and they and he wanted to know the truth: was I 'practising thought control on my pupils', which the writer of the letter had asserted? Yes, I was, I said: every morning I stood in front of 1300 children in our assembly hall and I expected them to be silent. Was that what he meant by 'thought-control'?

Common-sense rode to my rescue, especially as the poor deranged boy had amalgamated my authoritative person with a speaker who had come to the school the term before my arrival. Shirley Williams was informed that the pupils of Island School had nothing to fear from alien forces invading their minds with evil thoughts.

There was a sequel. A year or two later there came another letter from the same boy. He was returning to Hong Kong, he told me, and was proposing to take over as Principal of Island School. He named a date for his arrival, and advised me to have cleared out of my office by then. In high humour, I showed the letter to Dr Bill Green. "It's not funny, Jonty", he said. "This is serious stuff. If this madman comes to Hong Kong, he might well try to get rid of you." Apparently, a warning was issued to the Immigration Department that this was one British citizen who should not get through passport control.

There was one other moment of high drama quite early in our stay (we were then still living in Stanley). The school had been running a series of talks in assembly on religions of the world. We had already had a group of evangelical Christians talking, then a Jewish speaker, then a pupil whose mother who was an advocate of the Baha-i faith, and the next day two Muslim pupils, a girl and a boy, were going to talk about Islam. I was looking forward to their talk, because they were both highly intelligent pupils from an extended family I was fond of.

Late in the afternoon, my secretary put through to me someone who after a few moments I realized was purporting to speak (somewhat incoherently) for a radical Islamic group. They had heard, he asserted, that the speakers in assembly were going to unfurl a portrait of the Prophet. I knew enough about Islam to realise that would be regarded as a ghastly blasphemy. Of course it wasn't going to happen, I said; he was talking nonsense. However, the man on the other end of the telephone went on to say that my family and I would be killed if the assembly went ahead and that the school would be bombed. I treated the call as I would any nuisance call, and put the 'phone down.

As it happened, on my way home that evening I had been invited to a diplomatic cocktail party, given I think by the Japanese Consul-General, who was a parent of a pupil in the school. I had been to enough of these parties already to know that most conversations there were impossible for someone as tall as me: rather small men and women would stand necessarily close in front of me to address their remarks vaguely upwards – and I could hear every conversation in the room except the one I was meant to hear.

In self-defence, therefore, there was nearly always a corner of the large room where a group of tall men would congregate. I saw the group with relief, and worked my way across to them. One of them I had already met several times at parties like this; he was the very tall Chief of Police, and we enjoyed our face to face conversations. "Oh, I'm very pleased to see you," I said. "I had a hilarious telephone call today from some idiot saying he was speaking for a mad Islamic group."

The policeman suddenly stopped smiling. "What did he say?" he asked. I told him.

It turned out the police had had a series of warnings that a group of radical Moslems – Shi-ites, were they? I think so – were planning a coup of some kind in the colony. By the time I got home that evening, there was an armed guard of policemen outside our flat, and they stayed all night; when I got into school next morning the whole school was being held in the road outside while the police scoured the premises in search of explosives. Eventually, staff and pupils were allowed in, but the police told me I would have to cancel the assembly. No way, I said: we are going ahead as planned. There will be a talk on Islam by two very good Moslem pupils, who have gone to a great deal of trouble to prepare what they want to say. After more discussion, we were allowed to go ahead as planned, except that, in every alcove of the assembly hall – which included a large gallery - stood a policeman armed with a sub-machine gun. I think it was the quietest assembly I ever knew in any school, not even a single cough.

The teaching staff of Island School were, in the main, excellent, and a few outstanding. The nature of Hong Kong itself, its proximity to China, the richness of the mix of a great international city, tended to attract teachers who had 'oomph'. When we interviewed potential teachers in London, we tried to be careful not to appoint people whose first ambition was to travel; the people we wanted were those interested in teaching in a first-rate international school based in an exciting city. Of course, there were possibilities of travel, at any rate in the holidays. The staff we appointed had to be fit and well, and we required medical clearance; so we tended to attract applications from younger staff. We interviewed very few people who applied in the belief it might be fun to work somewhere warm and sunny for the last part of their careers.

The so-called 'teachers' action' of the late 1970s promoted by some of the teaching unions had an effect, though not as damaging as it was to many maintained schools in the UK. A few of the staff were members of the NAS/UWT (as it was then still called), and thought that therefore they too should 'take action' by withdrawing from all extra-curricular activity. I was still, as it happened, a member of the NAS/UWT myself, and it was clear there was no requirement on people working abroad to take action.

Our pay and conditions in Hong Kong were very little to do with those in the UK. Despite my union membership, I thought the teachers' action almost entirely foolish, and desperately damaging to the profession. It wasn't action at all, it was inaction – and by giving up on all extra-curricular activity relationships between staff and pupils were damaged, in some ways irreparably.

However, since only a handful of Island School staff seemed to think they should follow the bad example of their colleagues at home, I could pretend to be equable. Most out-of-school activities continued; what had been a delightful canoeing club operating on Saturday mornings out at Deep Water Bay was discontinued – much to my disappointment, since my sons and I had been enthusiastically involved ourselves.

The staff representatives on the governing body decided they should withdraw their labour, which seemed to me entirely satisfactory, as I disliked having staff representatives at Council meetings; I did not enjoy having to be secretary of the Council myself, as I thought I should be its servant, not its voice. Still, I made sure I was always on the side of the majority in Council, if matters ever came to a vote, which they hardly ever did. Most staff who had given up time to running extra-curricular activities continued to do so, and gradually the whole 'teachers' action' petered out, in Hong Kong at any rate.

I wish I could say the same of what happened in the UK, where I share the view of commentators like the late Chris Woodhead, sometime Senior Chief Inspector, that the teachers' action did probably more damage to relationships in schools than anything else in that period. Certainly, when I went back to Matthew Humberstone School from Island School, I was dismayed to find that many of the activities that had made the school seem such a special place in my time had been discontinued.

Clubs and societies had died. There was no staff-student team playing in the local basketball league. There were no school plays – my 'leaving present' to the school had been to produce, with the A level English sets, in a week, a Shakespeare play: a cut version of Henry IV i. There were no longer any school cricket teams. Even school football had ended. If boys and girls wanted to play games out of their PE lessons, they had to join local clubs – and inevitably that meant boys and girls whose parents weren't themselves involved in local activities had less incentive to get involved. I remember asking a young PE teacher at MHS, whom I recalled as an enthusiastic coach of all sorts of games, "But what do you do on Saturdays now?"

"Oh, I run a market stall; it supplements my income nicely."

Perhaps it did; but that was one of the reasons a school which had been so proud of its record of sending pupils to Oxford and Cambridge ended up in 'special measures'.

That, fortunately, didn't happen at Island School. Indeed, the extra-curricular side flourished. One of my happiest memories of those years is of going in 1979 with an Island School rugby team on a tour of South Korea. It might well have been a disaster, as while we were waiting for our flight at Kai-Tak airport the news came through that the President of Korea, President Park Chung-hee, had been assassinated. After some delay and a telephone call or two, we decided we could risk going after all; it was a ghastly thing to have happened, but it didn't seem to be the start of a revolution.

When we arrived in Seoul, we discovered that the declaration of a period of national mourning meant all public events had been cancelled: this included the three matches against various youth teams that we had scheduled. So we turned our tour into a training-camp in the national stadium, aided by four members of the Korean national team and the national coach.

We visited the countryside, we ate Korean meals, we met a number of Korean dignitaries; and, on the last day, we quietly played a match, 14 a side, 20 boys, four Korean internationals (good enough players and nice enough men to moderate their physical strength to take account of the schoolboys) and four members of staff, including me: the last game of rugby I ever played, and one of the happiest, not least because the dry surface and the dust were such a reminder of my home-country.

෨ஃ

Given the kind of the population the school served, remembering what a success the Saturday morning classes for parents and pupils at Sevenoaks had been and how useful the WEA classes at Matthew Humberstone, and conscious that for part of each day, most weekends and every holiday, the school buildings were unused, I decided it would be worthwhile trying to set up some sort of night school to cater mainly for adult members of the international community. What I thought would be a simple matter turned into an administrative quagmire: a night school would have to be a separate institution, registered with the Education Department, with a 'manager' and all sorts of rules and regulations.

Still, the enthusiasm of people like Nan Robertson and Claire Clydesdale made me persevere, and in due time we set up the Island School Evening Institute with me as the manager (effectively the chairman) and a member of staff, the head of the economics department, Richard Abrahall, as principal. A brochure was published, offering a range of courses, some utilitarian, some artistic, some intellectual; people signing up for courses were warned that, if there weren't enough takers, a course wouldn't happen. Teachers (some Island School staff-members, but mostly volunteers from outside the school) were to be paid, and there were course-fees (though, since the school didn't charge rent for the use of our premises, these weren't huge). At one stage of its history, there were more people enrolled in Evening Institute courses than there were pupils in the school – and I think it gave the reputation of the school a considerable fillip.

Another of the innovations of those years was what we called 'mini-sabbaticals'. I admired greatly the fact that Australian schools were generous about allowing teaching staff regular sabbaticals, usually as study-leave. Knowing that, every seven years or so, they would be offered a term's sabbatical encouraged Australian teachers to stay in their posts, rather than to seek promotion in other schools. Given the nature of our contracts, there was no way the ESF would be able to do something as apparently profligate as that. However, I instituted what I called mini-sabbaticals, whereby for a year a member of a particular department would be given four periods a week 'off' teaching so that he or she could do some form of research.

I remember as particularly successful some research done by the very able maths department. Acting on what I think was initially a hunch, two members of the department looked at how well the top sets knew the four main mathematical functions: addition, subtraction, multiplication and division. They discovered a significant proportion of these clever children didn't actually know how to do long division. Instead, they did their dividing by a process of intelligent approximation, the accuracy of which they checked by multiplication.

The researchers then extended the scope of the study to discover that these were pupils who had moved schools at the stage where long division was being taught. When they started in their new schools it was assumed that they had already learned long division. They hadn't; but they were clever and so worked out a strategy to make up for the lack of technique. This had an obvious bearing on why the not-so-clever pupils might struggle. Given the nature of our school population, one dared not assume that 'the basics' had always been covered.

I need to record three changes in my own life which happened during these years, one bodily, one spiritual, and one imaginative.

Aged 38, I took up distance running and gave up smoking, and nearly a year later, at Eastertide 1979, I ran the Hong Kong marathon, a full 26.2 mile course, finishing somewhere near the end of the field in just under four hours. Nature did not intend me to be a distance runner, as I am very tall and big-boned; but the solitary self-discipline of long slow distance running suits my temperament – and if I hadn't got fit and stopped smoking I would probably have died at roughly the same age as my father did: 52. Thirty-eight years later, I am still addicted to that form of exercise, even if now I have downgraded my description of it from 'running' to 'jogging', and will no doubt soon have to call it 'shuffling', as I am regularly overtaken by fast walkers, even when I think I am sprinting.

Round about the same time as I started running, Ann and I began going regularly to church again. Ann had been brought up a Roman Catholic but was happy to go to Anglican services. I had too many reservations about too much to be entirely happy in a Catholic service – but the longer we lived on the edge of China the clearer it became that we were both Christians in something of the same way that our Jewish friends were Jews. It wasn't really a choice: we both came to recognise that we were Christians whether or not we wanted to be. Our way of seeing the world was Christian. It wasn't simply a matter of belief, or even of faith; it was what we were, whether we liked it or not.

For instance, Ann was by now working as an occupational therapist for the Hong Kong Spastics Association, helping design homes in such a way that people with cerebral palsy could live independently, and trying to persuade businesses that the physical handicaps of cerebral palsy did not make 'spastics' unemployable. Talking to a Chinese social worker about one of the children she was concerned with, Ann mentioned her worry the child seemed to be very bruised; yes, her spasticity made her clumsy and liable to fall, but the bruises were worse than that alone would explain. Was she perhaps being beaten by someone in her family?

What you don't understand, Mrs Driver, the social worker explained, is that for us Chinese these damaged children are a punishment; something the family did in a previous time, a previous existence, has brought misfortune on the family. This child brings nothing to the family, indeed is merely a drain on the family's resources, its well-being.

You don't need to believe in the miracles of the New Testament, nor in the Virgin Birth, nor even in a supernatural God, to find yourself returning to a belief in the value of individual lives; it was embedded in every fibre of our moral imagination.

Of course, this was more than merely 'the religion of our tribe'. A good many of the great English hymns I could sing without bothering to open the hymnal; the Book of Common Prayer was as familiar as my mother's face; my knowledge of the Old and New Testaments from countless divinity lessons and church services had been supplemented by my having read through the whole bible from beginning to end, twice, while I was locked up in solitary confinement in South Africa. When the congregation stood up to say "We believe...", that was what 'we' did believe; how trivial the small voice of the "I" seemed in that context. "We believe, although actually I don't..." The poor forked individual was subsumed in the larger collective, and the broad church of Anglicanism seemed to make room for doubters, even for agnostics and atheists.

The other change which happened wasn't really a change at all, but more like a recurrence. I had never been a productive poet: if I finished two poems in a year I would be pleased. Before we came to Hong Kong, and indeed when we first lived there, I had begun to think I might not write poems again. Although I had forced myself to finish the novel I had been working on before we left England, it wasn't entirely a surprise when Faber & Faber rejected it; and I seemed to lack all desire to write any more novels.

What brought poetry back from my imagination I am still not sure of. Was it there all the time and just needed heat and dust to tease it back to life? Sometimes it seemed simply that I was living again in a hot climate, where for all the differences of the Far East the smells, sounds and tastes were often like those of my childhood.

I had thought, too, that my interest in character – in the variety of humanity – could find its expression only in novels; but suddenly – and for me rapidly – I wrote twenty-four 'Hong Kong Portraits', some of real people, some of imaginary, which were then broadcast on the local radio station, RTHK. I had also been reading (in translation) as much Chinese poetry as I could find, and had realized that for centuries Chinese rulers had been using exile as a weapon against writers they disapproved of. Exile was a constant presence and a perpetual threat in Chinese poetry.

107

One word against the system and even a poet might be sent away to live 'in the water-margins'. That became the title of my next book of poems after Hong Kong Portraits.

ॐ॰॰

It had been my restlessness which had driven us to move from Cleethorpes to Hong Kong; it was Ann's desire to have 'one dear perpetual place' for the family that took us back to England after five and a half years in the Far East.

In many ways, I would have liked to stay longer in Hong Kong or to have gone on working in international schools, of which there were more and more, all over the world. The relative smallness of what I think one has to call the 'ruling class' of the colony – the city-state – meant we knew lots of people outside the always rather narrow confines of school-teaching. Our point of view was still a semi-derelict house, but it was a house. Ann saw much more of the real Hong Kong than I did, because she regularly visited the massive housing estates in the new territories and learned to speak Cantonese, but we both enjoyed the range of our friendships and acquaintances.

It was also the first time in my life that I hadn't needed to worry about money. We could afford holidays in China, on Bali, on a house-boat in Kashmir, in a hotel on the Malaysian coast; we could go regularly for family meals in restaurants; and if I wanted to waste money buying a Ralph Lauren tie or a multi-coloured shirt from Lane Crawford I could.

Ann was right, however. Our children needed to go back to England, and to finish their education in English schools. Using the need to catch up on what was happening in English education as an excuse, I extended into another week a week in London to interview potential staff for the ESF.

I arranged to talk to the Headmaster of a big London comprehensive school but was depressed to find him unwilling to see me on school-premises. I went to Rugby School to see Brian Rees, who had moved there from Charterhouse after the death of his first wife; that too was a depressing experience, first because the pupils I asked to direct me to the Head's house were so off-hand as to seem thoroughly rude, and then because Brian himself was clearly on his way to the breakdown which saw him resign from the school not very long afterwards.

I went to see Charles Martin, an old friend from Sevenoaks now running one of the maintained grammar schools that was part of the King Edward's School empire in Birmingham. He was in the middle of the 'teachers' action' that left him and a deputy in sole charge of the school except during actual lesson-times. I went to stay with a friend who taught in the education department of the University of Bristol; Fred Inglis was a doughty left-winger who sent his daughters to a local comp. When the elder girl came back at lunch-time, I offered her some of what I was planning to eat.

"Oh, I haven't got time for lunch," she told me. "I've got classes."

"But you were at school this morning, weren't you?"

"I go to school in the morning for my social education, and to private tuition in the afternoon for my academic education," she explained, with innocent honesty.

That evening, I asked Fred what the private tuition cost. He was friend enough to tell me: it cost him pretty well as much as day-fees in an independent school.

I went to Somerset to stay with Robert and Elinor Birley; Robert was more than anyone my mentor in education. He had been delighted to be knighted 'for services to education overseas', even though he had been Headmaster of both Charterhouse and Eton, and three times chairman of the Headmasters' Conference. Although he was confined to what turned out to be his death-bed, his mind seemed as fine as ever. I did not confess to him how depressing I was finding my recent experiences of education in England.

My last visit was to Canford School, near Poole. The Headmaster was Martin Marriott, who had invited me to visit him in England after he himself had arrived, unannounced, at Island School one morning. I was used to public school Headmasters and Headmistresses turning up in Hong Kong; occasionally I would be invited to a cocktail party in a hotel or at the Hong Kong Club to meet one or the other of them, and I had become cynical that all of them claimed merely to be visiting their ex-pupils, or fund-raising, never trying to recruit pupils.

To a couple of them who had dared to offer places to Island School pupils without asking for a reference beforehand I had written cross letters. Martin Marriott on the other hand was straightforwardly honest with me: he'd come because he wanted to recruit a few more pupils, had heard that Island School was a good place, and thought it might be worthwhile making my acquaintance.

When I told him about a colleague of his in an English boarding school who had unwisely taken a pupil of mine only to find that the boy was entirely unsuitable, which I would have told him quickly enough if he had asked for a reference, Martin suggested I should apply to become an overseas member of Headmasters' Conference (HMC). That way I might be able to prevent poaching; there might be other benefits too.

The visit to Canford made me realize that there were independent schools thoroughly worth considering. Not only was it extraordinarily beautiful in the springtime of the English countryside, it seemed to cater for a wider range of pupils than I had expected. I had already been warned, in London and elsewhere, that applicants to local education authorities (LEAs) from abroad tended to get short shrift. Letters to LEAs in Yorkshire and the West Country making polite enquiries about possible Headships, even of schools much smaller and less complex than Island School, had not even been answered. I remember asking Martin Marriott, bluntly and perhaps impertinently, whether he thought Headmastering of an independent school was a job worth doing. His answer, carefully considered, was a main reason in my decision to include some independent school Headships in my next round of applications.

Back in Hong Kong, I began looking carefully at adverts in the *Times Educational Supplement*. I applied to a few more comprehensive schools in places where I thought Ann and the family might be happy to be settled, explaining in my covering letter that, if I were called for interview, I would of course expect to pay my own airfare. Answers came there none. Applications to a European international school and three independent schools in England resulted in my being at once called for interview at all the schools.

The first to interview me was Berkhamsted School – then still for boys only. I liked the town, I liked the look of the school, and I liked the man who showed me round the school, the Second Master, Peter Gibbs. The Headmaster, John Spencer, was still recovering from a major heart operation, but gave me a good hour of his time, too.

I confess to enjoying being interviewed. There is, in almost all teachers, some element of the performer and being interviewed for a job one actually wants usually puts an edge on that performance. I had seen and liked the school, and had had time to find out something about it and about the governing body. The chairman was Sir Kenneth Cork, sometime Lord Mayor of London, an accountant, boss of a firm called Cork Gulley, nicknamed 'the undertaker' because he and his firm specialised in winding up companies in trouble.

The main financial governor at that stage was Anthony Tuke, not then knighted as he was a few years later, a Wykehamist of formidable intelligence, one of whose jobs was as chairman of Barclays Bank. The other governors included Colin Bertram, a Cambridge academic, and the Warden of All Souls' College, Oxford, which had an old connection with the school. The others were the usual mixture of local council members, old boys and old girls of both the boys' school and the girls' school, country solicitors, estate agents and successful businessmen.

As far as I remember, there were six of us gathered together for interview; one man I quickly decided I didn't like, simply because he looked a bit like Mussolini. The others were charming people, all of them working in good schools: Radley, Rugby, and so on, and it is an interesting commentary on that group that all of us ended up as Headmasters, somewhere or the other. We used occasionally to get together at HMC conferences to compare notes on our careers.

With so many people to interview, it was a very long day, especially as, after the last interview, the governors seemed to take such a time to come to a decision; and I shall be for ever grateful to the man who was then the Second Master at Radley, afterwards the Headmaster of the King's School, Worcester, for entertaining us during that long wait with a hilarious and indiscreet account of the TV filming of Radley which had happened earlier that year.

Eventually, the treasurer of the two schools, Colonel Jeremy Day, appeared and asked me to come back to the interview room. There, I was offered the job, and at once accepted. Kenneth Cork said, firmly, that the decision had been unanimous; the length of time the discussion had taken made it apparent it couldn't have been, and this was confirmed a while later when Anthony Tuke resigned.

He had apparently been deeply worried the appointment of a South African revolutionary would bring the school out on to the streets in protest against Barclays Bank and its policies in South Africa. I had known he was the chairman of Barclays and, when he asked me a slightly awkward question about my attitudes, I had taken the risk of teasing him a little in my reply. "For instance," I said, by way of explanation, "When I was asked to give up my account with Barclays, I refused..."

Kenneth Cork interrupted: "Are you aware," he said, "that Mr Tuke is involved in Barclays?"

"Of course," I replied. "I do my homework."

What I hadn't been aware of was that Anthony Tuke, for all his abilities, wasn't exactly a popular chairman of the finance committee. The others on the committee found it demeaning that, when he was chairing their meetings, he used to do the *Times* crossword with his left hand as he worked down the agenda with his right. I should report, for historical accuracy, that I got to know Tony Tuke a little better at a later stage of my career, and we got on perfectly well; I suppose by then he had realised that my revolutionary days were past.

I had one other bit of luck in that interview. Colin Bertram asked me what I thought the best form of motivation was. It was not a question I was expecting, but the answer came at once: "Oh, praise," I said. "Every time..." He grinned happily at me: "do you know the school motto? *Virtus laudata crescit...*"

Out of the depths of my Latin teaching at school and university there slid a translation: 'a pat on the back does wonders'. In the next few years, I got to know Colin better, and he told me that was the moment when he decided I was the man he wanted.

Something else I have never forgotten was Kenneth Cork's wisdom in making sure the decision seemed unanimous, when clearly it wasn't.

In future years, when I was involved in appointing Headmasters or Headmistresses, either as a governor myself or as a consultant to governors, I used to insist that, however fierce the debate, however close the decision, once the choice was made there had to be another vote, and it had to be unanimous – or, if it couldn't be, anyone not prepared to be unanimous needed to resign forthwith. The new appointment has to believe he or she has the backing of all the governors.

The unhappiest governing body I was ever involved in was one where there had been a fierce tussle between two rival groups of governors over the appointment of a new Headmaster. The group which lost – only just lost, apparently – never forgot their disappointment and, whenever anything went wrong in the school, there would be muttering about the mistake. If it had been a mistake – and I don't think it had been – those who thought so should have had the grace to resign. Responsibility for the big decisions has to be collective.

In some ways, I was sad to give up a career in international schools, and even sadder a return to a state-school in England seemed impossible. Having moved from being a housemaster at Sevenoaks to being a senior teacher in a comprehensive school, I thought a return from running a big international school, in one sense comprehensive, and funded mainly by government, to a local comprehensive school would be seen as acceptable. Clearly, it wasn't. No LEA was interested enough to reply to my letters, even though I had explained I would happily pay my own travelling expenses from Hong Kong in order to be interviewed.

I had seen enough of schools elsewhere in the world to realise how limiting and (often enough) plainly cockeyed is the view held by some British people (particularly 'on the left') that the division between independent and maintained schools is the root cause of the class-system, and not merely a symptom. When I suggested to British friends that, if they were really serious about getting rid of class, they'd need to start by imposing 100% death duties or by giving the state the ownership of all housing, they treated me as if I were mad instead of merely provocative.

Of course, the private ownership of one's housing – even notional ownership, with a bank or building society holding a mortgage – is deeply part of the British historical psyche, left-leaning as well as right. It becomes almost comforting to pretend that, by abolishing the independent schools, we would be able to get rid of class-distinction in a generation. We know perfectly well we aren't going to do anything so expensive – and, actually, when one asks the British people in surveys and opinion-polls, most of them admit that, if they could afford independent schooling for their young, they would choose it.

Sometimes, I have an unworthy suspicion the British actually rather like their class-system, and think it is better than elsewhere. One hears the pride in the defensive use of the terms: "working-class, and all the better for that", "middle-class and proud of it", "well, actually, I suppose upper-middle, but rather on the poor side..." and so on. When one points to other countries which haven't got independent schools but do still seem to have social classes, one is given patient explanations of how insidious the British system is. So one points to Australia, reputedly less class-bound than most Western cultures, and explains that, there, a quarter of all children go to independent schools. Ah, but Australia is different...

I find especially dispiriting a view that, until the wealthy upper- and middle-classes in the UK are forced to put their children into maintained rather than private schools, insufficient attention will be given to improving the former. Only 7% of the school population is in independent schools; do the other 93% not have parents and grandparents to care about their schooling? And, if they don't, why don't they?

I know there is much disputing about the extent to which the grammar schools actually provided more social mobility; and I know too the greatest failure of implementation of the 1944 Education Act was that the 'technical schools' – which so enriched German education – hardly happened at all in this country; but the range, the variety, of the secondary schools available was surely good for the society, and for intellectuals like Tony Judt the grammar school system provided the way to fulfilment of intrinsic capability. Would it not have been better if the United Kingdom had followed for instance the Australian model, and provided funds for all schools, those fully state-controlled and almost all independent schools too, but giving more funds to those schools which charged lower fees, or no fees at all?

The fact of the matter was that, in the UK in the 1960s and 1970s (and later too), there were some good schools and some bad schools, and a great range of quality between. What mattered was to make the not so good schools more like the good schools. Looking back on my career, I sometimes wish I had been lucky enough – and brave enough – to persuade an LEA to let me take on a rundown state school and to turn it into a school as good as – shall I say? – Sevenoaks. Instead, I went in another direction.

ॐॐॐ

One last story about Island School, Hong Kong: after I had announced my impending departure, the editor of the *South China Morning Post* (known as the *SCMP*) sent a journalist to interview me for a social column which she wrote. She happened to be Chinese, though her English seemed perfect. We had an interesting chat, during which I told her a story.

I had, as usual, been queuing for my lunch at the small canteen on one of the concrete playgrounds. I made it a rule that I always joined the back of the queue, and took my turn; often, I would get into interesting conversations with children whom I hadn't met in any other context. On this occasion, the queue was quite long. Two boys ahead of me, one of whom I had recently dealt with for misbehaviour of some trivial kind, hadn't noticed me.

"He's a bastard," the first boy asserted. His friend agreed. Then the first boy added, reflectively, "But fair".

"Yes," said his friend: "a bastard, but fair".

For once, I crept away without getting any lunch. Almost every schoolmaster in England knows the wonderful description of a certain Headmaster as 'a beast, but a just beast'. I told this (perhaps a little self-aggrandizing) story to the Chinese journalist.

The editor of the *SCMP* arrived a little late at the governors' meeting the next night, clutching a press-cutting. "Look at what I've just 'pulled' from the proof-copy of tomorrow's edition," he crowed. It was a story about the fact that the Principal of Island School was leaving. The headline? 'End of term for a Fair Bastard'.

Chapter four

Berkhamsted School

I hope it will not give a wrong impression if I say that my six years as Headmaster of Berkhamsted were the easiest of my professional career. It was however not a simple place, and grasping the complexity of the institution took a while. What local people called "the boys' school" or sometimes "the grammar" was actually divided into three: a prep school (80+ boys from five to ten) with its own premises and its own Headmaster, a junior school (200+ boys from ages ten to thirteen) sharing the campus of the main school, also with its own Headmaster, and then a senior school (440+ boys from 13-18), of which I was directly the Headmaster, though I also had oversight of the prep and junior schools. Total numbers (725, plus or minus) were a little more than half the number of pupils I had been in charge of at Island School.

What I wasn't was Headmaster of the girls' school; it was a slightly smaller school, in two sections, with its own Headmistress, on a separate campus, a third of a mile away, but the other side of the town-centre. There had been a move to amalgamate the boys' and the girls' schools a few years beforehand, but it had foundered, partly for financial reasons, partly because of the ferocious opposition of the staff of the girls' school. Roger Young, who had amalgamated a boys' school and a girls' school in Edinburgh, had been brought in as consultant, but his report and recommendations had been shelved. However, there was a consolidated governing body, and a treasurer who looked after the finances of both schools, a delightfully courteous retired soldier, Colonel Jeremy Day (as it transpired, an Old Wellingtonian).

There was a junior boarding house for boys (St John's, about 45 boys) and two senior boarding houses for boys (Incents and School House, each housing about 50 boys). Once upon a time, it had been more of a boarding school than it was when I got there, but the boarding ethos still dominated the arrangements of the boys' school. For instance, there were lessons on Saturday mornings, there was Chapel on Sundays, and the Headmaster lived in a house on campus – indeed, all three Headmasters and the Headmistress had houses provided by the school. I had made it clear to the governors in interview I would very much want the boarding side of the school to flourish – and the fact that more than one of my pupils from Island School transferred as boarders to Berkhamsted gave earnest of that intention.

Back in England on leave after my appointment but before I started work there, Ann and I had spent a few days staying in Wilson House, the Head's residence in the middle of the school, with John Spencer, my predecessor, and his wife, Brenda. He provided me with a photograph of the whole staff, assembled for his farewell. Carefully, I cut each face out and glued it to a card, and then gradually added to the card a surname, a first name, a subject, and whatever details I had gleaned. I hadn't had that recourse when I went to Island School, and now became very glad of it.

The other thing John Spencer provided was a lump sum in cash in the school accounts. "By the way," he told me, "when you look at the bank balance, you will see that I have managed to save up a bit of cash for you to spend." I can't now remember precisely how much it was, but it was tens of thousands, perhaps as much as £175,000 – in those days a substantial sum. Most Heads inherit overdrafts.

Of course, there was a downside of this munificence. John Spencer had been the Head of a north country grammar school before his appointment to Berkhamsted, and had there been his own bursar. He retained the habits of frugality and control he had learned in a tougher environment. A few weeks after my arrival in the school there appeared in my study a large and irascible head of department. "How on earth do you expect me to run a department without paper?" he demanded.

"Why don't you order some?"

"You know I can't; and the bursar says I can't have any…"

"Surely you have a budget?"

"No, I don't."

I discovered there were no departmental budgets at all. Everything – down to the supply of pens and paper – was centralised. Even quite minor expenditure required the Head's signature – and he signed nothing without an interview and explanation.

Quickly I realised something very basic about Berkhamsted School: this was a fine stallion, marvellously muscled, but he had forgotten how to run. The reins had been held so tight the school thought standing still was the only mode. All I had to do was to let go of the reins, and give the place a gentle nudge in its ribs.

Part of the reason for there not being that much work for the Head to do was that most of the recruitment of pupils was done by either Phil Bailey, the Head of the prep department or by George Pitman, the Head of the junior school. Very few day boys came into the school at 13, so I could thus concentrate on recruiting pupils for the senior boarding houses. My Far Eastern connections meant we always had a few Hong Kong boys anxious to join us. We developed a strong link with Malaysia and, later, through an admirable organization called the Commonwealth Linking Trust, with India. The school already had several African boys, and keeping and strengthening those links was a joy to me.

One of my favourite recruits was a large Nigerian, Adinbola Adediran ("but you can call me Peter, sir"), one of the sons of a former Chief Justice of Nigeria. Adinbola called Peter happened to be a black belt in judo; early on in his stay at the school he was set upon by a gang of local yobs, who thought it might be fun to beat up a black boy from 'the grammar'. Adinbola deposited them, one after the other, over a convenient wall; the result was that small boys from the school, whenever they were threatened, had only to turn their heads to yell, "Peter, help," for the attackers to fade away.

Since Adinbola could also run 100 metres in swift time, I had hoped he might become a deadly weapon for our 1st XV; however, he was actually such a gentleman he would rather have handed the rugby ball to someone in front of him than to run over him on the way to the try-line.

The two senior boarding housemasters were John Davison in School House and David Pearce in Incents (named after Dean Incents of St Paul's, who had founded the school in 1541). They were both English teachers (David was head of department), had both served the school for many years, and were, quite simply, among the great schoolmasters of my acquaintance: intelligent, compassionate, intellectually rigorous, although without any of the arrogance that sometimes accompanies rigour, energetic and good-humoured. They went on being friends long after I was no longer Headmaster. Keeping boarding going in the school was made much easier by having such admirable housemasters.

They were by no means the only excellent people on the staff. Because I didn't have that much actual work to do, I could afford to spend time showing parents around the school. Indeed, I made a habit of doing so. Invariably included in the tours was the science department, and the physics department especially. With any luck, John Hughes – Dr Hughes, whom the boys knew as 'Doc' Hughes – would be doing an experiment. Sometimes, parents would be so intrigued I would have almost to drag them away – although I too would willingly have stood quietly with them at the side of the lab to watch teaching of a kind I wished every pupil in every school might get.

'Doc' Hughes wasn't an exception, either: the chemistry department was just as lively. Keith Roberts, the head of the chemistry department, had a first-class honours degree in his subject and was an outstanding all-round schoolmaster. Biology, modern languages, classics … all were good departments, and I knew there was hardly a classroom in the school where I would ever find bored or badly behaved boys.

Of course, some teachers were better than others; in which school will this never be true? However, Berkhamsted had more than its share of excellent teachers, and hardly anyone who didn't have some quality which would inspire the young. Sometimes I would stand outside the classroom of one of the most flamboyant of the teachers in the school,

Some of the buildings of Berkhamsted School, from a painting by the late Harry Sheldon. Deans' Hall is on the far left; the Chapel straight ahead; a side view of the Library on the right. The staff are in gowns after Chapel, Jonty in the front with the Second Master, Dennis Beard; stalking behind them is the towering and stooping figure of J A Davison, the long-serving housemaster of School House.

David Sherratt, just for the vicarious enjoyment of his classroom performance.

Sherratt's flamboyance extended beyond the classroom. A year or two before my arrival, he had been involved – as he always was – in a night exercise (for the Parsons' Trophy) of the Combined Cadet Force (CCF) in which groups of boys from the various houses competed to find the way most rapidly along a set route to a campsite. Sherratt was positioned to intercept the groups and to try to persuade them to reveal their names and their routes. If they succumbed, they lost points, and probably the competition.

This year, he dressed up as a general, in full military regalia, and posted himself on top of a haystack as an observation point (or so he said; another version of the story had it that he had kept out the cold by liberal use of a hipflask, and had gone to sleep on a haystack). As one of the groups came past, Sherratt started to climb down to try to elicit information from the boys; unfortunately, as he did so, he slipped and fell heavily, breaking his arm. The boys weren't sure what to do: give away their position and their identity, or help their schoolmaster. Decency prevailed, and the boys got help from an Old Berkhamstedian who lived nearby. Sherratt was taken to hospital, still in his uniform.

It was the time of the 'troubles' with the IRA and death threats to Army officers abounded. So the hospital put Sherratt in a private room, and kept his presence a secret. On the Monday morning, he didn't turn up to teach, and no one knew where he was. The Head telephoned local hospitals but could get no information. Eventually Sherratt returned, his arm in plaster, and very worried in case he found he had to pay for his private room because his identity as a general was bogus.

The accident didn't deter Sherratt from his involvement in Parsons' Trophy. I remember that, when I went out myself one year to check on its progress, I found Sherratt dressed as a butler and holding a silver tray, on which was a bottle of sherry and some glasses. As the groups came past, he offered them sherry and asked which they were. The only group which didn't lose points that evening had spotted him and crossed ditches, climbed hedges and skirted round fields to avoid temptation.

Sometimes, 'characters' in a common room aren't very good teachers; I remembered several from my own schooldays, whose characterful behaviour concealed empty teaching. That was not true of David Sherratt; he was a brilliant, resourceful and rigorous teacher.

The games-coaching was of a high standard, too. I was especially impressed by John Francis Davis, whom everyone called Fran. He had played both cricket and rugby at county level, and was a first-rate coach of both games, with able assistants ready to help if required. A vivid memory is of Fran's trying to help a 1st XV half-back improve his kicking. The boy, who had an unusually high opinion of his own abilities, was not convinced that this aging schoolmaster actually knew much more than he did himself.

Patiently, Fran coached him, fielding the boy's kicks, and then sending the ball back for the boy to try again. Eventually, the boy managed a half-decent torpedo kick back to his coach. Pleased as anything with himself, he stood, hands on hips, and said, or rather sneered, "Do you mean like that, sir?"

"No," said Fran, "I meant like this." And then he kicked the ball himself, so that it swivelled in a perfectly timed torpedo flight, a good 30 yards farther than the farthest the boy had managed, way over his head and into touch.

There was only one subject where I saw a problem. The head of the art department was a long-serving schoolmaster, a popular member of common room, a charming and talented man who had made a considerable reputation for himself as an artist both locally and more widely – and that reputation certainly did the school no harm. However, when I went into the pottery classroom, there didn't seem to be much pottery going on, and I realized quickly there was more clay on the ceiling than on the work-benches. "How does the clay get up there?" I asked one of the boys.

"Like this, sir," he said, and demonstrated. A lump of clay was placed on the end of a ruler; the other end was placed over the edge of the workbench. Down came a fist, and upward went the lump of clay. Some lumps stuck to the ceiling, some came back down. The (admittedly only part-time) teacher of pottery seemed to see nothing peculiar that this was happening in his class, or that a pupil should think it permissible to demonstrate the skill involved to a peripatetic Headmaster.

A conversation with the head of art assured me the man was in fact a first-rate potter; "I don't want a first-class potter," I said. "I want a first-class teacher." The necessary arrangements were made, we interviewed, and the next term we had a new young teacher of pottery – more than simply pottery, in fact, because the work in clay which she got out of the boys was brilliantly and hilariously various.

Since I liked the man and his wife personally, I thought a kindly way round the larger problem might be to bring into the department an artist in residence, someone who needed the extra income of teaching a day or two a week, who would enjoy the space and time afforded him or her to work on his or her own paintings, who might in that process inspire the boys with new ideas and fresh techniques, and indeed might bring into the department some new ideas. It wouldn't cost a great deal of money. I had approval in principle from the governors, so proposed the scheme. It found no favour.

In those days, the pension arrangements for teachers to take early retirement were still quite generous. I had already arranged for the early retirement of one member of staff, who had once upon a time been a fine schoolmaster but whom deafness had now subverted. I was encouraged by his gratitude when I made the arrangements for him to get a pension and retreat from what he could see but couldn't hear was ever-present disorder in his classroom.

There was another who needed to go, too: he had gradually been shunted from one department to another, and was now teaching mainly juniors, but clearly and audibly wasn't coping with them or his subject. He was however a delightful man, and I was dreading having to suggest early retirement to him, too. Sitting at my desk one day, worrying exactly about this problem, I heard a diffident knock on the door. I called out for whoever it was to come in, and the man concerned looked round the door.

"If you're busy, Headmaster," he said, "this can wait. It's not important."

Finishing the London Marathon, 1985.

"Come in," I said. "I'm not busy, and I'm glad to see you. What can I do for you?"

"Well, Headmaster, I don't want to trouble you, but there is a rumour going round common room you are making it easier for some of us who think we are nearing the end of the road professionally... well, to get our pensions and ...um... retire early. I really don't want to cause a problem for you..." and so on.

If only all 'early retirements' had been as easy as that. The main speech at the staff leavers' party at the end of the year was not flattering to the new Headmaster; but I was able to make over the next few years appointments that reflected what I had learned at Sevenoaks about how important in a school the teaching of art can be. All visitors to a school should ask themselves questions like these: where is the art? Is it on display? Inside the art-rooms? Around the school? Is it worth displaying? How various is it? How wide-ranging? Is it dominated by the imagination of the teachers, or does it reveal the imagination of the pupils? Are the young learning skills which they will be able to take with them elsewhere? A flourishing art department can help transform a school very quickly.

The other problem for me was the chaplaincy. On my visits to the school after appointment, I had met and liked the chaplain, Bill Hussey (unfairly nicknamed 'Fussy-Hussey'). I knew he was coming to the end of his time as chaplain, but hoped he would stay on long enough for me to make my own appointment. To get the right kind of chaplain was important; although the school wasn't specifically Anglican, it had been founded by an Anglican clergyman, and Chapel was central, not just architecturally. Moreover, I had in my mind's eye the ideal my own father had represented in his role as chaplain.

Unfortunately, Bill Hussey decided he must go when John Spencer went. The school had to have a chaplain, not least because he doubled up as head of the department of religious education (R E, as it was called, rather than 'divinity' or 'theology') and therefore taught most of a timetable. So John Spencer had appointed someone, with whom (he wrote to tell me) he was quite sure I was going to get on.

Almost immediately, we did not get on. One of my father's habits as chaplain had been to visit the sanatorium every day. When I did my own weekly visit to the san sister, a wonderfully forthright Scot called Flora McIsaac, I found out the new chaplain hadn't yet been to see her or the san. When I suggested to him he might be at least an occasional visitor there, he made it clear he didn't think it part of his duties. Bad start, as far as I was concerned… Worse followed.

Like most schools in the U K, Berkhamsted had lost a good number of its ex-pupils in the 1914-18 war. One of the most heart-breaking documents I know is the list of prefects which Charles Greene, Headmaster throughout those years, had meticulously kept. As one after another of 'his' prefects were killed, he ruled a red line through the name and recorded the date. On some pages there are as many names ruled out as are left.

Where Berkhamsted was unusual was that, especially at the start of the 1939-45 war, many of its immediate ex-pupils had joined the RAF; its casualty rate was therefore higher than it might have been and, as a consequence, the annual Remembrance Day service was even more special than in most schools. Numbers of older Old Berkhamstedians would turn up for chapel that day, many wearing their decorations.

A few days before Remembrance Day, the Second Master came to see me. Had I seen, he wondered, the order of service for Remembrance Sunday? No, I hadn't. He thought it might be wise if I were to do so. I went to the chapel to ask. Although the appointment of the chaplain required the blessing of the Bishop of St Albans, the Rt Revd John Taylor, the Headmaster was in fact the 'Ordinary'; in other words, temporal authority over the activities of the chapel rested on me, not on the chaplain himself. Rather unwillingly, he showed me the order of service he had had printed. Immediately after the two minutes of silence, he had arranged for a recording to be played of John Lennon's singing, *Give peace a chance.*

I instructed him to scrap that order of service, and to use whatever the form had been the year before he arrived. He wasn't happy, so we compromised to an extent, in that I allowed him not to have the hymn with words by Spring-Rice and a tune by Holst. It's theologically a bit shaky, anyway. I never did persuade him that *Onward Christian Soldiers* is one of the great hymns of the English hymnal, not militaristic, and that the Salvation Army loves peace as much as he does.

We had other disagreements, mainly to do with his work-load; he thought it wrong he should be both chaplain and head of department and wanted me to split the roles, employing someone else as well as him. He wanted to introduce A level R E and I said we couldn't really afford it, but if enough boys wanted to take the subject I would see what could be done. He thought no boys would opt for it until it was actually time-tabled. I tried to explain the mechanics of staffing and timetabling, but he thought I was merely against the study of theology. I explained my father's degree had been in theology.

The final straw came when I heard a rumour he had refused to baptise the grandchild of one of the non-teaching staff. Apparently the baby's mother had neglected to marry the father before the baby was born. I went to chapel at once.

"There must be some mistake," I said. "No clergyman would refuse to baptise a baby, surely."

"I believe in the sanctity of marriage," he said.

Before I could stop myself, I burst out, "But the baby's not married".

"If I baptize the baby, it's as good as saying I don't care whether its parents are married or not."

"I tell you what: if you don't baptise that child, I'll bloody well do it myself."

"You can't do that," he replied.

"Oh yes I can."

With that I left, knowing my next recourse was a visit to the Bishop. Incidentally, I was technically right; any professing Christian may baptise a child, though it is usually done by non-clergy only in extremis. Midwives, faced with a child they know is going to die soon, are allowed to – and sometimes do – baptise their charges.

After an interregnum, when another clergyman on the staff bravely took on the role of chaplain, and did a much better job than he at first thought he would or could, I was able, with the approval of the Bishop of St Alban's, to make my own appointment. Initially, it seemed one of the best appointments I had ever made: a young, bright, lively, happily married clergyman, with children of his own and oodles of energy, and we were able to arrange for him to act as chaplain not only of the boys' school but the girls' school too. His teaching was excellent. Sadly, however, I must report that, the year after I left Berkhamsted, everything fell apart in the chaplaincy on which I had placed so much hope. It is one of the stories which can't yet be told.

Heads should, I think, teach. It is often seen as one of the ironies of the profession that, the more skilled you are in a classroom, the more quickly you are promoted out of it. If you want to be paid more, you have to become a head of department, a head of year, a housemaster or housemistress, a deputy head, and eventually a Head – and usually each step up the ladder means an increase in pay. There are teachers who refuse promotion, who won't even be heads of department because that would take them away from teaching actual classes. Understanding – and indeed admiring – that scruple, I had tried, at Island School, to see if there was a way of using what were known as 'senior teacher' posts to reward people who seemed to be especially effective in the classroom; but judging effectiveness was (in those days anyway, before evaluation became more normal) largely subjective. The classroom teachers who were not rewarded with higher status and more money were often resentful; and collegiality suffered.

Robert Birley believed passionately even the Head Master of Eton had to teach. Indeed, he thought his teaching of history was more important than his administration of the school, and he had managed to keep up his scholarship, particularly in the College library, as well as teaching a substantial timetable. I knew I wouldn't be able to emulate his skill as a teacher, but, at Island School, I had taught, usually, one class up to O level, and two half-classes of A level. I thought that, at the very least, a

Head should demonstrate he still had some of the capacity which had presumably earned him promotion in the first place. Perhaps ever more importantly, I thought a Head who didn't teach might lose sight of the fact the most important activity in a school is in the classroom.

There were however problems. First, I enjoyed A level teaching much more than O level teaching (though in some ways the best teaching I ever did was with 11 and 12 year olds); however, especially at Berkhamsted, there were several teachers who enjoyed sixth form teaching and were very good at it; if I taught at that level, I would be displacing someone at least as competent as I was.

Secondly, a Headmaster is necessarily a figure of authority; if he isn't, the school is likely to be shaky. But teachers of English shouldn't be 'figures of authority' if they want to do their jobs really well. Outside the classroom, what I said went; inside the classroom, what I said needed to be challenged. Thirdly, when the inevitable crises happened, I would get pulled away from the classroom. It simply wasn't fair on classes to have their teacher miss periods, or fail to get their essays marked because he had to go to a meeting in London.

Of course, all professions face that dilemma. As you gather authority and experience, so you are removed from the actual work of the profession. Engineers become managers, cardiac consultants become departmental bosses and then advisers to a government, researchers become accountants. One of the most interesting training courses I did in my years at Berkhamsted was called 'Action Learning for Chief Executives' at the Ashridge Management College.

A group of six managing directors of 'middle-sized companies' met regularly in the company of an experienced facilitator to talk about the work they did: what went well; what they worried about; what they thought their successes; what they knew were their failures. Although the course rather petered out in its second phase, when at least one of our number found himself shifted abruptly into another role, it was thoroughly useful experience, and perhaps made me less worried I had a role as a manager as well as those of a teacher and leader.

❧❦

One of my innovations at Island School had been to extend the library and employ a full-time librarian. While the library in Berkhamsted School was of an inconvenient design (because a librarian couldn't easily supervise both floors at once), it was placed where I thought a library should be, right in the middle of the main school. In the kind of teaching I believe in, where a main object is to fit the pupils to learn to work independently, a school library has a central purpose, and a full-time librarian a crucial role.

Has that changed, I wonder, when there is so much information available which one may get merely by trawling the internet? I suppose, in the old days, the very difficulty of finding the information you needed was part of the way of ensuring its likely truthfulness; now, masses of information is available, though often unreliable and always indiscriminate. Yet a library – even an increasingly electronic library – is where we need to train our young to look critically at all the knowledge available.

How do you make sense of this? How do you distinguish sense from nonsense? Information from disinformation? The cry, Is it relevant? seems to be of very little help. I don't know yet, the wise man answers. It may become relevant when I know a bit more. For me, it's still much harder to look anything up in an electronic book, because I know how to use an index and the contents pages, and how to skim a book, backwards and forwards, until I find what I need; but the young type in a keyword and tell me what I need to know very quickly.

My first appointment of a librarian at Berkhamsted didn't work out but the next appointment was a success: Harry Spry-Leverton had been in the army from 1976-82, reaching the rank of Captain in The Light Infantry. His service had included a time in Belfast. In 1982 he had married Tessa, a sculptor, and had sent himself to university, although he continued to serve in the Territorial Army. I actually appointed him before he had finished his degree, with the consequence he couldn't start work until he had taken his finals. Once installed, Harry did a little bit of teaching and helped in the CCF, but mainly concentrated on sorting the library out and getting the boys to use it profitably.

Graham Greene, one of the sons of Charles Greene, Headmaster from 1911 to 1927, had never failed to give the school a copy of each of his books as it was published. The result was that the library had an extraordinarily valuable collection of presentation copies. One of Harry's coups was to load all the books into his car one summer and to drive to Antibes, where Graham Greene seemed delighted to sign each one.

I wish I had met Graham Greene myself; oddly enough, I did meet two of his brothers, Hugh of the BBC, and Raymond the mountaineer and doctor. I lost count of the number of times people said to me, when they heard I was Headmaster of Berkhamsted, "Oh, isn't that the school where Graham Greene was so unhappy?" It wasn't until late in my time there I devised an answer: "where do you think he would have been happier?"

Another success at the school was making the old Tudor hall in School House back into a graceful as well as a useful space. John Spencer's frugality had furnished the hall – a marvellously beamed and paneled school-room, with tall windows on both sides – with some cheap office furniture bought in a sale of surplus equipment; this the School House boys used as their study (though it did look as if they had used the plywood furniture for football practice, too). Lighting had been provided by fluorescent strip lights fastened to the underside of the beams, so ugly that, on my very first tour of the school, I had exclaimed to the Second Master I didn't much like them. "Neither do I, nor does the housemaster," he said.

One of the ways we used John Spencer's carefully saved surplus was to turn the old-fashioned dormitories in School House from a series of iron beds interspersed with small lockers into individual study-bedrooms. Careful design meant we did so without having to cut numbers or despoil architecture. Since the boys now had studies, we could get rid of the office furniture in Old Hall and the strip lighting; concealed lights were installed to point upwards to show off the beams, and more attractive hanging lights added.

Round the walls, there were benches concealing the heating and, a year or two later, an old boy of the school who was a master-carpenter built in oak a series of glass-fronted bookshelves for the end walls, into which we put various of the precious books from the library, as well as the Halsey Library, presented by a member of that distinguished local family. On the floor were two big carpets, one bought with money raised from sponsors when I ran the London Marathon, one with money raised when the housemaster and I together ran the Berkhamsted Half Marathon. On the walls were hung portraits of past Headmasters.

One portrait I noted was missing: C R Evers, headmaster from 1945-53. Strangely enough, I had met Ronnie Evers years before, when he was Headmaster of Sutton Valence School in Kent, to which I had taken a rugby team from Sevenoaks. He noticed my tie, and I his: we were both old members of Trinity College, Oxford. Ronnie had left Berkhamsted in 1953 at the behest of his governors; rumour had it the final straw was when he (suitably rotund and rubicund) had played Humpty Dumpty in the local pantomime.

Some wit had called him the "acting Headmaster", and the governors had declined to add his portrait to the pantheon. I thought that a great shame, so persuaded the present governors to employ Andrew Festing to paint Ronnie's portrait. I thought too we should be honest enough to paint Ronnie as he was now, long since retired, rather than as he must have been in 1953.

At the same time, since I admired a group portrait which hung in the entry hallway of the City of London School, we used a small legacy to get Derek Fowler, head of art at the City of London School, to paint a group portrait of the four living Headmasters of the school (Ronnie Evers, Basil Garnons Williams, John Spencer and myself) and the three living chairmen of governors (Major Adrian Hadden-Paton, Sir Kenneth Cork, and Bobby Furber). Nowadays, three more individual portraits have been added: my own (also painted by Andrew Festing), the Revd Keith Wilkinson, and Priscilla Chadwick, who amalgamated the schools into one complex institution, known as Berkhamsted Collegiate School, though under her successor it reverted simply to Berkhamsted School (even though actually it comprises six schools).

More controversial than getting portraits painted was a decision to create more space in an old school jampacked into the middle of town by putting a mezzanine floor into the school hall, known as Deans' Hall (two deans, Dean Incent the founder and T C Fry, Headmaster 1889-1911, afterwards Dean of Lincoln). The original idea for the horizontal division of the cavernous hall came from David Sherratt, teacher of English and producer of spectacularly lavish school-plays.

One could never be sure with David when ideas were serious or not; but this would give us for relatively little expenditure four new classrooms in the base of the hall, as well as an upper hall considerably better lit and more airy than the sombre version of 1912. The treasurer, the bursar, a governor and I went to look at Uppingham School which had done something similar with its Victorian hall, and came back enthused enough to face down those who thought this proposal a desecration.

Eventually, we carried the day, though the building work did mean ripping out the elegant paneling from Deans' Hall. That was the only time I had qualms about the operation, though various irate Old Berkhamstedians threatened never to set foot in the school again. I don't think anyone now thinks it was a bad decision: the new Deans' Hall is both more useful and more beautiful than the old version, and the four classrooms in the middle of the school are valuable, too.

આ૰ન્

For a couple of years in the 1980s I was asked to represent Headmasters' Conference (HMC) on the 'English 18' section of the Secondary Examinations Council (SEC). It was a thoroughly dispiriting exercise, and I contributed nothing to the advancement of education in English (language and/or literature), merely wasted time getting to and from meetings in London, and then sitting there listening to what sounded more like posturing than arguing.

My only contribution was to ask for a change of wording of the minutes of a meeting to which I hadn't been able to get myself: the minute said the object was to examine pupils' work 'unclouded' by any teaching. When the ratification of the minutes came up on the agenda, I stuck up a hand to ask the chairman, Professor Arthur Pollard (of the University of Hull), if we might possibly find a metaphor which didn't regard teaching as 'clouding'. It was apparent from some of the stares and comments of others there they really didn't understand what I was talking about. Fortunately, the chairman had a brain and a sense of humour, and agreed we might do better.

I hadn't been held in much esteem beforehand, and thereafter seemed to be regarded as openly opposed to the views of most teachers there, even when I said nothing for or against what was being debated. There seemed to be an assumption that, as the Head of an independent school, I wouldn't really understand anything, almost as if my present role gave me a cloak of invisibility to cover up my experience in other schools and other countries. Fortunately, my appointment was for two years only, and I was relieved to be excused from attendance. The SEC didn't last much longer, and its demise was not I think widely mourned by anyone.

❧❧

I am conscious I have written very little about the curriculum, about what I think should be taught in schools.

In part this is because, like most teachers, I get exasperated at the assumption, every time a social ill is perceived, schools are expected to set the problem straight by adding something else to what they already have to teach, when there is already more than enough to fill the timetable. So crowded does the school-week get that either specialisation increases or the weekly timetable has to be spread out over a fortnight.

We are instructed that somehow we have to fit in more health education; so what do we do? We will cut one period a week of physical education, so there is now just one period a week – and by the time the boys and girls have changed out of their P E gear and had time to have a shower afterwards they have only 20 minutes of actual physical activity.

Or we are instructed that any decent curriculum must include some teaching of history; so we shall no longer be able to teach physics, chemistry and biology as separate sciences, but must combine them into something called general science. It is thought appalling that children leave school knowing as little as they do about the careers open to them, so we must include at least one period a week of something called 'careers education'. To do that we shall need to amalgamate history and geography into a single subject, which we shall call social studies.

And so it continues, with more and more getting jammed into the curriculum, and more and more needing to be cut from the curriculum to make room for all that we should be doing. It is scarcely surprising, therefore, some boys and girls leave school seemingly barely able to write a coherent paragraph: there are so many subjects to be taught we are in danger of forgetting that, underlying all of them, there is the need for literacy. Similarly, boys and girls who have been taught to use calculators will happily show that 10 x 10 = 1000, but not have the almost instinctive numeracy afforded by the knowledge of multiplication tables to spot an obvious error.

Yes, of course we must have computer studies in the modern curriculum; yes, we must have craft, design and technology, too; we must have personal, social and health education; and what about political education or civics? How can we expect our country to run as a democracy when we have taught our young so little about political and civic theory and practice?

My own school education provided me with a degree of scepticism about the curriculum. My father was deeply influenced by his reading of Plato, and insisted I should study the sciences as well as the arts (though my inclination was to the latter). Ideally, as far as my father was concerned, I would have done what Plato recommended, the arts first and the sciences second; but in modern times if you didn't have a grounding in the sciences you couldn't (usually) start them later.

Anyway, the 'top set' at St Andrew's College – the 'clever boys' – did in their matriculation years physics and chemistry, as well as maths, Latin, English, and Afrikaans (and optional additional maths, too, as well as compulsory divinity). My father wouldn't let me do history, since he thought the version of history offered by the South African matriculation boards was corrupt; if I wanted to read history, I could make the decision at the university, where I'd get a wider vision of the past. Biology was regarded as rather a soft science. Art? It was a subject I loved, but it wasn't available to clever boys except as a leisure activity. Geography? In those days it was seen as a soft subject. I could learn enough history, geography and indeed biology merely by reading.

As it happens, I suspect what I now see as the poverty of much of my school education (not, I hasten to add, in English or in Latin, in both of which I was brilliantly taught, nor to an extent in maths, where I had at least one good teacher) was a function not of the curriculum (which, considered objectively, was quite broad, relative at least to the narrowness of the English A level system) but of the actual teaching. The function of most of the teaching was merely to get us through the matriculation system.

So, when I was in a position of sufficient authority to have some say over the curriculum (not complete sway, because the examination boards and the universities or professions were the dominant forces, and because no sensible Head ignores the views of his or her heads of department), I always tended to shrug my shoulders when it came to questions of what subjects the school should teach. What mattered was not what the subjects were, but how well they were taught.

Sometimes, when I was feeling naughty, I would argue that anyone could make a perfectly adequate school-curriculum from a set of subjects, none of which was usually taught in school: statistics; linguistics; social and physical anthropology; astronomy & cosmology; human physiology; psychology; logic & metaphysics; dance ... Of course, what was vital was literacy, the ability to read carefully and write cogently; but the generations which had studied the classics almost exclusively were actually quite well educated in their way. They could read and they could write. Add to that numeracy, and there was a chance of a school's producing well-educated youngsters.

More seriously, I would point to the centrality of philosophy in the curriculum of French schools. While there are schools in the Anglo-Saxon tradition which teach philosophy in one shape or the other (the Critical Thinking paper in the International Baccalaureate is essentially an introduction to some aspects of philosophy), it isn't generally seen as even an examinable subject at school level.

Often, my attitude to the curriculum must have appeared as at least traditional, and probably conventional. Yet our division of what was regarded as worthwhile knowledge is, for better or worse, largely a matter of convention. The old joke about Jowett, Master of Balliol, applied: My name is Jowett, / I am the Master of this college. / What I don't know / Isn't knowledge...

What was regarded within a subject as worthwhile knowledge might be a matter of debate, but was largely a matter of historical accident; what was regarded as worthwhile within the school-curriculum was equally an historical accident. Why on earth had the newish subject of craft, design, technology crept into most schools, but not philosophy? Well, there were good reasons, but they were largely pragmatic: teachers of carpentry and cooking could become quite easily teachers of design and household management. It was much harder to make a teacher of history into an adequate teacher of philosophy.

I was by no means against changes to the curriculum, any more than I had been against change in the syllabuses of the English departments in which I taught. Some change was necessary if only to force especially more hidebound teachers to widen their range, to read something new, to renew enthusiasm, rather than to go on merely repeating their lessons year in, year out. Computing, for instance, was an unavoidable addition to the curriculum; but we cannot go on adding subject after subject to what we want to teach the young, without turning some subjects into no more than tasters. One term of Latin in five or seven years of a secondary school isn't an education. So I would suggest the addition of this rule to all curricular reform: thou shalt not propose an addition to the school curriculum unless thou also specify the subtraction of an equal element.

The idea of information now being so instantaneously and freely available on the world-wide web that content-free teaching is possible seems to me merely hilariously sentimental. You can't teach someone how to read a map unless you put a map in front of him or her to read. You can't teach someone how to read a novel critically unless you give him or her novels to read.

I would add one complication about the teaching of modern languages. It seems obvious the best way of teaching anyone how to speak another language is to immerse him or her in that language. The wonderful Trudi Berger, for many years a teacher of languages at the University of York, used regularly to get classes (admittedly of motivated university undergraduates needing to add an O level in German to their preliminary qualifications so they could match the matriculation requirements of the university for a degree in modern languages) up to the required standard in 11 days, by taking them on a crash course which started with the singing of nursery rhymes. The standard way of teaching most subjects – four or five periods a week for three or four terms, and so on – works well for many subjects, but doesn't work so well for modern languages.

However, immersion courses are very tricky in a school. I was always very keen on sending groups of pupils away to France or Germany precisely so they could get that immersion; but the system was (properly) disliked by most heads of department because it disrupted the teaching of their own subjects – and by the coaches of teams who didn't want to lose star players because they were doing something as trivial as spending a fortnight in Bordeaux. I thought myself the disruption was worth the success in promoting the study of especially French; but it was not a popular view in common room, though we seldom had any problem getting pupils themselves to volunteer.

࿔

Headmasters' relationships with their immediate predecessors are famously fraught. It is all too easy for a new Headmaster to bridle when he pours out generous glasses of Australian chardonnay at his party to thank the staff at the end of his first term, only to be told by some old hand, "Your predecessor used to serve champagne on these occasions." Your predecessor had a considerable private income, but you don't say that.

Nor do you say anything when your predecessor mentions he would appreciate knowing why you decided not to follow his recommendation about who the next head boy should be. I remember being told by a Headmaster of Christ's Hospital School of an occasion when, to his relief, a meeting in London had at the last moment been cancelled. He could, after all, go to morning chapel. He arrived at his customary stall only to find his predecessor sitting there, and showing no inclination to move.

"So what did you say?" I asked.

"I told him to hop it."

I was fortunate to have none of those problems. The Spencers had bought a house in a village about half an hour from the school, but were scrupulous about leaving me to run the school as I thought best. John was there when I wanted advice, but never offered it. We saw them socially, and they came to Wilson House contentedly, even though it had been their home for 11 years. Ann and I have a happy memory of a dinner party in Wilson House given for all three of my predecessors.

Our relationship with Basil Garnons Williams, Headmaster from 1953-1972, and author of an admirable history of the school until 1972, was particularly close. When he wanted – after the death of his wife and in his old age – to come back from Lavenham in Suffolk to live in Berkhamsted, Basil took the trouble to ask for permission to move back. Of course he didn't need anyone's permission, but it was typical of his old-fashioned courtesy; and in fact it was wonderful to find him most mornings sitting in our kitchen with my wife and (often enough) her mother. I have always thought the relationship between a current Head and his or her predecessor's predecessor is a bit like that of a grandfather or grandmother. The immediate responsibility within the family has passed, but the affection is still abundantly there.

I was fortunate too in the succession of head boys I had. It was one of them whom I asked to make the vote of thanks when we invited the local MP to speak to the sixth form. We had a general studies period just before lunch on a Friday, which I used for the occasional outside speaker; and I had felt for some time that the boys needed to be more aware of party politics, so had invited the MP, warning him that he really shouldn't talk for more than half-an-hour, so that there might be 15 minutes for questions. In fact he talked and talked and went on talking, mainly about himself and his life-history up to the time he became an MP. His career had included some years of selling motor-cars, about which he spoke for several minutes.

When, eventually, he stopped, I asked if there were any questions. Since it was now ten minutes into the lunch-break, there were none. I nodded to the head boy. I have been known to say, more than once, if a job is worth doing, it is worth delegating; now, to my alarm, the head boy turned and nodded to another, a clever boy known for being occasionally outrageous. He stood up, grinned genially, spread his arms wide, then said, "Gentlemen: I have only one question to ask you all: would you buy a used car from this man?" He paused, and paused. Then, just as I thought

I would have to intervene, because the MP was looking thunderous, he went on: "Of course you would." There followed some brief applause; but I thought I might safely abandon any future attempts to bring local politicians into the school, even though one of our celebrated ex-pupils was the Labour Party MP, Michael Meacher.

∽◈∾

One of the harder things to explain about a school is the quality of the common room. I use that term, 'common room', deliberately; I don't mean simply the room where teachers gather, where they may go when they aren't teaching; I mean the collective spirit of the teaching staff, its 'commonality', its collegiality. It's not simply a matter of the accumulated abilities of the teachers, as if one could add up all the degrees and certificates and multiply that by the years of experience to get a total. It's something more complicated than that; it is how the teachers co-operate with each other, how they play as a team. In part it derives from a confidence in its own abilities, a sureness of touch in its dealings with pupils and their parents; but it is mainly to do with the treatment of each other.

A Head sees this quality partly in how the teaching staff treat him. For instance, are he and his family included in the social life of the common room? Are he and his wife asked out to dinner by the staff in the same way as he is expected to entertain them? Are the Head and his family invited to take part in school outings and expeditions when the staff and their families are invited? If a Head decides for instance he'd like to go on an awayday tour with a school team, would his presence be regarded as intolerable interference or as a welcome addition?

And how do the teachers treat each other? Are there cliques and social exclusions? Is there moaning about X's laziness and Y's arrogance? Of all the schools I've worked in, indeed all I've known, the common room of Berkhamsted School for Boys was the happiest. There was a lot of laughter and very little bitterness. There was a great deal of co-operation and (if needs be) of occasional covering-up for each other.

I heard some gossip from senior members of staff that a young married man on the staff was having a fling with a young unmarried woman who had joined the school recently, a fine teacher but one who was having

141

some personal problems settling. In a sense, her private life was hers and nothing to do with me, any more than his marital infidelity was. But I wasn't having the school disrupted, and I wanted the young teacher to calm down and teach systematically, as I thought she'd be able to do. I did not want her professional career to get confused by messy personal complications.

So I called into my study the man whose name had been attached to the rumour and, without inviting him to sit down, gave him from my headmagisterial chair what is best called a bollocking. There was no way the school would put up with this; he was jeopardising his own career as well as his marriage. He was putting the young woman into danger, too. I was not interested in discussing the matter; I was telling him to put his house in order. I finished what I had to say, and sent him away.

In fact, I had the wrong man, and he knew who it was I should have been reprimanding. But instead of saying anything, he accepted the reprimand, told me he understood what I was saying, and left. As far as I was concerned, the gossip stopped, the rumours abated, the young woman settled down to teaching, and nothing more needed to be said or done. It was months before I realized I had got entirely the wrong person.

That sort of loyalty showed in the kind of support the staff gave each other when there were other problems, for instance when someone was ill and needed covering. In some schools, the question of cover for illness or other absence is fraught: it's understandable, because a teacher's occasional free periods are valuable. They are times when one may get some marking done, or some chores covered, or merely 40 minutes of respite from what can be a physically and mentally exhausting job. But, dammit, here's a message from the deputy head that Y has a migraine and has had to go home; this is the period when I had planned a quick visit to the bank to sort out the problem with the cheque-book; but would you please go to supervise Form 5C while it does the work Y himself should be supervising? Do you grin and bear it? Do you moan madly? Do you cite your union rep's advice that cover isn't part of your duties?

At Berkhamsted co-operation was the norm. There was teasing, there were practical jokes, there was often leg-pulling – but it very rarely had any edge of nastiness. Laughter was everywhere.

Why then did I once again move on after six years? Ann made no bones about the fact she didn't want to go. Although she had not gone back to being a JP as she had been in Cleethorpes, she was deeply involved in her work in the local hospice (she had gone back to her original profession as an occupational therapist, and was helping patients find good and useful ways of filling their days, even when they were the last days).

Our daughter was happily in the Girls' School taking her A levels (and indeed on her way to becoming head girl of that school and getting a place at Oxford). Our eldest had his place at Oxford, and the second son his at the School of Oriental and African Studies in London. The town was pleasant, and we had made some good friends in and out of the school. Our house was comfortable, our garden delightful, and Ashridge accessible. London was half an hour away by train.

I had told the governors when I was interviewed I would be unlikely to see out my career at Berkhamsted. I promised to see at least a generation of boys through the school. There was nothing about the place I disliked, and much about it I enjoyed. Within the boys' school, there were the occasional difficulties to be dealt with, but they weren't insurmountable.

Part of the larger problem lay in the relationship with the girls' school. The Headmistress was Valerie Shepherd, who had come to the school from Wycombe Abbey School, then as now one of the pre-eminent academic schools in the country. The same governors governed both the boys' school and the girls' school. Before my arrival, the custom had been for each school to take it in turn to have its own business dealt with; so for this term's meeting the agenda would be: the girls' school, then joint business, then boys' school, and for the next term's meeting a reversed order. That was fine, except when the Head of one school arrived to find something which actually affected both schools had been decided in the first part of the agenda. Having cleared the idea with Valerie herself, I suggested to the chairman it might be sensible if both Heads attended the whole meeting. This was agreed.

More tricky to deal with, even than the temperamental differences between the Headmistress and myself, were differences in working conditions: the girls' school didn't have lessons on a Saturday morning, and there was a long-standing arrangement all the teachers in the girls' school got a half-day off each week, it was claimed to allow women time to run their homes.

The obvious way to make the working conditions in each school more equitable was to give the boys' school teachers the same privileges; but to do that would mean cutting both our curriculum and the extra-curricular side. It would increase the pressure to introduce weekly boarding, too; I was convinced it would be harder to get full boarders from overseas if all the English boarders went home for the weekend.

Moreover, while the top teams would undoubtedly keep going, I thought the lowlier teams – the fourth XI, the third XV, the second string cross-country runners – wouldn't get the fun of inter-school matches. Most important of all, without the four lessons on a Saturday morning, there would be less time for an expansive curriculum during the five remaining days of the week. So I set my face firmly against giving up lessons on Saturday mornings.

(This was, incidentally, a constant theme throughout my professional life. At Sevenoaks, when some of the staff wanted to abandon Saturday lessons, I had led the opposition to any change. At Matthew Humberstone School, where nobody would have dreamt of there being lessons on a Saturday morning, I used often to go into school to clear my desk. Indeed, in my first term there I had a major row with the school caretaker, when he found me in my office and told me I wasn't allowed there over weekends. At Island School, I had encouraged the so-called Evening Institute to have classes on Saturday mornings. At Berkhamsted, and later at Wellington, I refused to accede to those staff who thought it would be pleasant to go shopping with their wives or husbands on a Saturday morning. What were holidays for? I would ask.)

Co-operation between the schools became more difficult after the retirement of Jeremy Day as joint treasurer. There were bursars in both schools, working independently; but Jeremy Day was responsible for the finances of both schools, though sufficiently a diplomat to allow me room to push ahead with my impatient innovations and to cajole Valerie Shepherd into the occasional concession to modernity. When he retired, his replacement almost immediately caused a problem by sending a report on some matter to do with the boys' school to the chairman of governors without showing it to me first. The chairman's immediate reaction was to copy it to me. I explained to the newcomer it would be wise if he were to consult me before he wrote reports on what I regarded as 'my school'.

He paid no attention, it seemed, and a week or two later sent another report without checking it with either the Headmistress or me. Now, the chairman didn't bother even to consult us. He terminated the new treasurer's contract immediately.

My own view was we could manage without the joint appointment. However, it seemed equally plain, particularly at sixth form level, we needed greater co-operation between the schools; and that wasn't going to happen without greater co-ordination, especially of timetables. If the two sixth forms were amalgamated into one, both would achieve so much more: was there any point in having a Latin class of three boys, and just up the hill a class of nine girls? Surely one class of 12 made more sense? Quiet discussions with crucial governors made it apparent what I saw as necessary was not going to happen, at least for many years; the governors weren't prepared to risk renewing the wrath of the teachers in the girls' school, though perhaps it was more the financial implications that worried them.

More and more I began to feel like Alice in the drawing by Tenniel when she has nibbled the mushroom, and grown and grown, her head out of the cottage chimney, her arms out of the windows, her legs out of the doors. It was a lovely cottage, but I was too big for it. Perhaps if the governors had agreed to let me run both schools, or at any rate to bring the two sixth forms together into one more rational institution, I might have been less restless. But there seemed at that stage no possibility of a change.

I knew that most Heads retired at 60. I was coming up to 50, and guessed that each year thereafter I would be less likely to get a third headship. I knew too that, whether I liked it or not, any thought of a return to a maintained school was merely silly; I had become friendly with two

Headmasters of comprehensive schools in the area, and had been to those schools to meet staff and to talk to pupils. I had got to know, too, the Headmaster of one of the remaining grammar schools in the county.

All three of them had confirmed my feeling I was too used to independence to cope with being ruled by an LEA. So I made a list of 20 independent schools I rather liked the look of, for various reasons (reputation, location, history, whatever) and then I looked up their Headmasters in *Who's Who*, and noted their dates of birth. Who would retire when? Which schools might be looking for a new Head in 1989 or 1990? My list was reduced to about ten.

I can confess, now, that Wellington College wasn't on that list.

Chapter five

Wellington College

What made me apply to Wellington was neither its history nor its educational eminence. Indeed, its reputation as 'the Army school' seemed to preclude my even thinking of applying. My own military experience was minimal: despite my grandfather (killed in France in 1917), my mother's brothers (killed in North Africa in WW2) and my father (a POW until 1945), I had avoided as much as I could of military training in South Africa.

When I was appointed a prefect at school, the master in charge of the Cadet Force (my much-admired Latin teacher) had taken me on one side to say he didn't want me in the ranks any more, making (he said) a misery of the lives of the sergeants trying to teach us to drill decently; he was promoting me to the rank of lance-corporal, but at once putting me to work in the armoury, so I wouldn't have to be drilled any more. My inability to tell left from right has always been a problem; at one stage, I tried carrying a pebble in my left hand when I had to parade, so I would turn that way when commanded to do so – but then I used to forget if the pebble was in my left or right hand.

By the age of 17 I had decided that, if I were called up in the ballot to do national service in the South African armed forces, I was going to refuse to go, whatever the consequences. It was one of the my first conscious political decisions, brought about by a brief experience of the instructors at a cadet camp at school; they made no pretence about what we were being trained to do: to kill blacks (whom they called "kaffers") if they got out of hand in any way.

In 1988, on a train journey back from an outing to some Headmasterly meeting in Cornwall, one of the other Heads said quietly he had been visiting two friends at Wellington; the present Master had announced his intention to retire, so they had asked him to sound me out on the possibility I might be persuaded to apply. I was flattered, if puzzled. I didn't think I had met any Wellington staff; then I remembered I had met two of their rugby coaches at an early season tournament at Douai School and had liked them, as well as admiring the team they coached. Wasn't it the Army school? I asked Chris. Not any more, he assured me. So I promised to think about it.

The next weekend, Ann and I drove from Hertfordshire to Berkshire. Eventually, we negotiated a way into the school-grounds and then found, half-hidden by thickets of overgrown rhododendrons, the main school building. Even from the outside, it was spectacular, a huge English version of a grand chateau in the Loire, red brick with white woodwork, oval windows and wrought-iron balconies, bronze pineapples and steep turrets above the roofs. Embarrassed in case someone thought we were trespassing, we didn't stay long, but I had decided I would at least take the suggestion seriously.

More research followed. I skimmed through David Newsome's history of the school, and looked up the entries in the *Public Schools' Yearbook* and various other educational guides. It seemed so unlikely such an outsider would get anywhere I thought I might as well apply.

How many applications there were I have no idea (I do remember hearing that one came from a female deep-sea diver); a dozen of us survived on to the long-list, though someone withdrew at that stage. Thus, eleven Heads and their wives were invited to visit the school, to meet the Master and Mrs Newsome over lunch, and to be shown round the school. I think our visit must have been during a holiday, perhaps the half-term holiday of the Michaelmas term of 1988, because I don't remember seeing any pupils or meeting other staff. David Newsome was a wonderful talker, and his knowledge of the school, its history, its buildings, its people, encyclopaedic.

Especially impressive was the visit to the Chapel. Unlike the French rococo of the main buildings, which had been designed by John Shaw, the Chapel of the Holy Spirit was designed by one of the great architects of Victorian Gothic, Gilbert Scott; an aspect of his architectural skill was how the ovals of French rococo were subtly modified as they progressed into the perpendicular, thus allowing the transition not to offend the eye. However, what struck me most was when David Newsome pointed at the various plaques in memory of the Masters, from Edward White Benson, the first Master, later the Bishop of Truro, then Archbishop of Canterbury, through to the Hon Frank Forman Fisher (whom I had known slightly). Then David Newsome pointed at a space on the Chapel walls; "and that is where," he said, "one day there will be a memorial plaque naming me."

I am not much given to believing in premonitions, but at that moment in 1988, standing in the Wellington College Chapel weeks before the final interview, I had a weird certainty that I was going to be Master myself, and that one day I too would have – as David Newsome does now have – a plaque in my memory on that wall. (Of course I shall not see the memorial myself, although I do hope it doesn't include any phrase beginning "Ex Africa...")

David Newsome had quietly let me know it was likely I would be interviewed again, which gave me a little more time to prepare myself. I had a list of the governors, and used *Who's Who* to find out what I could about most of them; one of the differences between Berkhamsted and Wellington was that only about three of the Berkhamsted governors appeared in *Who's Who*, whereas at Wellington only about three did not. Once upon a time, an inspector from the Board of Education had said, "if at any time the Governors of Wellington College tired of administering the affairs of the College, they were well qualified to undertake the charge of the British Empire".

While the governors of 1988 were no longer quite as high-powered as their predecessors of the 19th and early 20th century had been, they were still a formidable body of men and women. HRH The Duke of Kent was the President (though he didn't attend meetings). The Duke of Wellington and the Archbishop of Canterbury were *ex officio* governors.

The Vice President (in effect, chairman) was Admiral Sir Anthony Griffin; others included his successor-designate, General Sir Roland Guy; Sir Robert Gatehouse, a QC elevated to the bench; Professor Michael Howard (not then knighted), the military historian; Sir Richard Buckley, who had been The Duke of Kent's private secretary; Douglas Fox, the estate agent; the Hon Lady Waley-Cohen; Air Chief Marshal Sir Neville Stack; Michael Hoban, some time Headmaster of Harrow; the Rt Hon Sir Michael Palliser, former head of the FCO; the Rt Hon Sir Humphrey Atkins (Lord Colnbrook); and others of comparable distinction if less fame.

Ann wasn't to be interviewed, but had been invited to have tea with three of the lady-governors while I was being interviewed by the other governors. I had written on a series of cards the questions I thought I might be asked, including the questions I rather hoped I wouldn't be; with Ann's help, I had rehearsed and refined my answers. I remember deciding I wouldn't treat the governors as if they were a public meeting: I would concentrate on answering directly the person who had asked each question.

One of the cards listed what I thought were gaps in my experience which might count against me: for instance, I knew very little about the prep schools which fed pupils to Wellington. I had also prepared carefully an answer explaining what I thought I might do at Wellington. I suppose the list would have numbered about ten or 12 things but, when I was asked the question and had got to the seventh point, I said to the person who had asked me the question, "Do you think that's enough for the time being?"

Suddenly, apropos of no other question, Frank Giles – whom I knew had been the editor of a Sunday newspaper – asked me, "Mr Driver, would you have been a Roundhead or a Cavalier?"

Frantically, I tried to remember some snippets of 17th century English history. Having failed, I decided a teasing answer might be better than evidence of ignorance. So I answered, "Well, I've always preferred Wordsworth to Coleridge."

"That's clever, Mr Driver, but it's not an answer."

The 11th Master and Mrs Driver outside South Front,
Wellington College.

"On the other hand, I've always preferred Disraeli to Gladstone."

"Mr Driver, I do want an answer."

"I would have bought an estate in Lincolnshire and retired from the conflict."

"Still not an answer…"

"Oh well, when I was younger I did wear my hair quite long. Is that an answer?"

A man who had been introduced by the chairman as Michael Howard leaned forward and quietly said to Frank Giles, "Frank, old chap, even in those days there were shades of opinion."

Years later, General Sir Roland Guy – Roly Guy, who succeeded Tony Griffin as Vice President, and who stayed a loyal friend and ally for the rest of his days – remembered that exchange, and told me he and other governors had thought, if I could cope with Frank Giles's question, I might cope with some of the other things likely to be thrown at me.

Quite what they were to be I hadn't realised yet. I was offered the job, accepted, and this time no governors resigned. Before the news was official, David Sherratt pinned a large Wellington boot on the Head's section of the noticeboard in the Berkhamsted staff-room; I am not sure how many people twigged the joke. The Berkhamsted governors accepted my resignation, the Wellington governors announced my appointment, and the process of beginning to find my successor at Berkhamsted was begun. The choice was the Revd Keith Wilkinson, then the Conduct (senior chaplain) of Eton, a married man with two daughters, on the surface a calm, clever man, I guess thought by the governors of Berkhamsted likely to be a safe pair of hands, a peace-maker.

ॐॐ

Before we moved, there were family matters to sort out. Dominic, the eldest son, had his place at Hertford College, Oxford; Thackwray, called always Dax, had been turned down by the same College, even though he was the most academic of the three children, and was destined for the School of Oriental and African Studies in London, from which in due course he got a doctorate; our daughter, Tamlyn, was halfway through her A levels. Having met her, David Newsome offered her a place in Apsley, the girls' house at Wellington; "do you mind, Dad, if I say No? I'd rather stay at Berkhamsted," she said, for which I was many times thankful during the next year. So we arranged for her to board in Berkhamsted with the family of a friend of hers, and to come back to us for weekends.

A Master's Lodge had been built originally for the Benson family after they had spent a few years living in lodgings within the main College; naturally enough, it was designed as a Victorian vicarage, and the old cellars of that building were still there. However, in 1940, a stick of German bombs had been dropped along the south front of the College, blowing all the windows of the Lodge inwards, and bringing down the entry porch on top of the Master, Robert Longden, killing him instantly, the only casualty of the raid. When The King visited Wellington a year or two later and saw the ruined house next to the virtually undamaged College (it had lost only some windows and part of a garden wall), he said it should be pulled down lest it depress the boys.

Some years after the war, the Lodge had been re-built, on more or less the same floor pattern, but this time the front door and the porch were placed the other side of the house, facing away from College. I was told the then Master had wanted parents to be able to come to see him without advertising their arrival; I suspect it was more to do with a memory of Bobby Longden's sad death. One of the first things we did was to put an extra door directly into the Lodge kitchen to make it easier for people to get to see the Master's wife. The front entrance was used very seldom, except for Royal visits.

Our children noted something else than the position of the doors. On their first visit, they rushed about the house, and then down to us: "Mummy, Daddy," they whispered. "There are SEVEN lavatories". Though our children weren't going to live with us full-time, except in holidays from school and university, we did have the advantage of bringing Ann's mother to live with us. The governors had agreed to our converting two rooms downstairs into a flatlet for her, and her gentle presence made it easier for the Lodge to become a home.

David Newsome's handover document could have not been more different from the tape given to me at Island School: 76 pages of handwritten notes on every aspect of the school, including comments on members of staff and their attributes. He had also written to me regularly since the announcement of my appointment, telling me what was going on.

I remember in particular a letter from him about rugby. The first XV had apparently not been beaten for three seasons. However, in his last Michaelmas term, that record fell: Wellington was beaten by Marlborough. David Newsome wrote it was actually very fortunate for me it had happened while he was still Master and before I took over. I remember being mildly astonished so minor a matter seemed to loom so large.

Two people close to David Newsome were uncertain whether to stay on. One was the Master's secretary, Janet Harding. She knew a great deal about the school, but was not happy with some of the developments in secretarial technology. For instance, she used a typewriter, not a computer; if any document needed correcting, she re-typed it from scratch. Hong Kong had already begun to convert me to the advantages of the word-processor, and Berkhamsted had confirmed the conversion. I was beginning to work on a personal computer myself, and I really did want a secretary who did the same.

I had spent too many years re-typing whole poems because I had left out a comma somewhere to think a typewriter, even an electric one, was always an ally. Janet decided to leave, and the post of Master's secretary was offered to Jacqui Radford, then the Head's secretary at the Wellington prep school, Eagle House. After visiting me at Berkhamsted, she accepted the post, and served as my secretary for all my years as Master.

John Robson, the Chaplain, had come from Christ's Hospital at the same time as David Newsome; they were close friends, indeed, John Robson sometimes called himself 'The Master's Chaplain'. It was quickly apparent John Robson and I were not likely to agree about a good many things. For instance, his response – and the Master's – to increasing indiscipline in Chapel had been to have fewer and fewer full school chapels, to which all boarders were expected to come, unless they were Roman Catholics going to mass in the local Catholic church. Instead, there was a voluntary Communion service after prep (homework) on a weekday evening, and

Winston Nagan, Professor of International Law at the University of Florida, talking to Jonty and Ann at Wellington, 1998.

only on two Sundays a term was there a full school chapel service. On the other Sundays, there was Matins, attended by some staff and their families, and by very few boys and girls.

Of course, I was going to change nothing before I arrived; but I made it clear to John Robson I had never felt any compunction about compelling pupils to do what I thought was good for them. They had to attend classes; they had to play games; they had to do their homework; and, since this was a 'Royal and Religious Foundation', I could see no problem about compelling attendance at Chapel. Indiscipline in Chapel would be treated as indiscipline was going to be wherever it occurred. Would I compel attendance at Communion services? he asked. Of course, I would never – and could never – compel a pupil to take communion if he or she didn't want to; but, if it was the central sacrament in the Anglican liturgy, surely making boys and girls experience it, even vicariously, couldn't be wrong?

In the circumstances, John Robson decided he would retire from the school before I arrived. Although I was nervous a new chaplain might be appointed with whom I had as little in common as I had experienced at Berkhamsted, the then assistant chaplain at Wellington, the Revd Michael Outram, was available, so he could be promoted to the senior post, and we found a new assistant chaplain, the Revd William Cameron.

There is more to say about Chapel, but I must tell other bits of the story first.

ন্ট&

Soon after our arrival in Wellington, some of what I was going to have to do other than the list I had given the governors in interview became apparent. On the first evening of term, Ann and I went for a stroll in the dusk. Not far from the Lodge, on a path down the edge of the railway line which ran in a cutting through the grounds, we saw approaching us two boys, both with lighted cigarettes in their hands as they strolled along, chatting. Seeing us, they dropped the cigarettes on the ground.

"The Master isn't meant to come here," one of the boys said.

"The Master goes where he wants; and if I catch either of you smoking again you're in trouble. Back to your houses, gentlemen, and pass the word round."

In assembly next day, I said to the school, "I need to make this absolutely plain. If there were once, there are no longer any 'no-go' areas in this school. I shall go wherever I want, whenever I want; and if I catch you breaking rules you can expect punishment."

It can't have been more than a fortnight later that a sixth former came to interview me for the school magazine. He was clearly seething with rage, even to be in my presence, and I could barely persuade him to sit down to ask me the questions he said he had. He asked me some innocuous question and then, almost without meaning to, burst out, "Are you aware just how unpopular you are with the sixth form?"

I hadn't realized I had managed to do enough yet to make myself so immediately unpopular, although it was already becoming apparent I was going to have to do quite a bit.

"Why do you think it's a good thing for new Headmasters to be popular?" I asked.

"You've made it pretty clear you think lots needs changing…"

"I've hardly had time to make up my mind about that, yet, have I?"

"But you are going to make changes, aren't you?"

I had forgotten that, however revolutionary they like to think they are, most adolescents loathe change. I can't remember where the interview went after the initial anger, nor what was published. I would certainly have told him what I have said often enough: that being a white South African, but so deeply anti-apartheid I was prepared to go into exile rather than compromise with the system, was very good practice for being unpopular. I really didn't care whether I was popular or not; I was going to do what I thought the school needed. What the school itself – certainly in the shape of the sixth form – thought it needed seemed immaterial.

There were however still many things I didn't understand about the place. For instance, how was it possible a school so magnificently handsome was beset with litter which would have disgraced a slum?

For instance how could pupils who claimed to be proud of their school treat it so abjectly? One evening, walking through a quadrangle, I came across a senior boy casually urinating into a corner when there was a lavatory within 20 yards of him. I came so close to striking him in my outrage I forgot to deal out an actual punishment. For instance, when we had the prefects into the Lodge, we were shocked by the grossness of their manners; some of them helped themselves to the wine we had provided with an oafishness unlike anything we had experienced with sixth formers in any of the four schools we had known intimately since 1968. Behaviour in the dining room was worse than bad-mannered; food-fights were common, and some of the girls from Apsley (the girls' boarding house) refused to set foot there.

There was a particular problem in the common room too, although about this David Newsome had warned me. He had – he said – promoted Noel Worswick from being a head of department to being director of studies, and he now chaired an academic board that did more to poison relationships than solve problems, partly because it excluded some heads of the academic departments from its deliberations.

David Newsome said he had hoped, by promoting Noel Worswick, he might make him less of a problem; the error was acknowledged. That was easy enough to sort out: I was (I explained) going to chair regular meetings of the heads of department myself, so we wouldn't need an academic board any more. The problem of Noel Worswick himself would take me a while longer to sort out.

There was something else wrong with the school, and I didn't know what it was. Frank Fisher had written somewhere that Wellington was a peculiarly difficult school to master, mainly because of the great mass of boys living in close proximity in College, in the centre of the school. They could be led, but not driven.

The overcrowding had been eased a bit by moving one house, the Anglesey, out into a separate building, but the governors had also taken the decision to close down the so-called 'holding houses' into which first-year pupils had gone before being fitted into the main boarding units. The last two of these, Heathcote and White Cairn, were closed in my third year as Master, but still the central College was like a huge ocean-liner, steaming ahead on a fixed course, difficult to slow down, even harder to steer.

The houses in the central College weren't known as 'houses'; they were called 'dormitories', and their housemasters were called 'tutors'. It was regarded as a promotion for a tutor to move to be a housemaster of a house in the grounds: the Talbot, the Stanley, the Benson, the Picton (still sometimes thought of as a 'dormitory' because once upon a time it had been connected to the main College by a tunnel, and it didn't have its own dining room); and now the Anglesey. The first three named had their own dining arrangements.

The girls' house was called just Apsley, without a definite article in front of it. In College the boys' dormitories were named after various of Wellington's generals: the Hill, the Murray, the Lynedoch, the Hopetoun, the Blucher, the Beresford, the Orange, the Combermere, the Hardinge. Total numbers in the school were usually a few above 800, 760 boys, 40 girls (in my time, we budgeted on 799 altogether, which meant that any excess made what the accountants called 'the bottom line' look good). Frank Fisher had allowed some day-pupils, but they had places in the boarding houses: two dayboys were generally allocated the space allowed for one boarder. There was an obvious case to be made for instituting a separate day-house; but it wasn't a priority. There were advantages including the day-pupils in boarding, especially as they stayed at school until quite late in the evening.

One Monday morning in my first term, the housemaster of the girls' boarding house, Rashid Benammar, a French-Algerian by birth, appeared in my study before Chapel, to tell me that, the evening before, he had caught two boys climbing into the girls' house. He named the boys, and I asked what the standard punishment for the offence was; it was apparent this wasn't the first time Rashid had had the problem. "Rustication," he said.

I had already learned the distinction between suspension and rustication in Wellington parlance: suspension was *sine die* – no day fixed for return; rustication was for a set period, usually a week. I had decided I really didn't like the notion of rustication. I didn't want pupils thinking they were definitely going to return and knowing when that would be.

I wanted them out of school, wondering if they would be allowed to return – and I would require them to write to me saying that, if they were allowed to return, they would behave. It would give me the opportunity of explaining a return was conditional.

I asked Rashid to send the boys and their housemasters to see me as soon as possible. When they arrived, I checked there was no dispute over the facts: yes, they had climbed into Apsley, and they had been caught. They knew it was against school rules, and a serious matter. "Very well, then", I said. "I am suspending both of you. You are both demoted as prefects" (one boy was in fact head of house) "and your housemasters will arrange with your families how you get home. Once you are home, you may write to me asking if I am prepared to re-admit you to school. Clearly that won't happen if I don't have an assurance of better behaviour in future. That's all. Thank you. You may go." The boys left; the housemasters left; and I was puzzled. There was some undercurrent I didn't understand, some mystery in the responses I had had, from the boys but also their housemasters. Something was not being said.

I got my secretary to type a notice for the common room saying the boys had been suspended. Shortly afterwards, the Second Master – a charming, courteous schoolmaster, a teacher of modern languages called Peter White, nicknamed 'Pog' because of his initials, POG – appeared in my study. Could he talk to me? Of course; he didn't even have to ask. Wouldn't he sit down? No, he was rushing; but he had just seen a notice in common room that I had suspended two senior boys. Yes, that was so. Was I aware, he wondered, that one boy was hooker, and the other loose-head prop, for the first XV, and we had a big match on the Saturday? Yes, I was; I had watched them playing several times, and jolly good players they were; wasn't it a good thing we had a strong second XV, too? His response was to wonder if I had discussed the suspension with the master in charge of the first XV.

I hope I didn't actually growl as I replied I hadn't; I probably didn't add I had absolutely no intention of discussing anything of the kind with the master i/c the first XV. After a moment or two of silence, the Second Master left, and I returned to my paper-work.

Some time later there was another knock on my door. This time it was the master i/c the first XV. I need to explain, at this point, that John

Martin was one of the two Wellington staff I had met before Chris Saunders suggested I should consider applying; moreover, he was one of the masters keen on long-distance running whom David Newsome had asked to take me out to show me places to run when I visited the school. We had run together two or three times, and I liked and admired him; he had been an outstanding games-player in his youth (a hockey international and a county cricketer) and now was a first-class coach of rugby, and the best kind of all-round schoolmaster. Nevertheless, when he came into my study that day, I did not invite him to sit down. "What can I do for you?" I asked; by now, the growl may have been noticeable.

"You know these two boys you've suspended..." He named them. I nodded.

"Well, they are in the front row of the first XV." I nodded again.

"Well, I just wanted to thank you. There is now a chance I shall be able to keep control of the 1st XV for the rest of the season."

"You'd better sit down, John," I said. "I clearly need to understand some things a bit better."

And so it became apparent one of the problems in the school was the rugby-players in the first XV had been regarded as such an elite they could do no wrong. The season before, the captain of rugby (actually a very nice boy, son of an Eton housemaster) had been caught in the girls' boarding house. He had merely been gently reprimanded by the Master and then asked what he thought the score in the next match was likely to be. That explained Rashid's diffidence in telling me what had happened, and the Second Master's query; and it explained something more about the school.

An even more serious problem became apparent later that term. One of the senior housemasters, taking his dog for a stroll during prep time, heard some noise coming from a clearing in the woods; when he investigated, he found five sixth formers, all of them fairly obviously high on something. He took their names, and sent them packing back to their houses. After collecting a porter and a torch, he went back to the clearing to investigate. It was apparent there had been some rapid covering up of whatever had been going on there.

Next morning, the five boys were paraded in my study, with their housemasters. I offered them a choice: they could go at once to the sanatorium, where the school doctor would take urine samples for testing, or they could go home. Glances were exchanged, and the five boys chose to go home. "Very well," I said. "You are suspended from school for the time being, while we investigate what was going on. I hope you will explain to your parents what you were doing."

Remembering from my days in Hong Kong the higher up the chain of command you went, the quicker the action, I telephoned the Chief Constable. A squad of police from the drugs squad came, with a sniffer-dog. Very soon there was evidence of illegal drugs, and not merely cannabis. I consulted the new Vice President, General Sir Roland Guy, to tell him I didn't think there was any alternative but expulsion. I'm not sure if it was then school policy, but it was certainly mine that, if I suspended anyone, I at once informed the Vice President, though I did not ask for permission to proceed. However, before I expelled anyone, I required of myself I should consult the Vice President; it was one way of ensuring I moved slowly before imposing a school's ultimate sanction. With Roly Guy's backing, I wrote to the parents, and informed the school.

The reaction within the school, from both staff and pupils, seemed to me almost one of relief, as if they had been waiting for something like this to happen, and were glad it now had. In the newspapers, there was the usual shock/horror about misdeeds within a 'toffs' top school'. I had prepared a press statement, which my secretary read out or faxed to anyone who enquired; otherwise we tried not to field enquiries, except from worried parents. I suspect myself many people knew perfectly well there was a considerable drug-problem at Wellington. After all, we weren't the first school to have it, and the year before, one of our ex-pupils, a young woman, scion of a celebrated family, had died apparently of an overdose of drugs in an incident at Oxford.

In a sense, the most instructive reaction came from one of the housemasters. He told me he had been to the Master the year before to warn him there was a problem with the abuse of drugs in the school.

"Oh," David Newsome had replied, "The Wellingtonian doesn't take drugs." And of course the Master was right: the ideal Wellingtonian, the person described in the last chapter of his history of the school, the brave, outgoing, generous-hearted military type, bolshie in captivity, faithful in friendship, loyal beyond reason … oh, he would never take illegal drugs; indeed, he'd probably avoid all drugs including aspirin, except a dram or two of single-malt whisky, and then only when appropriate.

There were boys like that at Wellington in my time and, if I ever have to be locked up in prison or detention again, I'd choose as many Old Wellingtonians as companions as I could; but to suppose all the boys and girls were like that is merely sentimental. A few were like that by their very nature. Some weren't like that, but would grow into that as the school influenced them. Others were made of ordinary clay, and could be led, either into decent and sensible behaviour, or into foolishness, and worse than foolishness.

At first, I hoped these five boys were merely one isolated group. All too quickly, it became apparent this wasn't the case. The school was riddled with little groups who thought, because nothing had been done to stop them, no one really minded they occasionally broke the law by smoking cannabis, eating magic mushrooms, downing amphetamines, or whatever. The first thing I needed to do was to be absolutely explicit about the policy I intended to enforce.

At the start of every half-term from then on until the end of my time at Wellington, even after I thought we had the problem contained, if never certainly beaten, I made sure everyone in the school heard me say, plainly, that any boy or girl who got involved in illegal drugs in any way must expect, as a result, first suspension and then expulsion. The same policy was stated explicitly in letters to parents. No one could have had any doubt where the line was drawn and what I would do if the line was crossed.

My end-of-year letter in 1990 to parents included this:

> boys and girls now know that (a) I will not hesitate to call the Drugs Squad if I suspect the law is being broken. (b) I shall not waste time discussing whether drugs like cannabis are addictive or not, better or worse than alcohol, or whatever (though I have my own very strong

views on the matter): they are illegal, and a conviction on a boy's or girl's record could blight his or her whole career. (c) If a boy or girl is found passing illegal drugs to another pupil, or in possession of illegal drugs, or under the influence of illegal drugs, he or she must face immediate expulsion, as well as a report filed with the Drugs Squad.

There is no question of our bringing in random blood-tests for drug abuse. At the heart of a school like Wellington is a social contract based on trust, affection and generosity; we run the College believing that we are all on the same side, agreeing to co-operate in the best interests of everyone alike. Sadly, we often fall from our own high standards; but if we were to introduce random blood-tests we would be deliberately breaking the basis of trust on which we think we depend. And, practically speaking, what would we do if a boy refused to be tested? Expel him? On suspicion he might be guilty? The ethical and legal consequences hardly bear thinking about.

At the same time, all parents of all boys and girls (and I do mean all) must be aware that we are going back into a phase in which illegal drugs are easily available. Your children will be exposed to drugs: they will be offered drugs at parties, and a few are bound to experiment. It is very important to keep channels of communication with your children open enough so that if they do experiment, they can talk to you about it without feeling you will not listen, however much you disapprove. There is some evidence that those whose already smoke are more likely to accept smokeable drugs (another reason for trying to prevent the habit); there are serious warnings that cannabis may be mixed with smokeable heroin… and both cocaine and crack are beginning to be available. Problems with drugs are just as likely to happen during the holidays as at school. I would urge you all to be vigilant, as well as loving.

Was I wrong to take such a stringent line? Of course, once I had said what I would do, I had to do it, or risk anarchy; and it turned out I expelled (with the consent of the Vice President and the subsequent approval of governors) 32 boys and girls in my first two years for various kinds of offences mainly involving illegal drugs, although there was some serious bullying I had to deal with too (more of that later).

They were by no means inadequate pupils, either: several times we were astonished whom the latest culprit turned out to be, for instance, a dayboy in his last year at school, an outstanding games-player heading for a good university, who had been buying cannabis in a local pub and selling it at a profit to other pupils... But that was the case; so out he went. He was lucky he didn't go out via the police, too, though I was always scrupulous about informing them.

And what about the boy who said this was the very first time he had tried pot, and it was only because the other boys in the group were doing it, and he promised never to do it again, if only I'd give him a second chance? There were schools which tried a more liberal policy, whereby so-called 'first offenders' were put on to a regime of occasional surprise testing, as professional athletes are tested for drug-abuse. My judgement was a good many Wellingtonians, given one free shot, would take it, just to see what happened.

I am sure, however, there were boys I expelled who were shocked enough by what had happened never to stray again. I have a particular memory of one case, where a father, an ex-soldier and a faithful OW, had been to see me when his son arrived in the school, specially to tell me how much he approved of my policy on drugs; he was sure the stringent policy was good for the school and its reputation. Less than a year later, he was back again, to plead his young son's case after he had been found experimenting with cannabis. I would have fought for my own sons if they had been in similar trouble; but, if I had relented for one boy, surely I would have had to relent for everyone. I hardened my heart and hoped I was right.

I doubt if we caught everyone we could have caught; and I know I made mistakes, though I am as sure as I can be I never expelled anyone who had not been involved in drug-taking in some way. Because I often found myself, especially early on in my time at Wellington, trying to find other schools for boys I had expelled, I felt I had to accept the occasional boy expelled from another school, though I said I wouldn't take boys expelled for drug-abuse. The Headmaster of another famous school, a friend and ally, persuaded me to take a lower sixth boy whom he felt had been unlucky to be caught breaking bounds in quite a minor way, but after a final warning; no, he assured me, there was no suggestion illegal drugs were involved.

I consulted a housemaster, and we interviewed the boy; he seemed surly, even by usual teenage standards, but was clearly an able all-rounder. We had room for him, and so took him on. Within half a term, it became apparent that the breaking of bounds at his last school must have been because he was dealing in drugs – and of course by the time we caught him he had dragged two other boys in the house into his own misdemeanor. All three had to go.

The parents of the home-grown boys were understandably furious with me; why had I risked taking into the school a boy so clearly a 'wrong 'un'? It seemed very wet of me to plead that the recommendation had come from a man I trusted implicitly; and when that man himself telephoned to apologise – because he had now discovered that his original recommendation had been misinformed – I was doubly mortified.

Even worse was the case when I took on a black boy from South London, the much loved son of a single mother; he had been reluctantly expelled by the Head of Christ's Hospital School, not for any heinous offence, merely a multitude of small ones. The Head was sure he had learned a lesson, and the case for compassion was strong; the boy's fees would continue to be paid not by the hard-pressed mother, but by a charity. I liked the boy, felt sorry for him, and found a sympathetic housemaster to take him on. Reformation was apparent; success looked likely; then a small group in another house was found with cannabis and a home-made hookah. One of the group had bought from outside the school some cannabis resin, but didn't know how to use it. Who could they get to show them? That new boy from South London? Blacks knew about dope, didn't they? So they persuaded the boy to show them what to do; of course, living as he did, where he did, he knew. He showed them, but didn't join in himself. Still, there was no way I could chuck them out and keep him; all had to go, though I did wish I could chuck the boy who had bought the cannabis resin into school a little further than I chucked the others.

The black boy's mother – a sister in a hospital in South London who worked night-shifts because she earned more that way, and who was clearly exhausted - sat in my study, weeping as she begged me to forgive her errant son. He wasn't a bad boy, was he? No, he wasn't. Couldn't I give him another chance? Please? Just one more chance? No, I couldn't, though I too wept as I hardened my heart.

In my second year, I began to detect the first signs my tough policy might be beginning to have an influence. The head of school told me that, at a party in London over the Christmas holidays, he had been offered a joint; he had refused, he said, and told me, grinning, he had cited as his reason the fact I was such a fierce Headmaster that, if I found out he had taken a single puff, even if he managed to do it without inhaling, he'd certainly get expelled. I had made it easier for my pupils to say No. Though I clearly wasn't popular, I no longer felt quite so hated, as I had done sometimes in my first year, when I had gone home to the Lodge one day to tell Ann I thought I might have made a terrible mistake coming to Wellington. She had been inclined to agree with me.

However, as the second year went on, I realised that, whatever the newspapers said, I had the support of most parents, almost all staff, indeed most of the boys and girls, and certainly all the governors. I asked Roly Guy if he would mind telling me why the governors had appointed me. "Oh," he said, "Simple really: you have a reputation of being a bastard about discipline."

Having had their official help several times, I now made an arrangement with the local drugs squad that they could use the school for the occasional training exercise, searching the grounds and the dormitories. Their sniffer-dog, a friendly spaniel, had one unfortunate habit: when he found drugs, he always got so excited he never failed to drop a turd. The training exercise had found nothing in the grounds; however, in one of the dormitories, the dog had suddenly got beyond himself with excitement about something under a boy's bed, and gave his handler the usual evidence. When the police dug under the bed, they found, not a cache of illegal drugs, but something else secreted there: a tightly rolled up pair of old and very smelly rugby stockings.

More often, what we heard was tragic: the ex-pupil from a famous landowning family whose experiments with so-called non-addictive cannabis had resulted in a psychotic breakdown which ended with his sectioning in a hospital; the ex-pupil who took LSD at a London party, was therefore sure he could fly, and whose body was found next morning on the roof of a car, three floors down – and then his sister, also an OW, committed suicide apparently because she couldn't forgive herself for introducing him to drugs.

It did interest me, in those dreadful years, to discover from the registrar of Wellington, Sue England, that considerably more than half of the pupils I had expelled came from just one prep school. The school concerned had an excellent reputation, though known as somewhat liberal; was that why so many of its ex-pupils got themselves into trouble at Wellington? Or was it that the school directed towards Wellington those of its pupils whom it thought needed good discipline? I've no idea. It was not a question I could ask, though thenceforth I did look warily at pupils applying from that school.

∽∾

Illegal drug-taking was not the only problem which needed to be dealt with. There was clearly bullying going on, especially in some houses and dormitories. Fagging – the practice of making younger boys work for the senior boys, for instance, by cleaning their shoes, or making their beds, or washing their games kit – had been forbidden years before; but there were still some collective duties that first-year boys were expected to do within each house. There was also something known as 'the fags' test', which was in theory a way of ensuring new boys learned a necessary amount about the school and its people in a hurry when they arrived. Both the remnants of fagging and the fags' test were innocuous enough, unless senior boys in a house abused them.

Initiation rituals were outlawed, but still crept back in if housemasters were not vigilant: "this was done to me when I arrived," said one senior, "so why shouldn't I do it to the new boys in their turn?" 'This' turned out to be to make the new boys run the gauntlet down the passage of a dormitory, while the seniors buffeted them with pillows. A pillow-fight in a dormitory? Hardly bullying? Yes, but running the gauntlet when some sadist among the seniors loaded his pillow with boots?

As I knew from my own schooldays, bullying, especially in a big boarding school, was almost impossible to stamp out unless one had the co-operation of the senior boys in each house. At Wellington, the prefect system had become obese. Almost everyone in the second-year sixth form would expect to be a house or dormitory prefect; all heads of house or dormitory would expect to be college prefects, and often their deputies too. Only the top three or four office-holders were still selected rigorously, to make what was known – for historical reasons – as 'the upper ten'.

It was beyond my power to tell housemasters who to choose as their prefects, though I was glad when they consulted me. It was however perfectly within my power to refuse to have too many college prefects; and it became normal a head of house was no longer automatically made a college prefect. I wanted 'my' college prefects to be boys and girls I could (within the bounds of common sense) trust utterly. In this way at least, Thomas Arnold had been right: the Head had to have prefects on whom he could rely.

To make my choice less arbitrary, less whimsical, I introduced a system whereby all members of the common room (that is, the teaching staff and a few others) and all members of the lower sixth (the first year A level pupils) were given an opportunity to vote on a list of boys and girls nominated to hold College office, to guide me in the final selection. Since those College officers carried the authority of the Master, it was essential the final decision rested with me; but advice from the staff and senior pupils struck me as worth listening to.

In fact, what at first surprised me was that the guidance offered by the boys and girls was often more sensible than the guidance of the staff; but, when I thought about this, it seemed less surprising. The teaching staff knew very well the people they taught, but few of them had even a vague acquaintance with a full range of the year-group. The boys and girls of the lower sixth had a shrewd idea of who would be fair, honest and even-handed. There was (it transpired) hardly any voting which might have been regarded as frivolous.

As well as introducing an electoral element, I set up a School Council, technically chaired by the head of school, although the Second Master and I made sure we were always present. Each house chose two of its members to represent it, as well as the head of house, and there was a termly meeting. There was no embargo on the raising of any matter, though I made it clear there were to be no comments on individual teachers. The meetings were open to spectators, and a few staff used to turn up to listen.

It was actually too big to be an effective body: 15 houses, each with three reps. Yet to make it smaller would have defeated one of its purposes, which was to give younger boys in a house more chance of speaking up. Occasionally, the agenda alerted us to a problem which we had not already perceived, but most of the usefulness of the Council consisted of the questions asked under AOB. Usually, they were trivial (*ie* could there be second helpings of popular dishes in Hall?) but occasionally significant.

At the same time, we began to put in place a system of 'leadership training'. To a great extent, this was based on my observation of the selection processes used by the military in choosing young officers for training. Ignorant as I was of most things military, I had got myself invited to watch the selection of young officers for Sandhurst and the Army, and then also selection for the Marines, the Navy and the Air Force. What I was watching, I quickly realised, was not just a process of selecting the right people, but also the beginning of their training – and some of the youngsters I watched being selected were going to be, in two years' time, leading platoons of soldiers on the streets of Belfast. I was immensely impressed, not just with the care taken to select the right people, but the lack of prejudice in the process.

What I had suspected about the prefect system became obvious as I watched the military at work: we gave some of our boys and girls at school considerable authority as prefects, but we trained them virtually not at all. Oh, the housemasters and housemistresses gave advice and offered support; but it was casual rather than systematic. We thought one of the functions of our education system was to produce leaders; but we relied on its happening willy-nilly, rather than logically. Since I had myself (now in my 50s) learned things about my own nature when I watched the selection processes (for instance, that the physical timidity of my weedy youth was still there, deep in my make-up, and – more prosaically – that my reaction-times were so slow I would never have made it as a pilot in the RAF), would we not be contributing to the education of the young by trying to teach them more about how to lead?

I managed to get a substantial grant, spread over several years, from the Rank Foundation. This we used (in the first place) to send each year two or three or four of the Wellington staff on a week's course at the Leadership Trust in Ross-on-Wye and (in the second) to send the whole of the lower sixth, in two batches, on a weekend of leadership training based on the St Catherine's Foundation at Cumberland Lodge in Windsor Great Park.

The Leadership Trust was run mainly by ex-Army officers, several of them from the SAS, and was very much influenced by the principles established within the SBS and SAS. Leadership involved skills that could be taught and fostered. Participants on courses were divided into groups, often quite disparate groups, and had to learn to work together in a hurry. There was a strong physical element: for instance, there was a choice of three or four activities: diving; caving; climbing; and sometimes canoeing. You were expected to choose the activity you found most terrifying, because part of the function of the course was to make you confront your own fears.

Another group activity consisted of taking one person from a group and putting him in charge of another group, with very little notice, with that group being given a specific task to achieve. Yet another activity consisted of the group having to deal with a crisis, when information relating to that crisis was dished out very sporadically and often in contradictory form, so that decision-making was necessary but then shown to be cockeyed after all. Most Wellington staff found the courses thoroughly useful, and some found them inspiring.

After some staff had done the course, I was told I should go myself. Of course, that was itself one of the principles of the Leadership Trust: you should not expect your subordinates and colleagues to do what you weren't prepared to do yourself. So I went, in considerable trepidation: I wouldn't have minded learning to canoe, even on white water, but that option wasn't available, so I had to choose diving (I am terrified of drowning and am no longer the reasonably strong swimmer I was in my youth); caving (I am entirely without agility, very tall, stiff and big-boned, and I suffer from claustrophobia); or climbing (I have very little upper-body strength and am frightened of heights).

In the end, I chose drowning. I did the abbreviated diving course, and survived, even managing to sit at the bottom of a diving pool sharing one breathing apparatus with five other men. At one point, I forgot my own terror enough to help a colleague who was having a panic attack under the water.

Perhaps the most interesting day for me was not 'confronting my fear' but being put in charge of the board of management of an international company. Apparently, the owner of the company had got so fed up with the constant bickering of the directors (each based in a different European country) that he had paid for them to spend a week at the Leadership Trust learning how to co-operate. It seemed they had learned little by the fourth day, when I was put in charge of getting them to co-operate enough to build a bailey bridge (which really cannot be done without a whole team working together, under a degree of direction).

We didn't win the competition, but we got very close, and actually got a bridge built, though rather a flimsy version. There was one hilarious moment, early on, when one of the more volatile members of the group – from a southern Mediterranean country – shouted I was a fascist, and stormed off to collect packed lunches for the group. His explosion helped make the rest of the group cohere and, when he returned, somewhat shame-faced (because it turned out we would have got lunch even without his initiative), he too became more co-operative. One of the group, forbidden to do any strenuous work because of a heart condition, had been an international yachtsman, and his skill with ropes and knots was a godsend.

I came away from the course with three main things learned. First, I was better at getting on with a strange group of people than I had realised; I had always seen myself as somewhat aloof, not at all hail-fellow-well-met. Without being anyone other than I was, I had managed to get along very happily and peacefully with a motley crew of other professionals.

Secondly, even though I was 'only a schoolmaster', I had managed to get the international board of a European company to work together in such a way that, afterwards, they complimented me on showing them how it could be done (I never found out, of course, whether the effect of the course lasted longer than the week). All teachers fear, in their hearts of hearts, the old adages deriding the profession may actually be true:

'he who can, does; he who can't, teaches' and 'a man among boys, a boy among men'. The 'Action Learning for Chief Executives' at Ashridge had helped me understand my work as a Headmaster wasn't all that different from the work other 'managing directors' did; but the Leadership Trust course confirmed I could lead, even outside school.

Thirdly, for the rest of my days, I shall try to act on one of the adages of the Leadership Trust: 'confront early'. The longer you wait before you confront a problem, the worse it will get. If you have a member of staff you think is out of order, see him today, not next week. Sometimes, early confrontation will make it apparent there wasn't a problem at all. More often, early confrontation will prevent a pimple becoming a boil.

With the staff better trained, and the selection process refined, I think the prefect system at Wellington got much better than it had been. The leadership training in the Great Park helped, and both staff and pupils enjoyed themselves. I was able to delegate almost all aspects of 'leadership training' to other members of staff.

I had made it plain to the school that, although I would not tolerate bullying of any kind, I couldn't do anything about bullying I didn't know about. Every morning before school began, I would be in my study and available to be seen. If the door was open, boys and girls could walk in to talk to me, to ask me questions, to complain. It is, of course, easy enough to say that but how many 13 year-olds are fearless enough to go to talk individually to the Master face to face? Nearly always, if there was a real problem, it would be a group that came.

I knew there had been a problem over the stealing of sweets from younger boys' tuck-boxes. I could see how the pattern would go. Here's a small boy eating a chocolate bar. Heroic head of house goes past and says, "That looks nice." Small boy says, "Have a bite, please." Head of house laughs, and takes a nibble, then leaves.

Not-so-heroic sixth former standing nearby says, "I'll have a bite, too", and takes more than a nibble. Third definitely-not-heroic sixth former says, "I'll have the rest of that." Small boy resists, and maybe saves the rest of his chocolate bar. Bullying sixth former says, "Cheeky little bugger," and raids the small boy's tuck-box.

So here is a group from that house, at my study door. "X has been stealing our sweets, Master", someone in the group tells me. I have come across X already, and know he is quite capable of stealing small boys' sweets, but how can I act without evidence? I explain this to the group, but they have prepared their case. They have taken to marking their chocolate bar wrappers with three little ink-dots. When the bars disappeared, they searched the waste-paper baskets in the senior boys' cubicles. X is such an arrogant swine, he hasn't even bothered to hide the evidence of his stealing.

X is already on a final warning about his behaviour. When his housemaster brings him to me, X doesn't try to deny the thefts, but actually manages to sneer at me: "do you mean to tell me you're going to expel me for stealing a chocolate bar?"

"Yes," I answer – and I confess that was one of the few occasions I got rid of a boy without the slightest compunction.

❧❦

I had learned, not from anything that happened at Berkhamsted itself, but from helping govern a local prep school which needed to change its Headmaster, that the local trouble-shooter of the teachers' union could be a useful ally in dealing with tricky professional problems. Yes, the officials were there to defend the rights of their members, and they would not tolerate unjust dealings or unfair dismissals; but they also knew there were professional standards which needed upholding.

Several times I've asked to have union reps brought in to help resolve disputes with teaching staff; I try to take them aside at some stage to ask, first, if those of us 'acting in authority' have been fair and have done all we should have done, and then to ask for advice about what they reckon should be done next. However strident the public pronouncements of the unions may be, the private professional advice has always been level-headed, and – surprisingly often – outspokenly on the side of the school and its needs.

The problem of Noel Worswick's continuing career at Wellington had been made worse by an accident in school-grounds. Walking from the Lodge to my study one morning, I came across a group of boys laughing their heads off.

"Do you know Mr Worswick's new nickname, sir?" one boy called out. "It's Harvey Wallbanger, sir."

More laughter. I shrugged and made my way to the study. I seemed to remember a Harvey Wallbanger was some sort of cocktail; adolescent humour, I guessed.

When I went to Chapel, 40 minutes later, the reason for the joke was made clear. Noel Worswick's car stood outside Chapel, one wing stove in and the front right wheel bent inwards, and the parapet wall against which the car had come to rest demolished. Straight after Chapel, I saw the bursar and asked him to arrange to get the car shifted and the wall tidied up and repaired as soon as possible. Apparently, coming back from dining with other staff in school grounds, Noel had failed to see the wall. Early retirement was becoming imperative.

I asked to see the representative of the union I knew Noel was a member of. No, an afternoon meeting wasn't convenient; I wanted a meeting at 9 in the morning. I knew that meant the union rep would have to spend the evening before in Noel's company, and possibly as a guest in his spare room.

When the union rep duly appeared, our meeting was over in very few sentences. All he wanted to know was whether I would be generous. Of course, I said. Noel had served the school long (since 1971) and – according to his lights – faithfully. Very well, said the rep: he may as well go to talk to the bursar straight away, and not bother me with the detail. I walked him round to the bursar's office, asked that useful man to settle generous terms for early retirement, and left them to the deal. At the end of the year, Noel left peacefully, and went to live in Oxford.

When I asked the union rep. afterwards why he had been so co-operative, he told me: "well, the moment Noel poured gin on his cornflakes, I knew..."

I had already started to re-shuffle and strengthen the senior leadership of the school. First, I brought in as senior tutor a long-serving member of staff, whose value had I felt been overlooked after he gave up his housemastership. Worswick's retirement, and the departure of the Second

Master, at the end of my third year, gave me the chance to re-organise what I called (not altogether happily) the 'senior management team', soon enough called the SMT. Some Heads like to bring in younger people from outside the schools to enliven their leadership, and often a deputy head will be brought in, almost as a trainee for a headship somewhere else in the few years' time. In the context of the school I had found, I didn't think that would be sensible: what we needed was to use wisely the talents we already had.

Over the 11 years I was at Wellington, I appointed some 95 members of the academic staff. If that seems many, I note that my predecessor appointed 74 over nine years. I would count about two-thirds of those I appointed as successful, and about a half as very successful. In general, the successful staff stayed, some for the rest of their careers as teachers. Not all those who didn't stay were unsuccessful; several who moved on after a year or two or four I would have liked to stay longer; but if it was clear in the course of the first two years staff were not going to be long term successes, it was sensible for them to move sooner rather than later, even if they didn't particularly want to go.

What I must now regard as the worst appointment I made in any school didn't become apparent until after I had left Wellington: he is now serving an 11-year sentence for abusing boys in his care. When I appointed him, I knew there had been trouble at his previous school, because its Headmaster warned me he had suspended the man from his post, after some younger boys had accused him of abuse.

However, I had already offered him the job at Wellington by then (he had a degree in physics, but was going to teach maths, always a difficult subject to find teachers of); so, when his previous school re-instated him after an enquiry had shown the accusations as apparently groundless, I had no reason to withdraw my offer, even if I thought I should. As I have noted already, the predelictions of a teacher are of no real concern; what matters are his activities.

A male homosexual need be no more a threat to boys than a heterosexual to girls. What matters is not what people are but what they do. Now, I may regret having appointed him to the staff, and I certainly feel sorry for the boys he abused; but during the years he served when I was his

Master he did not, as far as I know, behave improperly. Indeed, part of the tragedy is that he had given every appearance of being a very good all-round schoolmaster, however gross his eventual lapse was.

I am not sure if the story I am about to tell is sad or funny. Perhaps it is both. It was always quite hard to find people to appoint as teachers of the relatively new subject of craft, design, technology (CDT). In the old days, in boys' school, they were nearly always teachers of woodwork (even carpentry). Often, they were jolly good teachers, not necessarily that academic, but practical men, loving their work, and good at teaching pupils how to use their hands to make beautiful and useful objects (a tray I made my mother when I was a schoolboy is still in use in my brother's house).

The new technologies (of plastics, of computers) made the subject very different; and finding good teachers was so hard some schools abandoned CDT altogether. The third time I asked him to produce a plan to get his department moving better, the head of department whom I had inherited asked if he might take early retirement; I was then able to appoint an ex-pupil from Island School who did what I thought an excellent job, though he didn't stay as long as I hoped.

One of the appointments I made to that department we all knew was going to be what South Africans term 'chancy': in his way an experienced and well-qualified man, he might (all who interviewed him realised) not fit into the school, either socially or educationally. We risked the appointment, hoping he might adapt himself to our ways. Unfortunately, that didn't happen: fewer and fewer pupils wanted to be taught by him; colleagues found it harder and harder to work with him; parents seemed thrown by his lack of any kind of social grace.

In the end, as I had the perfect right to do, I terminated his contract before two years were up, giving him plenty of time to find another job, and knowing the fact CDT was a 'shortage subject' meant he was likely to get a job quickly. He wasn't happy with the decision, but he went.

Before the man's departure, the elected chairman of common room came to see me. He hadn't always got on well with my predecessor; but he and I had worked out a comfortable *modus operandi* and were open with each other about problems in common room. Now, he wanted to talk to me about Y whose contract I had just terminated. He agreed it had to be done, though it was sad; what he wanted to say to me was this: Y had clearly been a poor appointment, though I had made some excellent appointments since my arrival. What was apparent was this: whenever I consulted widely on appointments and listened to heads of departments, we got good appointments; whenever I went my own way and didn't consult, or ignored the views of those I consulted, we got poor appointments. The case of Y illustrated this clearly. I had appointed him while ignoring the clearly stated opposition of those whom I had consulted.

I was not – am not – a particularly meticulous keeper of files and records, relying perhaps too much on a reasonably good memory, at least for events, circumstances and arguments, if not for names and faces. However, when we were appointing staff, I tended to keep every scrap of paper, every comment by every person who had interviewed the candidates, which we always did *seriatim*, rather than collectively, so that, when it came to the final decision, I could marshal all the pros and cons.

"Hang on a moment, Paul," I said, and went into my secretary's office to collect Y's file. There, at the back of the file, were pinned together the comments of the various people who had shown Y round the school and the department – and crucially there was the comment of one particular man senior in that area. I forget the exact words, but they were to the effect that, though Y was rather an odd person, he was much the most interesting candidate, and could well make a good member of the department.

"That's extraordinary," Paul said. "That's not at all what he said to me. I was told you'd appointed Y by overriding everyone's objections, that no one had agreed with the appointment."

And so I came to a formulation of one general truth about a Head's decisions: the good ones are perceived as having always been made after collective consultation and agreement. The bad ones are perceived as made after he or she has ignored the advice of wiser colleagues.

There is however a corollary: to make no decision is nearly always worse than to make a bad decision. Towards the end of my time at Wellington, I faced decisions about staffing which I would happily have avoided; I shall get to them later.

Almost all the teaching staff – and indeed many of the non-teaching staff too – were housed on campus, on the 400-acre estate that was what remained after outlying bits of the original purchase of Berkshire heathland had been sold off over the years. While it was a great advantage in a boarding school, and a considerable supplement to incomes, it was also a complication for the Master; David Newsome had told me it was the part of his job he found most awkward. I confess I rather enjoyed the intellectual juggling involved, and it certainly wasn't as tricky generally as the juggling of married and unmarried, expatriate and local, I had dealt with in Hong Kong. But still it could present problems and cause disgruntlement.

Consider this (mainly fictitious) example: Mr & Mrs X had both taught at Wellington for nearly 30 years; they had started in a small town-house and gradually, as they had their four children, the Master had managed to find them larger premises, until after a few uncomplaining years jammed into a three-bedroomed house they had had allocated to them a five-bedroomed Victorian house with its own large garden.

This they looked after meticulously for 20 years and made the garden into a showpiece which they opened three or four times a year to fundraise for local charities. Their children – who had been successfully educated at Wellington, admittedly for a fraction of the usual cost – had grown up and left home, and now Mr & Mrs X enjoyed their lovely home and garden and still served the school nobly.

However, the Master had somehow to find a house for Dr & Mrs Z; Dr Z was the new head of the mathematics department, with a First, a doctorate, and excellent experience: a rare acquisition. The Master had had to promise him housing as good as he had had in his last post. The only suitable housing was the house that Mr & Mrs X had lived in – and loved – and furnished with antiques and decorated themselves, because they felt the works department rushed at jobs – for 20 years. No, they did not want to be moved to a new three-bedroomed bungalow which the College had retained as part of the deal on selling the land for development on the edge of the College estate; they wanted to stay where they were for the last five years of their service to the College.

৵৽

There was I guess always someone who would think any decision the Master made was bad. It was certainly a good thing the Master was not officially a member of common room. Although I went into common room three times a week for a break-time meeting, it was the only time I ever went in without invitation. A couple of times when I needed to find a member of staff in a hurry, I would actually wait outside the common room until I could ask someone if it was all right if I went in. I reckon the staff needed somewhere they could sound off to their colleagues about my lousy decisions and iniquitous misjudgements in the certainty I wouldn't turn up unexpectedly. For the occasional common room dinners, too, I would always ask if Ann and I might be invited, rather than assuming we would be welcome.

One of the unusual aspects of the College was its ownership of a social club in the grounds with its own licence: in effect, a private pub, where staff – both teaching and non-teaching – could gather for a drink and a chat or a game of darts or cards, often late in the evening when technically all the pupils were safely in their houses and dormitories. The social mingling of teaching and non-teaching staff was, I think, both important and unusual, and helped break down a barrier that may exist too easily in what I suppose must be inevitably hierarchical schools. Again, I was careful not to barge into the social club too frequently, although I did chair meetings of the committee that ran the place.

৵৽

The other major problem of my early years at Wellington was our relationship with the prep schools which fed us pupils. Am I right to remember Frank Fisher had governed 17 different prep schools? He had certainly been largely responsible for the purchase of Eagle House school on the edge of our estate. Although technically a separate institution, the governors of Wellington appointed the chairman of governors of Eagle

House and several other governors, and the Master served *ex officio* on the board.

However, Wellington needed to recruit at least 150 boys aged 13+ each year, and preferably a few more. Eagle House produced only a proportion of that intake at 13+. For years, entry had been built on the foundations which Frank Fisher had laid; David Newsome accepted the occasional invitation to preach at a feeder prep school or to give away the prizes at a speech day, but there had been very little effort needed to nurture the crucial relationship which would result in prep schools recommending Wellington. Nevertheless, in his time, the order-books were full, and often the lists for entry would be closed several years in advance.

I think it was the bursar, Colonel David Cook, who first told Ann and me he was worried about numbers; when I looked at the lists of pupils who had registered to join us, and the lesser numbers still on our books, he was clearly right. Quite suddenly, those easy passages from prep schools especially in the south, south-west and south-east to Wellington had begun to empty. It happened in other schools too, but Wellington seemed especially hard-hit. Was it the bad publicity engendered by the expulsions for drug offences? Was it the Lloyds debacle, whereby dozens (perhaps it was even hundreds) of effortlessly wealthy families found themselves no longer rich? Was it the economic crisis of 1987 called 'Black Monday'? Was it that Frank Fisher's influence had disappeared after his death?

I have no sure idea, but suddenly what David Newsome had referred to as lists full enough to close years ahead began to look empty, and a priority for the registrar, and especially the Master, was to get more pupils signed up. We had to do more to make especially the Heads of the prep schools which had traditionally sent pupils to us aware we were still a very good all-round boarding school; for too long we had been living on the bumper harvests which Frank Fisher's careful husbandry had nurtured.

A first step was to make our own housemasters aware of the problem. The tradition at Wellington was that, when a boy was registered, his parents opted at the same time for a particular house or dormitory. While we said we couldn't guarantee there would be a place in that house or dormitory, we knew perfectly well parents looked first at the school and then at the housemaster. It was he who would provide day-to-day care. The suggestion we should have merely a general list of those registered, and then ourselves allocate pupils to houses or dormitories, seemed likely to be self-defeating.

More sensible would be to give the housemasters some responsibility for filling their own lists. Of course, we could have waiting-lists; and some parents had no idea which house or dormitory to choose, so we could do some directing; but it was essential for the housemasters to understand keeping Wellington full was part of their responsibility. The registrar and I would do what we could, but their co-operation was necessary – and demanding of their time and energy. It wasn't just the Master who had to tour the prep schools and be nice to parents and Heads; it was all of us.

So we began a regular circus of invitations to prep school Heads and their wives (where they had them) to come to Wellington to be shown around the school, by their ex-pupils if possible, to meet housemasters and tutors, to be shown departments, and to be wined and dined. Most of the time it was great fun, and we met some admirable people. We also accepted as many invitations to visit prep schools as we could, however minor the occasion seemed to be.

Having spent part of my childhood in a prep school run by my parents, I think I have a special affinity with the small prep school deep in the country, catering for not that many pupils, often boarders, quite often eccentric in some aspect, nearly always loving and gentle. I know the image of these schools presented by some writers (who do often seem to find their experience of schools as awkward as I indeed found my own) as versions of Dotheboys Hall; but Ann and I used to enjoy being invited, especially to prep schools for Sunday evensong.

The pattern was usually this: we would arrive in time for afternoon tea, and then be shown a few empty classrooms and some dormitories. At six a bell would sound, and the pupils would gather for an evening service, often with the youngest in pyjamas, dressing gowns and slippers. The congregation would sing a cheerful hymn or two ('The day Thou gavest, Lord, has ended...'), the choir would sing an anthem, the Head would read a lesson and say some well-worn prayers, and then, as the visiting Head got up to preach, the Head's wife would slip out to make sure supper was ready for her guests; often, the school Labrador would follow her.

I invariably followed the old advice once given to a nervous young Head, who asked, "What shall I preach about?"

"About seven minutes."

Indeed, 'preaching' would dignify what I did: I would tell a few stories from my childhood, and perhaps one or two of my father's stories from the war. Then there would be some more prayers, a last hymn, a grace, and the choir would leave. Often, at that stage, the visiting Head would be introduced to the boys 'down' to join his school. Then supper, a glass of wine, and a journey home, with both of us struggling to keep awake, unless we had been sensible enough to get a driver to take us. (Frank Fisher had been told by the governors that they would not appreciate a headline in the press, 'Master of Wellington on drink-drive charge', and so had advised him to let himself be driven to functions where he might be given a drink or two; David Newsome had passed on the advice.)

Somehow or the other, we managed to keep Wellington more or less full to capacity until 2000. This does, however, bring me to the central paradox of my time as Master.

I arrived at Wellington just as the academic league-tables were beginning to be noticed. For all its reputation as one of the great schools of the United Kingdom, Wellington was in fact lower in the academic league tables than the school I had just left. Most of the great boarding schools we regarded as rivals in terms of recruitment of pupils (Eton, Harrow, Charterhouse, Marlborough, Shrewsbury, Rugby, Radley perhaps most of all) were miles ahead of us in the league-tables: we were low down in the third division, not even the second, much less the first. It was one thing for me to point out that our clever boys and girls still got their three, four or even five As at A level and their places at Oxford and Cambridge; a parent with a reasonably clever child and not much experience of schools would be sensible to choose a school where most pupils got good A results, rather than merely some.

The easiest way for a boys' school to improve its position in the league-tables was to take in girls (I know of only one girls' school which tried to take in boys). In a sense, Wellington had already done a little of that, when Frank Fisher had opened Apsley House. However, when I talked to our girls about opening another girls' sixth form house, they were unanimously against the idea: they survived in a big boys' boarding school because they had a single fortress to retreat to, where they did not have to compete. If there was another girls' house, competition would be inevitable. Anyway, even 40 more clever girls in the school wouldn't get us from the third division into the first.

At the governors' behest, in 1990 and again in 1995, I produced a paper showing how Wellington could go co-ed. Having run a co-ed school (Island School had a small majority of girls), having worked in another (MHS), and knowing that Sevenoaks had gone fully co-ed from 1983 when the Kent LEA stopped funding the grammar school intake there, I was personally quite keen on co-education.

If Wellington had been a day-school, to go co-ed would have been simple: from the next September, we would simply start recruiting girls in the same way we recruited boys. It wouldn't have made us popular with the girls' schools in Berkshire, but it could have been done. However, Wellington was 90% a boarding-school (most houses and dormitories had 11 pupils per year; usually, two of them would be dayboys, though often one of those would become a boarder in the sixth form). Moreover, it was designed as a boarding-school, not as a day-school.

So, to make Wellington co-ed without increasing its overall size – which of course we could have done, but that would have required more classrooms and a bigger dining-hall, and there was already not really enough room in Chapel for the whole school – one would have, over a five-year period, to empty one or two boarding houses from the bottom up; you could hardly start putting young girls into the first year of a boys' boarding house.

You could, of course, shut a boys' house down abruptly and transfer its pupils into other houses; but that required the other houses to have vacancies. And you wouldn't then at once fill that house with girls; they would need to be brought in, year by year. My paper showed the various permutations, and I worked out that, before Wellington could go co-ed, total numbers would have to be allowed to drift downwards to some 670 before you could begin seriously to recruit girls as boarders at 13+. Our present numbers were based on an entry of 799. Let us suppose fees were then some £20,000. 799 – 670 = 129 X £20,000 per annum... Even governors theoretically keen on co-education blanched at the thought of that loss of income.

The other way of driving a school up the league-tables was to admit fewer of the not very clever pupils. While Wellington was not at that stage a difficult school for boys to get into (if their parents could afford the fees), I did turn a few boys away every year. Sometimes, this was because, when we interviewed them, it was apparent they would probably hate the school. Sometimes it was because we thought they wouldn't cope with its academic or emotional demands; but it was seldom at that stage purely intellectual. We had a theoretical pass-mark at Common Entrance: 55% (other schools would say 60% or even 65%). Yet we all knew that was more or less meaningless, because schools marked the Common Entrance exams for themselves, and set the levels where they wanted.

Most reasonably intelligent youngsters from reasonably good prep schools would have been well enough taught to get at least that sort of mark – and, if they didn't, there were usually extenuating circumstances or a special talent we were interested in (we did not however give sports scholarships, and I set my face firmly against them; we already had more than our share of good games-players, so why spend money getting even more?).

Anyway, one of the real strengths of Wellington had always been that it was a school for all-rounders. We were not Winchester, nor Westminster, we were Wellington. When I spoke at banquets in the City, and explained that those who got academic results in the bottom 25% per cent ended up employing those whose results were in the top 25%, I invariably got a huge laugh of rueful recognition. Some of our best pupils had struggled to get 55% in the Common Entrance exams, but five years later got good enough A levels to find places in the better universities.

Could we, without going co-ed and without raising our entry-levels at 13+, push ourselves higher in the league-tables? I really did not want Wellington to become the kind of school that concentrated its energies on teaching merely for good exam results. When I had been a classroom teacher myself, I had resisted as fiercely as I could any notion that all we should do had to be relevant to the O or A level syllabuses.

It was not pretension to claim to teach beyond the exam syllabuses. It was bad enough the introduction of the AS level exams, taken at the end of the lower sixth, forced teachers to spend the lower sixth year teaching more formally towards an exam, when once upon a time we had regarded the lower sixth as the year when teachers and taught could follow their intellectual and imaginative interests way beyond any conventional notion of syllabus.

Of course, especially our boys should be made to work harder. Teachers too were encouraged to teach better and more systematically – and, when we measured the intellectual levels of our boys on entry, we were able to show that, five years later, they had achieved considerable improvements; but that is not what most league-tables were designed to show. They listed raw results, and Wellington stayed relatively low in those lists. Fifteen years later, more and more schools began to opt out of the league-tables, mainly without ill consequences; but while I was Master there was no escaping the brute fact: compared to our rivals, we seemed not particularly academic. Fortunately, there were enough parents who could see beyond the surface to keep our numbers buoyant, and we still had a decent percentage of very clever boys and girls.

The other brute fact was we were an expensive school. Of course, in that we were no different from other big boarding schools; but each year saw us further out of the financial range of the professional middle-classes, the local solicitor, the general practitioner, the sort of family which had traditionally sent especially its sons to boarding schools.

Wellington was in some ways fortunate: we had the Foundation, which (at that time) provided for the education of the sons and daughters of officers serving in the armed forces who had been killed or had died on active service. After wars, there were a good many Foundationers; in my time, there were never more than a dozen. It was also true military families were helped with allowances to cover their children's fees, because they were expected to serve wherever they were sent. The Old Wellingtonian Society had a fund to help a few of its members pay for their children's school fees (although, altruistically, the Society would pay fees for any school, not just for Wellington).

We had various other funds, out of which we provided a range of scholarships to help us bring clever boys and girls into the school, without having to pillage fee-income. Frank Fisher had raised a bursary fund to help parents with fees; for ten years or more, the governors had spent only part of the income, and had used the rest to build up the capital. When the extent of the downturn of the early '90s became apparent, the chairman of the investment sub-committee, David Hopkinson, asked me if, for the duration, I would like to have all the income to help parents who ran out of money to pay the fees; it was a godsend.

However, all in all, when I added up how much of our income came from fees, and how much from endowment of various kinds, it was apparent that about 93% was from fees, and only 7% from endowment. By way of comparison, one American private school I knew something about, Lawrenceville, got roughly half its income from fees, and the other half from endowment. In the long run, what Wellington needed to do was to build a proper endowment. While the governors started such fund-raising before I left the school, we did not achieve what I had hoped for in this regard.

I did at one stage propose as a possibility to the governors what I called the 'Christ's Hospital' alternative: to give up competing with other schools in terms of magnificent facilities, to settle for what we already had as more than adequate, to keep our fees as low as possible, and to concentrate our efforts on raising bursaries and scholarship so that more and more pupils from less wealthy families could come to us.

I don't think any governor saw the whole of that as a real possibility, but they did say I could have the equivalent of five fully-funded places to use at my own discretion, to hand out 'Master's bursaries or scholarships'. Over the years I used those funds (because I could split the five places as variously as I wished, under the watchful eye of the bursar) to get into the school some remarkable boys and girls: a Russian boy who got five As at A level before going to Oxford, where he got his First and a doctorate; one of the sons of the late Chief Abiola of Nigeria, who should have been its President (the boy became head of school and went to Cambridge); the stepson of Archbishop Ndungane of Cape Town, who had been at university with me and who had served a sentence on Robben Island for his membership of the Pan Africanist Congress before becoming an Anglican priest; and various English boys whom I wanted in the school for one reason or another but whose parents couldn't afford the full fees.

࿐

With numbers in the school steady if not buoyant, with the discipline of the pupils seemingly under more control, most of the time at least, with an SMT I felt comfortable with and a set of prefects on whom I knew I could rely, I could begin to do some of the things which I had told the governors I thought might be possible.

Oddly enough, what seemed to produce most controversy was a decision to dig out the rhododendrons that had once graced the front of the College but which had now reverted to a sprawl of overgrown *ponticum*, scarcely producing even the blue flowers of its old age. It seemed to me obvious that getting rid of the *ponticum* which obscured the view of the College from the lakes – and which had clearly been intended when the place was first built – was not only an aesthetic necessity but also symbolic.

The College needed to open itself up to public view. What was the point of rendering it almost invisible from the main drive in the grounds, known as the Kilometre? There were OWs and governors for whom the rhododendrons seemed almost sacred. Fortunately, the bursar found in the minutes of a governors' meeting in 1957 a decision that the rhododendrons were to be cleared, with a view to re-planting with new stock; the decision had never been implemented, presumably because of the same objections we now faced. By promising that, if it turned out the opened-up view of the College was not as splendid as expected, we would re-plant, we got governors to agree.

It was actually a bigger job than merely cutting down the overgrowth; the root-system was so established that the only way of clearing the ground was to dig down with excavators. Chopping away the accumulation of years made it apparent why some of the pupils and old pupils wanted to keep the weeds as they were; there were several quite elaborate smoking-dens in the bushes. Once the *ponticum* was cleared, and even before the lawns which replaced it were established, the decision was justified. College viewed from the lakes was a magnificent building, grandly symmetrical in a way which had been almost entirely obscured for several generations. It was still a pity cars had to be parked up the driveway which led from the Kilometre to Great Gate. The bursar found one alternative car-park near the science block, and then another between the Murray Rears and the Art School (I shall write more about those buildings later) but we had to accept that a proliferation of cars was part of how we lived in the second half of the 20th century.

My wife spotted how we might improve another of the features of the main College building. We had been to visit our daughter in Brasenose College, Oxford, and a day or two later, walking through Front Quad with its surface of broken cement, Ann said suddenly, "You know, this quad is the same size as the Brasenose quad; why don't we make it as nice?" So Ann, the bursar and a housemaster went off to look at quads in the Oxford colleges, and came back intent on making the quads of Wellington attractive. We were told we couldn't have a lawn in Front Quad, as fire-engines might have to be driven in; but we could have a design of stone-ware, with the Wellington crest as centre-piece, elegant planters for climbing shrubs and vines, and six big benches, tall enough for boys and girls to lean their heads back, and made from oak which had come down in the great storm of 1987.

In Back Quad we were allowed a lawn, segmented by decently paved walkways, and in the centre – thanks mainly to the generosity of Sir David Scholey, who succeeded General Sir Roland Guy as Vice President – we placed a large bronze fountain-like vase, with carvings on its base of various Victorian dignitaries, including Wellington. Upper Combermere Quad was given a lawn as well as decent stone-work and (after I had left) Lower Combermere Quad became the Princes' Quad (plural Princes, partly because the governors accepted on long-term loan a handsome marble statue of Prince Albert, and partly because the Prince of Orange came from the Netherlands to open the refurbished quadrangle). Since I often felt that, in honouring the influence E W Benson had had on making Wellington what it was, we underestimated the influence of the Prince Consort on the foundation, I was delighted both to have the statue there and at the renaming of the quadrangle.

South Front, too, was refurbished and re-surfaced. The brick balustrade edging South Front, which had been partly demolished by the stick of bombs that had killed the Master, Bobby Longden, in 1940, was at last restored. I had wondered for some time why there was a lovely wrought-iron gate, half obscured by bushy undergrowth, leading to the open-air swimming pool near the lakes. I discovered almost by chance these were the gates erected in memory of Bobby Longden, and I persuaded the governors we should move them to the centre of the South Front balustrade, facing the south entrance of College, much nearer the place where Longden had been killed.

The other side of the balustrade was what had been the so-called common room garden, adjoining the garden of the Master's Lodge, which Ann had already partly re-designed, with beech-hedges, flower-beds and an avenue of laburnum arches. The common room garden was intended as the garden for all those staff who lived in or near College, without the advantage of gardens of their own, but by 1989 it was more or less derelict; the College gardeners took very little care of it, because the common room was meant to.

When I told the chairman of common room I thought it a pity no one looked after it, he showed me a plan. I waited a year, and nothing was done to implement that plan. I made some mild suggestions and waited another year. Still there was no action. So I persuaded a new housemaster to take over the supervision of what we would now call the College garden. The members of common room would still have access, but the lawns would be mowed by College staff, and the garden would be recognised as for the benefit of the whole College. Within a year the garden was transformed, with paths opened, shrubbery pruned, trees planted and seating provided.

Enhancing the physical appearance of Wellington would have been of little use if the litter-spilling habits which had existed when we arrived had not been changed too. The Second Master divided a map of the estate into fifteen segments, and each house took responsibility for clearing the litter in one segment; once that foul job was over, we had more pupils on our side: when you have picked up other people's litter you are less inclined to drop your own. The bursar ordered more litter bins, and made sure they were elegant as well as utilitarian, black with gold lettering and a Wellington crest.

Under the enthusiastic chairmanship of a long-serving English teacher, a passionate environmentalist, the Green Society flourished. It had the added advantage of attracting some of the less conventional boys in the school, and Ann and I tried to set a personal example by never passing any bit of litter without picking it up and depositing it in a bin. It was surprising how soon what had been a very scruffy place began to look pristine.

One of the things I didn't need to do at Wellington was to appoint a full-time librarian, as I had done at both Island School and Berkhamsted. The Wellington librarian was so good it wasn't long before she was offered a post as librarian at Eton, on terms more favourable than Wellington could match. I was distressed to lose her services, but was able to appoint an admirable replacement, who then served the school for many years, and way beyond any notion of what her actual duties were. Between us, we extended the library by taking over various ancilliary rooms, and re-defining their purposes. In particular, there was a confusion about the room known as the 'Master's Library' – or was it the 'Masters' Library'? In fact, the schoolmasters made very little use of it, and the earliest reference to it seemed to make it the possession of the Master himself.

So we turned the Master's Library into the reference section of the main library, and it became a useful space again, especially when the room next door was turned into a computer room, as an addition to the main computer room in the CDT centre. While the library was thus a more disparate place, the careful use of CTC cameras enabled the librarian to keep a wary eye on all activities within the library complex.

No child should be made to go to boarding school who doesn't want to. At Wellington, when I was interviewing a family and realised a boy wasn't keen to board but had a father who thought such a move "might make a man of him", I would sometimes send parents out of the Master's study so that I could interview the boy on his own. "I promise you," I'd say, "that if you really don't want to come here I won't even offer you a place, whatever your parents want." More than once, I saw small boys burst into tears of relief at that news; and I would put up with fatherly anger if I got it as a consequence. Forcing a child to board is, simply, a form of bullying, even if it is done in the name of parental care.

Of course, a young child will often be anxious at the thought of being away from home. Parents may face the same concern. I always pointed out both to child and to parents that a boy or girl of nine or ten was very different from one of thirteen. Most adolescents want to be with their peer-group rather than with grown-ups, even their most beloved and trusted grown-ups. Often at Wellington we would find day-boys living nearby would come back into College for events on Saturday evenings or Sundays, and sometimes not even for events, merely to see their friends. Indeed, occasionally I had to make it clear to day-boys back for the weekend that school-rules still applied to them, not more relaxed home-rules.

There was (I discovered) an informal arrangement in most boarding-houses that allowed day-boys the occasional over-nighter in a spare bed or on a friend's floor. 'Sleepovers' in boarding houses must surely give the lie to horror-stories about the continuing iniquities of Dotheboys' Hall.

Only those who live in a small and crowded country think that boarding schools are somehow unnatural. If you grow up in a country as big as South Africa or Australia or India, and want an education, particularly a specialised education, you may well find that going away from home to a boarding school is the only option; fine if you live in a city where there are schools galore to choose from – but if you live in the Australian outback or on a farm in the wilds of Mpumalanga you may have little choice but to board for at least some of your schooldays.

Having been boarders ourselves, I in South Africa and she in India and later Derbyshire, my wife and I chose not to send our children to boarding school; we would have had trouble finding the money to do so anyway. Actually, however, both my wife and I think the eldest boy in particular might have been better off in boarding school than he was in a day-school, good school though it was; he and I were too similar to find living in the same household easy, especially in the latter stages of his adolescence. (I had had exactly the same problems with my own father. We loved each other; but we clashed furiously.)

What boarding offers (as well as sometimes sensible separation of powerful personalities, which may be daughter from mother as easily as son from father) is – above all else – time: time to study; time to play games; time to learn a musical instrument; time to sit in the library reading; time to socialise with friends; time not to have to make choices about what you have time to do. Of course, in a day-school one may get to do some of those things; but if your mother can't find the time to drive you to your dance-class on Saturday morning because she has to deliver your brother to his cricket-match, well, you will probably lose out. The gradual separation of a child from his or her home is a part of growing up; the alternative may be an undue dependence

Within some families there may be particular reasons that the best option for a child is to board: the kind of families which are required by their jobs to move every few years, or the kind where there is emotional upheaval following a divorce or a death. At Wellington, we thought ourselves specialists in looking after the sons and daughters of those in the armed forces killed in action or dying in service; they were the Foundationers whose fees were paid for by the school itself. After wars, there were quite a few of them; in my time there were never more than a dozen – but their existence and their presence gave the school an especial ethos.

In the old days, a child might be delivered to his school at the beginning of term and not have any contact with a parent other than the weekly letter home, until the first day of the holidays; that is more or less what my brothers and I had in our boarding school, three nights and two days away by train from home (though we were lucky enough to have a grandmother and an aunt living in the same town as our school) and there are overseas boarders who have something of the same experience; but, in general these days, there is constant communication between home and school – sometimes to an extent which is dangerous to the independent development of children. I am relieved that, in my day, worried parents had to write or telephone or make an appointment to see me, rather than to send an email demanding an immediate response.

☙ ❧

One of the things that had surprised me when I first started to look at Wellington was how disparate all its publications were. There was almost no sense of what businesses call 'corporate identity'. Wellington seemed a mess and muddle of component parts without any central purpose.

Soon, I realised it wasn't just the publications that were bewilderingly various: when it came to design, everybody did what he or she wanted. So there were as many letterheads as there were writers of letters, and signage around the school of every shape, size and description, often very ugly. I knew enough about design from my dealings with Henry Steiner in Hong Kong to realise I was a rank amateur, and amateur designers are usually not very good.

A housemaster told me about a talented young OW who ran a flourishing design company in London, and we arranged to meet. We talked about the parameters within which I wanted the College to be identified as a purposeful entity – elegant, restrained, modern – and he came up with appropriate designs for every aspect of collegiate life.

Not everyone in the place approved immediately – for inevitably some felt I was restricting their intellectual and aesthetic independence – but for them I had a simple if draconian answer: if you want College to pay for it, you are going to have to conform to the collegiate identity which we have chosen. Once again, it was surprising how quickly the change happened.

౼ఞ౼ళ

On the matter of attendance at Chapel, we (that is, the chaplain, the assistant chaplain, the director of music, the organist and choirmaster, most of the housemasters and the SMT) moved much more slowly and deliberately. Early on, I took what might have been a risk in telling the staff that, as far as I was concerned, attendance at Chapel was part of their duty; after all, they were paid by 'the Royal and Religious Foundation of the Wellington College'. If any member of staff had a conscientious reason for not attending Chapel, he or she was required to see me to explain the objection; I would then of course grant exemption on conscientious grounds.

Otherwise, I expected every member of staff to show up in Chapel at least once every week; and every house had to have a housemaster or a tutor present at every service. Hardly any staff (I remember only three or four) came to see me to plead for exemption; of course, they were given it. The pupils behaved better in Chapel partly and simply because there were more staff present.

There is a proper degree of scepticism about 'public school religion', that it may be merely formal and habitual, rather than in any way a matter of conviction. Remarkably, David Newsome and John Robson had raised by private endeavour (because the governors refused to put any College funds into the venture) the considerable sum of money required to convert an underground space near Chapel into a crypt-chapel, intended as a place for private prayer and meditation in the middle of a big, busy and often noisy school; and the crypt-chapel was used as such, and never in my experience abused.

In some ways, Chapel at Wellington was remarkable for the separation that seemed to exist between the disciplinary structures of the school and the religious habits of pupils. Pupils who were by no means regarded as goody-goody seemed comfortable in Chapel, and the voluntary week-night services were always well-attended. I avoided going to them myself, even when I wanted to, because I didn't want them to seem in any way official.

All the same, it seemed absurd that many pupils attending 'the Royal and Religious Foundation' might hardly ever attend Chapel. Even if their parents weren't church-goers, I thought their children should be. It was a significant part of their education. They might not 'get religion', but they would at least get the English hymnal, the Anglican liturgy, some bits of the Old and New Testaments, the anthems and the occasional memorable sermon. They would also learn how to behave in church.

Over the years, term by term, without ever announcing a 'policy', we quietly increased the number of full school chapels until, by the end of my time as Master, there was one every Sunday of the term. Moreover, some of the services were for Holy Communion, and only some of old-fashioned Matins. Of course, there was a conscience clause, whereby parents could ask for their children to be excused from attending Chapel.

It was very seldom invoked, even latterly in my time as Master, when Islam became more vociferous.

Jews, Hindus, Sikhs, Moslems, atheists and agnostics, all were welcomed into Chapel, and I cannot believe we did any of them harm by encouraging their attendance. The nominal Christians went because I told them they had to; I assume the practising Christians would have gone even if I had not told them they had to. I hope some of the nominal Christians learned better, and I trust none of the practising Christians were deterred.

I can't remember precisely when I risked saying what I shall now, in a paragraph or two, repeat, or even if there was a specific reason for doing so. In 1994, the head of school, an excellent and generally sensible boy, very popular with his peers, was noticed breaking a school rule by going into a pub one Saturday afternoon, and was reported to me. I can't remember now what his reason was, but he had not been drinking; still, he had to be seen to be dealt with, especially because he was head of school. I gated him for a week, and announced that I was demoting him from being head of school. I did however carefully not announce that anyone else was becoming Head of College, because all along my intention had been to re-instate him when the gating was done.

However, on Monday morning, in Senior Chapel, I suddenly noticed about half of the boys were not singing the hymn, but were ostentatiously standing silent, in some form of demonstration. I guessed it was to do with Ian Vitty's demotion, although he himself was not in Chapel, because he had an appointment in the sanatorium (he had told me himself when we discussed his gating and demotion).

The custom at Wellington was for the Master to stay sitting in his stall on the south side of the entrance to the Chapel (the Second Master was on the north) while every boy and girl in Chapel walked past him on the way out; it was actually a very useful custom, because it meant every week every pupil in the school walked past the Master at least once – and it was surprising how often you could tell from that simple procedure if there was a problem beginning in some boy's or girl's school-life. I asked myself: do I just ignore the demonstration? No, I wouldn't.

As the short service ended, I left my stall and stood in the middle of the nave. "The school will sit down", I said. "The staff may leave, or they may stay." Most stayed. Then I told the school, simply and directly, that I was for once ashamed to be their Master. They had a perfect right to be cross with me for demoting their head of school – but I could guarantee that, if he had been in Chapel, he wouldn't have taken any anger he felt out on the Chaplain or the Chapel by not singing the hymn. He had been to see me, and we had talked. If they were angry with me, why hadn't they been to see me in my study, where I had been since 7.30 that morning? They knew I was there, with the door open. They weren't helping Ian, and they weren't helping themselves; they were behaving like cowards. I was ashamed, and for once I was leaving Chapel before them. I turned and walked out.

There was another school, not far away from Wellington, which apparently went in for silent demonstrations by pupils who would refuse to sing the hymns in their Chapel. I gathered this protest had emanated from that example. Fortunately, it never happened again. The head of college was, as I thought he would be, mortified at what had been done apparently as a gesture of solidarity; he knew as well as I did any demonstration merely made it harder for me to re-instate him. Fortunately, since there were no more shows, I was able to re-instate him precisely as I had planned, and he went on being an excellent head of school (and, incidentally, got all As at A level when he had been thought of mainly as an outstanding front-row forward on the rugger-field).

Two or three years later, I took the risk of explaining in a sermon in Chapel that, although the pupils might like to think that they were there because I compelled them to attend, actually they were there because they chose to be. Attending Chapel was part of a social contract which being a pupil at Wellington made them participants in. If they thought about it, was there any way in which I could keep anyone in Chapel who wanted to walk out? Oh, I might be able (if I really wanted) to stop one boy from walking out by pinning him in his pew; but I wouldn't be able to do that if ten boys suddenly stood up to walk out? If a whole house stood up to walk out? They were there because they chose to be.

And at that moment I took what I guess might have been thought a risk, by pausing rather longer after my point than most preachers might do. My wife told me afterwards she had wondered if anyone might be brave enough to walk out. What would I have done? she asked. I think I probably would have resigned as Master. I guess I was testing that the school now was, not in my control, but in control of itself. There really was a social contract, whereby they knew they were there by their own choice, not merely because their parents paid the fees. Of course, there would still be disciplinary problems in the school; these were adolescent boys and girls, and they explored boundaries; but discipline in the school as a whole was secure, and depended on what had become, most of the time and for most of them, self-discipline.

જ⊷

I had told the governors that, if I were appointed, I would make the school more international, both in terms of recruitment and in terms of its attitudes. Inevitably, if they appointed an ex-South African who had run a school in Hong Kong, they must expect that. One of my favourite moments as a Head came at a conference of the Boarding School Association where I was standing talking to Gillian du Charme, who had been head of a school in New York and was now Headmistress of Benenden School. I had become one of her governors in 1988, when I was still at Berkhamsted, and in due course she became a governor of Wellington. I had only recently begun my time at Wellington. The Head of a famous English public school came up to say, "And how are you enjoying your second Headship, Jonty?"

"Very much", I replied, which was (as it happens) still very much a lie. "But, you know, it's not my second headship, it's my third. I was Principal of Island School, Hong Kong, for nearly six years…"

"Oh, I don't count that," said the man airily as he walked on.

Gillian turned to smile at me and say, quietly, "You know, Jonty, sometimes I think the English suppose there aren't schools in other countries."

Sometimes, I got exactly the same sort of feeling about attitudes at Wellington: if the exchange schemes I had in mind actually produced pupils, would they cope with an English boarding school? I had built up some strong connections during a spell I had in India in 1986 on a fellowship awarded by the Commonwealth Linking Trust, had made friends with a number of Indian Headmasters, and had visited their schools. Now, I found myself needing to explain that a boy from, say, Doon School would already have experienced a much more intense version of boarding than any English boarder, more in line with the spartan existence of a boy in a Victorian boarding school than that of an English boy in a liberal school in the latter stages of the 20th century.

The very first Indian exchange pupil to arrive at Wellington was already playing first-class cricket at home; he was offered a net with the 1st XI, and accepted. He was a quick bowler, and the first ball he bowled was a fraction short of a length. It lifted sharply and laid out the batsman – who happened to be that season's captain of cricket. I'm afraid my own reaction was delight. The exchange schemes were, I reckoned, going to succeed – and in general they did, though we had one or two failures with boys who had been poorly chosen in their Indian day-schools.

(As a matter of policy, we did not allow exchange students who were with us for less than a full two years of the sixth form to play for school first teams; it seemed unjust that a boy who had worked his way through school teams all the way up the school should now be deprived of his place by a Johnny-come-lately, no matter how talented he was. Unlike some of our rivals, we had no need to recruit games-players from overseas to strengthen our teams.)

Another early success built on the connection established at Berkhamsted with the Budhanilkantha School, outside Kathmandu in Nepal, until 1994 under the guidance of various English Headmasters, including most famously John Tyson. I proposed to Peter Lawrence, a master at Eton who was in charge of recruiting GAP students to go out to the school, an outstanding sixth former from Wellington, Tim Kruger. To my chagrin, Peter Lawrence preferred another boy from another school, whom I happened to know. The boy who went out didn't survive many weeks in the demanding atmosphere of Nepal, so I put forward Tim Kruger's name again, and this time he went.

So successful was he that, when he had finished his year there and his degree at Cambridge, he set up a school of his own and, to support it, a business exporting knitwear from Nepal to the UK. At one stage, Tim's company was employing some 700 local people and accounting for one per cent of all Nepal's exports. Unfortunately, after seven years, the combination of the Maoist uprising and the Crown Prince's murder of the Royal Family led to massive instability in the country, in particular the destruction by the Maoists of the school, and the closure of Tim Kruger's company.

We were fortunate to have a ready-made connection with Bordeaux. First, there was our old friend, Catherine Monroux, who had originally come to Ann and me and our babies as an *au pair* when we were in the International Centre at Sevenoaks. She had qualified as a teacher and had spent some years teaching English in an excellent Catholic *lycee* in Bordeaux, Grand Lebrun; now, as she had a gap in her career for domestic reasons, I persuaded her to come to Wellington from September 1991 for a year, to arrange exchanges and to teach French and some Spanish.

Secondly, I persuaded the governors we should have a French governor, and suggested Emile Nouel, a prominent figure in French engineering circles and in Bordeaux itself. He served as a governor from 1993 to 1999 and, though never vociferous, was a charming and useful addition to the board, as well as a delightful host when members of the school visited Bordeaux.

The exchanges with Grand Lebrun which Catherine Monroux set up involved ten English pupils and ten French spending a fortnight together, one week in England, one in France. The arrangements seemed in general to work well, and pupils enjoyed their experiences of France as well as improving their colloquial French.

The other exchange in Bordeaux was with a more experimental private foundation, known as ACADIS, set up and run by Daniel Peyron, who was intent on trying to broaden the purposes of the generally very academic secondary education in France by including work experience as an integral part of what pupils did. This was obviously of especial interest to Wellington, because it meant our pupils going to Bordeaux would get to meet potential employers. Since neither ACADIS nor Grand Lebrun were boarding schools, it also meant our pupils were accommodated with French families. There were of course some disasters; I have never forgotten the wayward French youth from ACADIS who arrived for a week at Wellington with his own plentiful supply of marijuana, which he had cheerfully carried through British customs. He went home very swiftly.

The funniest story concerned one Simon Preston, who had the great good fortune to be billeted with a French family who owned an imposing chateau on a wine estate outside Bordeaux. In answer to a question, Simon told the paterfamilias, whom he had realised was a count, that, yes, his father was keen on wine. The count therefore gave Simon a bottle of the estate wine to take back to his father.

On the boat taking the English pupils back across the Channel, one of his friends suddenly remembered it was Simon's birthday. They must celebrate. However, all their money had been spent. "What about that bottle sticking out of your haversack?" someone suggested. So they pulled the cork, purloined some plastic mugs, but didn't very much like the wine: too warm, and rather sweet. After a few swigs, the cork was shoved back in the bottle. We never heard what Father Preston said when his son presented him with a half-full bottle of Chateau d'Yquem.

The beginning of the official end of apartheid in 1991 meant that we could once again without political objection take on visiting teams from South African schools. I had a vividly unhappy memory of a touring rugby team from Bishop's (Diocesan College) in Cape Town to Hong Kong towards the end of my time there. The team's coach was Basil Bey, who had been captain of rugby at the University of Cape Town when I was there, and who had been something of a friend in the residence we were both in, Smuts Hall. Would Island School provide a team to play against the tourists from South Africa? Or, if we wouldn't provide a team *per se*, would we allow our pupils to play for a combined Hong Kong schools' team?

Before I could explain why I wasn't keen, I got a heavy-handed message from the Education Department, purporting to have emanated from the Governor's office itself: if Island School plays against the South African visitors, beware of the grant to the English Schools Foundation from the Hong Kong government. The threat wasn't necessary, although in other circumstances it might have had the usual effect most threats have on me.

Still, there was no way in which a school I was Head of would have played a South African touring team, even if that team happened to come from a generally liberal and increasingly non-racial school, like Bishop's. If however any of my pupils chose to play for a team not representing Island School I wouldn't dream of interfering with their freedom to choose, although with sadness I would myself refuse to watch any matches, even if players I coached myself had chosen to play. On the other hand, the boys from Bishop's were welcome to visit Island School – and a few of them turned up at a school dance and were made welcome.

Therefore, when from in 1991 onwards South African teams began to ask to tour English schools again – as in fact some had done surreptitiously before then – we were happy to invite them to Wellington. Often, they provided opposition of a calibre seldom found at home; English school-coaches found soon enough that South African schools tended to bring touring teams over to England only when they were fairly confident of winning.

I need, here, to interpose something more personal than professional. I have already explained how I moved from being South African to stateless to British. At some stage, the South African authorities probably wrote that they were according me the honour of putting me on the list of British citizens who required visas before they could be admitted to South Africa (most Britons were welcome there without visas). I never got the letter. When, however, I thought of trying to go back I took the precaution of asking advice from Helen Suzman, then the one Progressive Party MP in South Africa. She consulted the Minister concerned, then warned me on no account should I try to come back without a visa. When I did apply for a visa, to do some research for a biography I was working on, it was refused.

In 1986, when I was still Headmaster of Berkhamsted, I took the risk of going back without a visa, to see my younger brother, Simon, who was dying of cancer and who had asked me to visit him. I thought that, as a 'public school headmaster', I could take the risk. As it happened, when I arrived in South Africa, I was at first admitted, but then pulled back behind the entry desk, and held for eight hours while my claim for compassionate understanding was investigated. A kindly English-speaking immigration official told me, quietly, my file had stamped on it, 'Not to be admitted without the personal approval of the Minister.'

In the end, I was allowed in, though only for 24 hours (a day later, this was extended for a week). The next year, after my brother's death, I again applied for a visa, and was again refused. In 1991, I wrote to Denis Worrall, who had been South African ambassador in London until 1987 (I had known him since we were boys) to tell him I thought, in the circumstances, I might be allowed to travel home freely. Only then did I have an official letter telling me 'your visa exemption has been restored'.

So, from the summer of 1992, we began regular visits 'home', to see my mother, stepfather, sister, brother, innumerable cousins, and various friends. I have written about those visits elsewhere, especially in the sequence of poems called *The Journey Back* (first published in *In the Water-Margins*, Snailpress and Crane River Press, 1994). Midway through my years at Wellington, the governors gave me two half-terms as a sabbatical, so Ann and I could spend nearly three months enjoying the South African summer, and where I was able to write a long poem called *Requiem*, which I had been contemplating for several years (it was published by the Belgrave Press in 1997).

Probably the biggest step towards making Wellington more international came when, at my behest, the school applied to join Round Square, the grouping of schools from all over the world set up to honour the memory and propagate the ideals of Kurt Hahn, founder of Salem School in Germany and, after he had left Germany because of the rise of the Nazis, Gordonstoun in Scotland. I think there was some feeling among governors against the move, and I'm not sure the three other British schools already in Round Square were that keen on being joined by such a big boarding school as Wellington with its 'military' reputation. However, Gulab Ramchandani, former headmaster of the Doon School, and on the main board of Round Square, was keen for us to join; and Jocelin Winthrop Young, who had been Headmaster of the Anavryta School in Greece, came to inspect Wellington, and must have reported favourably.

There was, I thought, a coincidence between what Wellington stood for – or, to be more truthful, what I hoped it might stand for – and the stated ideals of Round Square: to be international and democratic; to care for the environment; to enjoy adventure, and to train the young in leadership and service. Uncertainty about the new venture was ended when a delegation of the Vice President, Roly Guy, a young member of staff, Jane Lunnon (she was still Jane Cullen then, I think), myself and some Wellingtonians went to a Round Square conference in Germany.

Our participation was a great success and, with the support of the governors now ensured, I relinquished any role as leading our involvement to the staff and to the pupils themselves. We became regular attenders of the annual international conferences and hosted them ourselves; we raised funds for schools less prosperous than ourselves, especially the Starehe School in Kenya; we hosted and encouraged exchanges of staff and pupils; we sent pupils off on work-camps in India and Africa.

Our involvement in an organization known as Global Connections was another helpful way of broadening international links, as was a connection with eastern Europe, which saw us getting regular student-teachers from Budapest. Another aspect of the promotion of internationalism came when Ann set up a branch of Amnesty International in the school, which met regularly in the sitting-room of the Lodge not merely to talk about unjust imprisonment in various countries but also to co-ordinate the writing of letters to the rulers of those countries appealing for the release of political prisoners.

かかぶ

Crucial to the success of Island School was the existence of a powerful and active Parent/Teacher Association. Most independent schools in the UK seemed suspicious of even the idea of a PTA. Wouldn't it try to run the school? No, not if you stipulated boundaries when it was set up. However, if you left out 'teacher' from the title, and put no compulsion on teachers but involved only those confident enough not to be afraid of parents, and then set up a Parents' Association, who could object?

Some parents themselves were suspicious a PA would be expected solely to raise funds, so we had to find functions broader than that. The Parents' Association at Berkhamsted had become a great success, organizing a variety of social and educational events, and especially welcoming parents new to the school.

So, when we got to our new school, we set about trying to create something similar. At Wellington, the suspicion came not so much from the teachers as from the Old Wellingtonians. Was this a way of narrowing the field of their operations? Of course it wasn't. Parents had to be seen as a crucial part of our constituency: after all, it was mainly their money which funded the school, and the education of their children which was our main purpose. It was they, more than anyone, more even than OWs, who passed on good news of the school's development and who encouraged other parents to enroll their children. We needed them on our side. Would it not be sensible to organise them into a coherent group, rather than leaving them voiceless?

In the end, we overcame all objections by the simple mechanism of making the first chairman of the Wellington College Association a governor who was also a more-than-satisfied ex-parent and a prominent Old Wellingtonian, one Johnny Yeldham. He made it clear to the committee – mainly of volunteers, though we did some judicious recruiting too – he would entertain no discussion of teachers nor of school policy; the former were the concern of the Master, the latter of the governors. One of the virtues of the WCA was that it allowed parents to go on being involved in the school after their children had left, and we had the support of some outstanding and energetic sympathizers, grateful for what we had given their children.

In some ways, the years from 1989 could be typified as the years of the Children Act, introduced as a response to some horrendous abuse of the young, especially the murder of two young girls by a school caretaker in a school in Soham. There was a part of me which deeply regretted the need for that kind of legislation; I had a sense that, if we – that is, the professionals running schools – had been a little braver, a little less cautious, perhaps even a little less English with our exaggerated concern for other people's privacy, the problems would have been tackled well before they reached a stage which required legislation.

If a teacher who abused a child had always known that, the moment he or she was found out, he or she would lose his or her job and never get another in a school, we might not have needed legislation. Of course, the world isn't like that: when we discover wickedness, we tend to try to push it further away rather than confront it and deal with it directly.

At Island School, for instance, before my time there, one of the senior teachers had been known to have had an affair with a sixth form girl. Nothing had been done about it – and how could I do something about it when it hadn't happened on my watch? In a sense, it was none of my business. And, anyway, we needed to let the teacher have his or her rights, didn't we? Suppose the accusation by the young woman had been fabricated? Or unjust? A set-up? And he was a very talented teacher. Still, I didn't want him anywhere our pupils any more, and I made my disapprobation sufficiently plain for him to decide for himself to shift out of teaching.

Even before the Children Act, and the later requirement to check the probity of references, I had been inclined to pick up the telephone to ask referees to expand. Some refused to do so: then I assumed "I've said all I intend to say" meant much the same as "I wouldn't employ this person if I were you". That is of course tough on the person about whom the reference is written, but better that injustice than the injustice of employing incompetents or abusers. There was – perhaps still is – an unwritten code within HMC: a last sentence of your reference which said, "If there is anything else you would like to know, do feel free to telephone", meant, "I'm not telling you everything".

Only a very innocent Head would not enquire. If you did telephone, you got the truth – nearly always. Only once do I remember telephoning, and getting ... well, not a lie, but a half-truth. I appointed, and the appointment was not a success, although it wasn't a disaster. Of course, the school losing the teacher was relieved of a small burden; we carried it instead. No, I can't say our pupils were damaged; but I do wish I had made a better appointment.

Of course, I now knew never again to trust that particular Head as a referee – and, when I checked with a couple of friendly colleagues, discovered I wasn't the only one to have been led a little astray. For myself, I would rather have a reputation for being unkindly – even brutally – honest, than for prevarication or even half-truths.

There was a time in the 1990s when it became regarded as somehow unfair to double-check on references. That made me cross; why on earth shouldn't I telephone a referee for a further explanation? Then, suddenly, we had a change, and what I regard as overkill, when school secretaries telephone on behalf of their employers to ask if the references I've written are actually confidential; there is an implication I may somehow have colluded with the person about whom I was writing. Have I perhaps asked the person to write his or her own reference?

As a matter of fact, I have never shown the wording of a reference to the person it was written about, though I am happy to make it plain whether or not it is a strong reference. Apparently, this practice was something forced on employers as a result of gross dishonesty by some referees.

I remember being enraged when I was first asked on the telephone, "Did you write this reference yourself?"

"Of course I bloody did; I signed it, didn't it?"

Poor secretary: I shouldn't have sworn at her, when she was only doing what she had been told to do.

These days, the world is murkier in some ways than the one I began in, where you were required by a code of personal conduct to tell the truth in references as clearly as you could. Then, you would not lie to keep a good member of staff; nor would you lie to get rid of a problem. If that is no longer the case, we should all be sad.

One of the side-effects of the Children Act of 1989 was to require local authorities to inspect boarding schools in their area. Some local authorities seemed not to realise that parents who paid out £20,000 a year for their child's boarding fees might do some of their own checking of what the school offered; others were more rational, and thus happy to work with schools to ensure standards were as high as we thought. Patience was sometimes required, perhaps not only on our side.

However, when inspectors from the Berkshire local authority realised we actually welcomed inspections – because we were proud of our standards of care and compassion – we were able to draw up what gradually became called 'protocols'. As far as I was concerned, they were written because they had to be written; but once they were written they served little purpose, other than to require regular re-writing to keep them up to date with changes in rules and regulations. I kept on being told Wellington had to have a 'Complaints Procedure'. I thought it nonsense, because how you proceeded with a complaint surely depended on what the complaint was. Were you complaining about the mashed potato served in the dining hall? Or about a housemaster bullying you?

In the end, I capitulated, and wrote a Complaints Procedure by imagining myself into the position of a first-year boy who had a complaint of any kind. He would start by telling friends in his house and year-group, then 'his' prefect, then the head of house. If the head of house didn't listen, there was a matron and a tutor, and above them a housemaster. There was also the chaplain, the school doctor and the sanatorium sisters. Above them all was the Second Master and the senior tutor, and then there was the Master, who tried to sit in his study with the door open from 7.30 most mornings until Chapel-time or assembly – or you could see his secretary to fix an appointment.

If you felt the Master didn't listen to your complaint, you could go to the governors via the clerk to the governors or the bursar or directly to the Vice President (name, address and telephone number supplied). If an appeal to the governors failed, the President was HRH The Duke of Kent; details of how to reach him were supplied. Point 24 (I think it was) said that above the President there was the Visitor, and she was Her Majesty The Queen. I gave details of how you could get in touch with her office. Point 25 was simple: 'If all other complaints have failed, you could emigrate.'

When I sent this to the local authority to check, it came back with the last three points excised. I suppose it is too much to hope a local education authority has much of a sense of humour.

One day, as I was on my way from the Master's Lodge to my study, passing through the gate called by some the 'Path of Duty' and others the 'Glory Gate', a crowd of small boys was coming through in the other direction. To my surprise, the group continued to push through the door ahead of me, forcing me to stop. I grabbed one of the smaller boys by the upper arms, picked him up bodily, and carried him backwards through the doorway. He and his peers looked astonished. "Hasn't anyone ever told you it's polite to stand aside in a narrow doorway to let older people through first?" I asked. Looking at his face, and at the faces of the other boys, I suddenly thought, they really have no idea what I am talking about; they've never been taught something I can't remember never knowing.

So, almost at first as a joke, I set about writing a succinct list of what I probably called at first 'Decent Manners', but which the Second Master amended to 'The Basic Courtesies'. He added a few points, and we decided we may as well try it out on the housemasters. In the end, with their approval, we decided to publish the list in the termly calendar, as a constant reminder of how pupils might be expected to behave.

All pupils at College are expected to be courteous at all times. Here is some particular advice.

1. Greet people: all members of staff, all visitors to College.

2. If you note visitors to College looking lost, offer help to them. "Are you looking for someone?" "May I help you?"

3. If adults come into your study or any room in which you are sitting down, or come up to you when you are sitting on a bench watching a game, you should stand up. (In the classroom, your teacher will direct you.)

4. If you are wearing any kind of head-gear, you should raise it – or at least touch the brim – to all adults. The Wellington 'Tick' is acceptable in this context; it is not reserved only for Speech Day.

5. If you approach a doorway at the same time as adults or visitors, you should allow them through the doorway before you go through. Do not push ahead. When walking in a group, be aware of other people going in the opposite direction.

6. Open doors for adults and let them go through first.

7. It is courteous to allow women to precede men through doors (the only exception is when one is getting out of a train or a coach), and for men to open doors of cars for women or the elderly.

8. If you do not know their names, it never gives offence to adults to call men 'Sir' and women 'Ma'am'. It is perfectly acceptable to call senior people by their job titles, *eg* "Good morning, Master", "Yes, Sister."

9. Take your hands out of your pockets when talking to members of staff, other adults or College Prefects, when singing hymns or the National Anthem, walking in and out of Chapel, when prayers are being said and on similar formal occasions.

10. Listen attentively to people when they are talking to you; look interested; do not interrupt until it is your turn to speak. Speak up clearly, and look up, when you are talking. In our culture, it is considered discourteous – and probably a sign of weak character – not to look directly into the eyes of the person who is talking to you. (A note on 10: I had discovered from Nigerian pupils that, in their culture, to look directly at someone who is addressing you, especially if they are reprimanding you or are senior to you, is taken as defiance.)

11. Respond promptly, in writing, whenever you receive a written invitation for a school or private function. A written note of thanks to your host or hostess is always appropriate when you have been entertained for a meal or a party. A written note to the organiser of a holiday or expedition is also an appropriate way to express your thanks.

12. The greatest courtesy of all is merely to add "Please" to all requests and say "Thank you" for all services rendered. "I am sorry", said sincerely, helps when things have gone wrong.

Ludicrously old-fashioned? Perhaps. Most school rules are decidedly negative; these aren't rules, and they aren't negative. I do notice, with pleasure, the list is still published in the school calendar, and I try not to mind that a journalist recently gave my successor's successor the credit for its invention.

Another version of the same lesson was this: early on in our time, we had some sixth formers to a dinner in the Lodge dining room, not a particularly grand room, but with a long oval table seating 16 (or 20 at a pinch). During the meal, one of the sixth formers leaned back to say, "You know, I've never been to a dinner party before."

Ann and I questioned him and then some of the other boys and girls present. It became apparent not simply that some of them – perhaps as many as half – had never been to a formal dinner party of any kind, but that some of them hardly ever sat down to a family meal. They grazed, rather than went to meals; they helped themselves to food from the pantry or the fridge, and then they ate on their own, in front of the TV or with a book propped in front of them on the kitchen table. No wonder table manners seemed a forgotten concept.

Ann and I had grown up in families where attendance was required, usually for three meals a day. If you were at home, you turned up; and that was where you talked. So now we resolved that, somehow, we would have every boy and girl in the sixth form into the Lodge at least once for a proper sit-down meal, with conversation. Our College prefects we tended to have to supper in the kitchen, since the chat there would be freer and informal.

Later, we extended this measure to hold, once a year, a formal dinner in Hall for the lower sixth. Did it do any good? I hope there was a greater degree of social confidence among the pupils as a result. Is a desire to give your pupils a sense of social confidence an aspect of snobbishness? Only in cultures where a lack of social grace is regarded as a virtue.

కళ⚘

One of the trivial things I insisted on as Head was that boys' ties should never be worn at half-mast, but must always be done up. Another was that their shoes should be polished. When I was taxed about my (boring) insistence on what were really very minor issues, I used to explain, if shoes were polished and ties done up, what was between them was probably in good order, too.

An unexpected advantage of my fussiness about ties being done up is this: when I am in London, if I see a man of a certain age coming towards me, who – as soon as he sees me – starts to check his tie is done up, I can be pretty certain he is an ex-pupil. I may not always recognise him or be able to attach a name to a face, but I have a starting-point.

ଚ୍ଚ ଔ୬

When I went to Wellington, I had hoped to go on being a teacher of English. It turned out the English department was as well-stocked with good English teachers as Berkhamsted had been, and I really wasn't needed for sixth form teaching. So I said I would teach a first year English class.

Fortunately, the head of English had been sensible enough to provide back-up. Timetabled to do the same class was a young teacher. When the various crises of my first year erupted, I had to keep saying to him, "Look, I'm sorry, Tim, but I shall have to ask you to take the class again for me today." After a while, it became clear pretending I was the English teacher for that class was unfair on them; they were getting confused, and the work was getting muddled. Tim Head took back his class, with great good humour and his usual successful efficiency.

I found other ways of seeing more of my pupils than some Heads are able to. First, we set up and ran from our sitting room in the Lodge a 'creative writing' group. Boys and girls would hand in poems, stories, bits of novels; we would make enough copies for everyone to have one, and then meet to have read to us, and to read to ourselves, the submissions.

The meetings were occasional rather than regular, and – as is the nature of these things – there was more dross than there were gems. There was, however, the occasional brilliance, and four or five of the boys and girls who were regular attenders may, one day, turn out significant writers. One already has: Greg Norminton was, right from his first appearance at these occasions, clearly a talent of considerable kind. There will be others too, I think.

I discovered from the bursar there was a fund which had hardly been touched for several years, the terms of which provided for the invitation to Wellington – and payment of – writers, who were required not to talk about literature but actually to read preferably from their own work. The money had been left by the sister of a young OW killed in the Boer War, Lt Nicolas Gifford Edmonds.

During my years at Wellington, we were able to have some excellent writers to read their own work: Christopher Fry (the playwright); Benny Green (reading from his book about P G Wodehouse), Gavin Ewart OW (reading his poems), Michael Meyer OW (reading from his memoir), John Fuller (reading his own poems), Jon Stallworthy (reading his poems), Sebastian Faulks OW (reading from his latest novel), Dan Jacobson (reading a set of his own poems), Eric Newby (the travel writer), U A Fanthorpe (reading her poems), Professor Hugh Brogan (reading from Kipling), and who have I forgotten?

Perhaps the greatest coup was to get Wilfred Thesiger, though because he was old and not very well we cheated a little by sitting him in an armchair in our sitting room and surrounding him with as many boys and girls as we could squeeze into the room, and then he talked and read aloud from various of his books, and answered questions. I doubt if anyone who was there will forget the experience.

We were able to have the occasional artist, writer or musician in residence too, such as Pete Churchill, a jazz musician, Alec Roth, a composer, Julian Grater, a painter, Sarah Dudman, who ran an educational theatre company, Simon Todd, a sculptor in wood, Lavinia Greenlaw, a poet, Dan Jacobson, novelist and academic, Greg Norminton as he was establishing himself as a novelist, Nick Maitland, a young painter, Jeremy Taylor, a song-writer, David Mansell, a photographer (whom I had known at Sevenoaks and who did the photographs for the first prospectus of my years at Wellington), and others.

We provided accommodation when it was necessary, space in the art school when required, meals in common room, and a small stipend, in return for some informal teaching and as much chatting to pupils as possible. It cost the school little and was, I hope, useful for the artists as well as fun for the pupils they came across; some of them were, I think, profoundly influential: David Mansell's vision as a photographer was clearly evident in a great deal of the painting done in his time there, and afterwards.

My other great good fortune came about in this fashion. As a boy I had inherited from my grandmother – a first-class amateur violinist who had, apparently, played in the Halle orchestra in its early days – a most beautiful violin, made by the Brothers Carcassi in Firenze in 1751. I had played it in a desultory way at school in South Africa, the only boy in the school orchestra, but I hadn't played it since then. A friend brought to the Lodge a man who was in charge of the selling of violins at Sotheby's. I mentioned the violin to him, and he expressed an interest in seeing it. I dug it out of its case, and showed it to him: all the strings and the bridge had collapsed. He cradled it, then started humming, as he turned it over and over, examining every aspect. "I could," he told us, "sell this for you tomorrow; we'd get £10,000 without any trouble."

We asked the children: would it help if we sold it now? They didn't at that stage need the money. One of them said to me, perhaps joking, "Well, Dad, I think you should start playing again." So, with encouragement from the Wellington Music School, I did. Once a week I had a lesson from a peripatetic teacher in the music school. It was fascinating what had stayed in my fingers and my brain from lessons 40 years before, and what had disappeared entirely. In the end, my teacher put me in for an exam, Grade Four – and, despite a massive panic attack which made me almost unable to play even the pieces I knew well, somehow the examiner decided he could safely pass me, without undermining standards for ever. I moved on to be taught by the head of strings himself, and even once or twice played duos with him in lunch-time concerts.

Soon after that, the head of music asked if I would like to join the school orchestra. Although I really wasn't up to the necessary standard, I did do so and, for the next five or six years, had great fun sitting with the second violins, miming furiously whenever there were more than about eight different notes in a bar. The boys who started next to me, and who used to point their bows to where we had got to when I lost my way on the score, steadily moved their way to the front row of the first violins, while I stayed in the same place.

Still, I saw the school from a place few Heads get to: the back row of the second violins. I toured with the orchestra (to France, to South Africa) and joined concerts in St John's, Smith Square, Bordeaux, Rheims, Johannesburg, Paris and elsewhere. The happiness of my last years at Wellington – especially in contrast to the early years – was as much as anything due to the orchestra.

Towards the end of my time as Master, I spotted another way in which I could return to being a teacher: I had always had a soft spot for the kind of boy who had opted to take English A level as his third choice because he quite enjoyed reading – and there was that nice teacher who had read poems to them in the first form. Now, given the demands of A level, that same boy was too often told he was in danger of failing to get a grade of the kind he needed, usually a C or a D. So, when I saw end-of-term reports that threatened failure, I sent the housemaster a note: would X. like to see me to fix some extra lessons, to see if I could help? Just half an hour every week, at a time to be sorted out. Most years, I would have two or three boys in that category of need. They would bring me their latest essays, I would look at them, and then with the boys would try to work out what was needed to improve their chances.

Often enough, it would simply be a matter of essay-writing technique. Sometimes, a basic understanding of poetic technique would be required, so paraphrase would not be thought an adequate substitute for analysis. It was often surprising how much sense even not-very-academic pupils could make of poems just by learning to look more closely at the words on the page.

I confess that, often, when the A level results arrived, I didn't start with the large-scale, but would search down the list to see if Jim and Harry had managed to get the Cs in English they needed, rather than the Es or Fs originally predicted.

My contract at Wellington required me to retire at the end of the year in which I turned 60. In fact, I turned 60 on 19th August 1999, and the year officially ended 31st August. I therefore said to the governors that, since I would be only 60 for the whole of my last year as Master, might I stay on for the year? Permission was given. I liked the idea of having served from 1989-2000, and I thought, too, the last year of service might be peaceful. School finances were all right. Pupil-numbers were satisfactory. Drug-abuse and bullying were, as far as I could tell, no longer the problems they had been. The appearance of the school – both buildings and grounds – was infinitely improved on what we had taken over.

While we needed to do still more to improve the exam results, we did have some schemes in place: a new fortnightly timetable rather than the old weekly one, which enabled the curriculum to be opened up a little, a tutorial system to mentor the pupils' academic work more directly, a more logical regime of prep in the evenings, and so on. We had moved another 'dormitory' – the Hopetoun – out of College into a purpose-built and very attractive house in the grounds; that gave more room in College for refurbishment.

We had decided that trying to refurbish the Talbot, a large Edwardian or late-Victorian house on the edge of the estate, while there were boarders – and housemaster and family – actually living there was going to be impossible, so we would build a new house nearby, then demolish the old Talbot, and thereafter build another mirror-image house next to the Talbot, with some shared facilities, into which yet another of the in-College dormitories could be moved, thus freeing up still more space in College for refurbishment. We had built two new physics labs, and a large residence for the non-teaching staff, 14 flats in what we named after a long-serving bursar as Bowman Court. The new art school was built and had been opened, and the old art school was being refurbished as a set of lecture-rooms.

The governors had decided the Millenium Project for Wellington would be to improve the lighting and sound-system of the Chapel, renovate the organ, and make some proper choir-stalls. Governors had also agreed that, at last, we would begin to make a nine-hole golf course on the estate; I am not a golfer, and the course was opened only after my time, but it was a splendid addition to facilities, and fulfilled a promise which had been made to some OWs years beforehand.

I always preferred refurbishing to new building, and look back with especial pleasure at projects such as converting the old gymnasium into a studio-theatre, turning the rather squalid bachelor bedrooms of Long Corridor with their shared bathrooms into eight studio flats with *en suite* bathrooms, making a changing room into a bookshop, and converting the resident matron's quarters into a new small dining-room. We also enjoyed renovating the so-called Pink Pavilion on the main cricket-ground, and re-painting it from green to an actual pink.

One of the most pleasurable projects of those last years was being able to shut down the squalid lavatories known as the Murray Rears. When I was first shown round Wellington, I had followed the advice of an old secondary modern headmaster in Yorkshire who had told me the best way of judging any school was to ask to be shown the boys' lavatories. I had been taken to the Murray Rears by David Newsome. Because I was much taller than him, as we left the building I was able to see it had another purpose than that for which it had been designed: above the lintel of the doorway was a great soggy mass of cigarette butts. Since David Newsome was himself a heavy smoker, he probably didn't notice how much the lavatories smelled of smoke, and he was too short to see the accumulation of butts.

Into what does one turn redundant lavatories? The outside of the building was attractive, with no evidence of its internal usage. It would have been silly to pull the building down, and anyway would probably have caused outrage in English Heritage or some other guardian of famous old buildings. I knew we needed new offices for the SMT; usually, any proposal to spend money on purely administrative convenience causes muttering, but if we gave the SMT offices in what had been boys' lavatories no one would object, surely? There might be some ribaldry, but that would defuse any moaning. Nowadays, that the SMT offices had once been a lavatory – and a smoking den – seems to have slipped from collective memory.

In 1990 I had succeeded John Blatchley (Headmaster of Ipswich School and treasurer of HMC) as editor of *Conference & Common Room*, then the house-magazine of HMC. It came out three times a year, didn't seem an onerous addition to my work, and I enjoyed trying to make the layout of the magazine more attractive and its content more literate. I wasn't paid for my editing, though I did try to pay our writers with book-tokens. A sadness was the sudden death of our publisher, Julie Belgrave, far too young; her widower kept the firm going, in her memory essentially, until it became too much for him to manage, when the magazine was returned to John Catt Educational Ltd, the original publisher, at round about the same time as I handed on the editing.

One of the disappointments of those last professional years was not being elected Chairman of HMC. I had been persuaded by various of the powerful figures in HMC I should allow myself to be nominated; I had forgotten there was a convention the boarding schools and the day schools in HMC took the chairmanship turn and turn about. After the election, I had apologetic notes from those who had persuaded me to stand – and, typically of the man, a kind note from the successful candidate, Patrick Tobin, saying he had voted for me (fortunately, I had voted for him, too). As the year went on, and I heard what the Chairman was having to do – mainly, it seemed, to defend colleagues from the ire of the governors who had appointed them – I was pleased to have escaped the honour.

❧❦

My hopes of a peaceful last year as Master – lots of pleasant dinner parties, a deckchair on the edge of the cricket field, time to practise before orchestral concerts, cheerful conversations with prefects, desultory wanderings around the quads and the grounds to admire the work of the gardeners, a few valedictory speeches – were increased by the appointment of a successor well before any deadline.

A good long-list of a dozen was reduced by governors to three; the governors' choice, strongly endorsed by me, was Hugh Monro, who had been Headmaster of Worksop, then of Clifton. Ann and I liked Hugh and Claire very much, and were more than happy with the governors' decision. Ann and I would arrange to move out of the Lodge as soon as possible after the end of the summer term, so as to give time for any alterations and renovations required.

Officially, I was still to be Master until the end of August, and – hating the thought anyone might call me demob happy – I was intent of finishing the job properly; but most of that I could do from our cottage in East Sussex, for instance, writing by hand to every A level candidate, usually to congratulate him or her, sometimes to commiserate, and where necessary to offer help and advice.

However, the hope of a peaceful end after the traumatic beginning were spoiled by three major problems with the staff. First, there was an increasing problem in one of the departments. Was sorting this something not best left for my successor? I wondered hopefully. No, said the Vice President: you must sort it out yourself. Under David Newsome, the department had been an academic flagship. Yet fewer and fewer pupils were being attracted to the subject; we had reached the stage when the two-year course had to be taught as a single unit, to justify the staffing. Although inspection reports were still mainly adulatory, I thought they missed the reality: each solution we found foundered on a kind of benign passivity. More and more I suspected the problem was in the leadership of the department. Sometimes one could fix that sort of problem by finding a change of roles – but I could see no extra place available in the management of the school.

For some time, the governors had, at my request, been building up a fund that helped provide for good schoolmasters and schoolmistresses who were running out of energy and enthusiasm to take early retirement from a profession which demanded never-ending energy and commitment. I suggested early retirement; while the man wasn't keen, he agreed I could discuss terms with his union rep. This I did. Yes, I was sure it was in the best interests of the school his client should retire earlier than required by his contract. Yes, the governors had authorised me to be generous. The union rep went off to discuss terms with the bursar and, at the end of the year, the man went. I don't suppose he was very pleased with the Master, but I thought it the right decision – and I hope his retirement has been fulfilled and my hunch about leadership right. My secretary told me she thought I had been very tough, and perhaps I was: he had once upon a time been an excellent schoolmaster.

About the next problem I must be even more discreet, despite the years which have elapsed. A senior member of staff (I shall call him A) came to see me because (he said) the wife of another senior member of staff (I shall call him B) had been spreading rumours A's wife was having an affair with B. It wasn't true, he told me, and I hoped he had the story right, not least because B was someone I liked as much as anyone on the staff, a cheerful, long-serving, all-round schoolmaster.

So I asked B to come to see me and took him for a companionable walk. I told him the rumour, said I hoped it wasn't true, but warned him, if it were, he might find himself looking for a new job. "What?" he replied. "In this day and age? When half our parents are themselves divorced?"

I began to fear the rumour was true, as indeed it was: two divorces followed, and the man finished his teaching career elsewhere, now married for the third time, and happily I trust. Boarding schools are not entirely like the real world; they are much more communal than most places in England now, and they are enclosed. The rewards of being in that community are considerable, but there are obligations about communal behaviour which can't be avoided.

The third problem was the one that hurt most. From 1998 onwards, it was becoming apparent that, for reasons I couldn't at first fathom, one particular house was becoming difficult to fill. Housemasters had a role to play in making sure their houses were in demand, and most did what they could, for instance in talking to prep school Heads and encouraging parents to register not just for the school but for a particular house, too.

There was no shirking of responsibility evident in the way this housemaster did his job (and as it happened I liked and admired him as much as almost anyone on the staff, not least because his experience before Wellington had been in maintained schools). When however I looked at the lists at the beginning of 2000, almost every house had a full complement on the books for entry in September, and this house had no one at all. We discussed what I saw as a problem but he didn't see it; he was sure somehow I would fill the first year of his house for him, for instance from the overseas intake – which, by its nature, tended to come in a little later than the home-grown intake. Of course, as I explained to him, we didn't want this to become a house mainly for overseas boys; it was essential we had a reasonable spread in each house.

Like all housemasters, he had been appointed for three periods of five years each, with an option on either side to break at five or ten years, and an obligation to retire from the house after 15. He had passed the first five year break-point without any worry; the next one was in 2002, two years after my departure. Could we not struggle on, I wondered in discussions with the SMT and the Registrar, filling the house as best we could, even if later than the other houses? We all liked the man personally; none of us could see any particular reason for the house's not being filled as easily as other houses. I suspect if I hadn't been leaving in 2000, I would have decided we must soldier on; but would it be fair to dump the problem on my successor's shoulders? The unequivocal advice of the SMT was that I couldn't duck the decision.

My handling of the announcement of the decision to the man himself, and to the present parents of the house, was I fear very clumsy, not least in its timing. My only excuse was I hated taking the decision and did my best to mitigate its personal effect, in terms of allowances and housing. There were nevertheless protests from parents – because for those actually in the house he was a fine housemaster.

The problem was outside the house, in getting pupils past the reputation the house seemed to have developed of being a happy place for mavericks – it was, and admirable for that; but who other than a maverick wants to join a house for mavericks? The protests reached the governors, and I found myself being questioned about the decision. I explained: it was a tough decision, and I had hated making it – but, actually, there had been nary a protest from other staff. They knew it was a decision I had to make. The governors, as they always did, gave me their backing.

For the next few years, when I went back on brief visits to Wellington, the man avoided talking to me. I am however pleased to report that, with both of us retired from schoolmastering for some years, he seems to have forgiven me, though whether he understands that apparently cruel decision I don't know. I console myself with the old adage: worse than bad decisions are no decisions.

There were of course good things about that last year. The governors decided the refurbished buildings of the old art school should be named the Driver Rooms, and the President, HRH The Duke of Kent, came to open them and to unveil a full-length portrait of me which hangs there, in my frilly Oxford gown and hood. I had persuaded the portrait-painter, Andrew Festing (who had painted my portrait when I was leaving Berkhamsted), to give me what I called 'an uncharacteristic grin'. Another version of the same portrait hangs with those of the other Masters in Old Hall. There were speeches and presentations, the Wellington College Association gave us garden furniture and other gifts, and members of the Old Wellingtonian Society clubbed together with the parents in the WCA to give us round-the-world 'plane tickets.

The governors gave us a marquetry writing-slope, with a picture of Wellington on the front and, inside the lid, a sort of circular summary of Ann's and my time at the College: a pair of crossed golf-sticks (drivers), a violin, the ever open door of the Lodge kitchen, the emblems of Round Square and Amnesty International, a map of South Africa and the South African colours, a pair of running shoes, a rugby ball, and a picture of our terrier, Robbie. In the middle of the circle, there is a quotation from *Love Song in Old Age*, one of the poems in *Requiem*: 'And then we were / Ourselves again'.

On the back of the writing slope is the only joke I've ever discovered in marquetry: a picture of a rhododendron, its leaves and flower, and a pair of shears and a spade.

By the same author

Novels:

Elegy for a Revolutionary

Send War in Our Time, O Lord

Death of Fathers

A Messiah of the Last Days

Shades of Darkness

Biography & Memoir:

Patrick Duncan, South African & Pan-African

My Brother & I

Used to be Great Friends

The Man with the Suitcase: The Life, Execution & Rehabilitation of John Harris, Liberal Terrorist

Poems:

Occasional Light (with Jack Cope)

I Live Here Now

In the Water-Margins

Holiday Haiku

Requiem, a sequence

So Far, selected poems

Citizen of Elsewhere, selected poems

Verse for Children:

Moose, Mouse and Other Rhymes